About The Au

Born in Dover, England in 1951, **Alan Clayson** lives near Henley-on-Thames with his wife Inese and sons, Jack and Harry.

Described by the *Western Morning News* as the 'AJP Taylor of the pop world', Alan Clayson has written many books on music – including the best-selling *Backbeat*, subject of a major film – as well as for journals as disparate as *The Independent*, *Record Collector*, *Medieval World*, *Folk Roots*, *Erotic Review*, *The Times*, *Discoveries*, *The Beat Goes On* and, as a teenager, the notorious 'Schoolkids' *Oz*. He has been engaged to broadcast on national TV and radio, and lecture on both sides of the Atlantic.

Before becoming better known as a pop historian, he led the legendary Clayson and the Argonauts in the late 1970s, and was thrust to 'a premier position on rock's Lunatic Fringe' (*Melody Maker*). The 1985 album, 'What A Difference A Decade Made', is the most representative example of the group's recorded work.

Alan is presently spearheading a trend towards an English form of *chanson*, and feedback from both Britain and North America suggests that he is becoming more than a cult celebrity. Moreover, his latest album, *Soirée*, may stand as Alan Clayson's artistic apotheosis if it were not for the promise of surprises yet to come.

Jacqueline Ryan, née Cole, lives in South London with her husband Liam and the youngest of her three children, Siobhan.

Jacqueline was born in Paddington, London in 1947 into a household where the piano and sing-songs were an integral part of family get-togethers. Her first sighting of The Troggs was around 18 years ago at the Fairfield Halls in Croydon. Their performance made such a lasting impression that the other acts at the concert are still unremembered.

In 1990, while writing for *The Beat Goes On*, a 1990s periodical for fans of 1960s music, Jacqueline noticed that there was no fan club listing for The Troggs. She promptly approached the group, and was delighted to be given the go-ahead to establish a Troggs society.

The first issue of *Trogg Times* appeared in July 1991. Since then, it has gone from strength to strength with subscribers all around the globe – and favourable reviews in such as *Record Collector* and Germany's *Good Times* (who published a recent article by Jacqueline).

Rock's Wild Things
THE
TROGGS
FILES

By Alan Clayson & Jacqueline Ryan

Helter
Skelter
publishing

London

Published in 2000 by Helter Skelter Publishing
4 Denmark Street, London WC2H 8LL

Discography and associated commentary copyright © Jacqueline
Ryan, 2000. All other text copyright © Alan Clayson, 2000

Design by Ian Welch

The publishers would like to thank Michael Heatley and Ian Welch at
Northdown Publishing.

The majority of photographs contained herein are from the personal
collection of Reg Presley, used with kind permission, and Jacqueline
Ryan/*Troggs Times*. Thanks is also given to John Walker, Richard
Reed, Doug McKenzie, Lothar Winkler, Barry Norman, Angelo
Valentino and Brian Sommerville. All attempts have been made to
contact copyright holders, where known, and apologies are offered to
any who proved uncontactable.

Printed in Great Britain by Redwood Books, Trowbridge

A CIP record for this book is available from the British Library

ISBN 1-900924-19-6

Contents

Acknowledgements

A legitimate market exists for 'showbiz' life stories, created by fans who, indirectly, pay the subjects' wages. Whatever our motivations for writing this present biography, we hope that it utilises your time interestingly – but remember, however we dress it up, it's only our opinions – and not always subjective ones either – about items of merchandise available to all. Your thoughts about 'Wild Thing', 'I Can't Control Myself', *Trogglodynamite*, 'Good Vibrations', *Athens Andover* and all the rest of them are as worthy as ours – and beyond all three of us, the only true approbation the Troggs need is from those who buy the records and tickets for the shows.

Nevertheless, *The Troggs Files* has been written with the full co-operation of the group, and we are grateful for access to privileged information and extensive interviews with Reg Presley, Chris Britton and other of the *dramatis personae* who both retold the old, old story for the trillionth time, and turned up new and rediscovered insights and information.

We have also drawn from conversations with Colin Frechter, Stan Green, Peter Lucas, Dave Maggs, Larry Page, Pete Staples and the late Ronnie Bond, and waded through Jacqueline Ryan's Troggs memorabilia, accumulated over seven years. There have also been exercise books of scribble to decipher and interview tapes to be transcribed as not a postal delivery seemed to go by without another Troggs-related package thumping onto the doormat.

For their co-operation and trust, we are also beholden to Brenda Ball, Elaine Britton – and, especially, Liam Ryan for patience that went beyond the call of duty.

Very special thanks are in order for our commissioning editors Michael Heatley and Sean Body for their faith in the intrinsic merit of this project; their battles on its behalf and their encouragement as we worked on it.

Let's have a round of applause to for Kaye Mapperson for location photography under very trying circumstances – and put your hands together again for Bill Jones, Ann Shaw and Joe Seicluna of the *Andover Advertiser* – plus all at the BBC Music Library, Andover Public Library, the British Library, Flying Music, the National Sound Archives, *Aldershot News and Military Gazette*, Colindale Newspaper Library and Andover Tourist Information office.

It may be obvious to the reader than we have received help from sources that prefer not to be mentioned. Nevertheless, we wish to express our appreciation for what they did.

Whether they were aware of providing assistance or not, thanks are also due in varying degrees to Ian 'Tich' Amey, Dave Berry, Stuart Booth, Carol Boyer, Bruce Brand, Alex Brown, Alan Burridge, Billy Childish, Gordon Clayson, Allan and Fiona Clewlow, Ron Cooper (of *Zabadak!*), Pete Cox, Don Craine, Carmen Czopp, Trevor 'Dozy' Davies, Dave Dee, Kevin Delaney, Piet De Rooy, Peter Doggett (of *Record Collector*), Ian Drummond, Sandra Dunbar-Stuart, Tim Fagan, Wayne Fontana, Pete Frame, Ann Freer, Gary Gold, Chris and Gill Gore, 'Wreckless' Eric Goulden, Oliver Gray, Penny Hicks, Marsha Hunt, Robb Johnson, Garry Jones, Graham Larkbey, Spencer Leigh, Peter Lindsay, Phamie Mac Donald (of Four Corners Vision), Steve Maggs, Angelika Mathieu, Jim McCarty, Sean McGhee (of *Rock'N' Reel*), Colin Miles, Zoot Money, Adrian Moulton, Mike and Christine Neal (of *The Beat Goes On*), Sandy Newman, Russell Newmark, Susan Oldbury, Chris Phipps, Mike Robinson, Charles Salt, the late Lord David Sutch, Mike Sweeney, John Tobler, John Townsend, Paul Tucker, Mark Turauskis, Twinkle, Chris Warman and Fran Wood – plus Barbara, David, Harry, Inese, Jack, Jan, Jenny, John, Samantha, Shiobhain and Sue.

Finally, we must mention *Trogg Times*, the quarterly magazine that was founded in 1991. For further details, please write to Jacqueline Ryan, Editor, *Trogg Times*, 56 Waite Davies Road, Lee, London SE12 0ND.

Prologue

'Let's Drink A Toast'

'We're a team, and I hate being singled out just because I'm the singer.'
Reg Presley

The most far-reaching occurrence to be reported in recent years in *Trogg Times* has been Wet Wet Wet's million-selling revival of 'Love Is All Around', which earned composer Reg Presley – the only original member of The Troggs still going the distance – three Ivor Novello awards and a huge swelling of his bank account, benefits that are, I suppose, the 'good karma' for the rip-offs, tax horrors and lean years following The Troggs' apparent farewell from the British Top 50 with 'Little Girl' in 1968, a few months after their own 'Love Is All Around' had peaked at Number 5.

No guitar-shaped swimming pool could be ordered by Presley on writer's royalties from a 1993 reworking of an earlier Troggs hit, 'With A Girl Like You', by Alex W Bettini, an Italian singer, but he expected at least a diving board's worth of returns from Wet Wet Wet, four Glaswegians who'd been making impressive chart headway since 1987. He'd got wind of their treatment of 'Love Is All Around' – not intended initially as an A-side – via The Troggs' then-manager Stan Green who was friendly with the Scottish outfit's road crew. Next, a tape came through the letterbox of Reg's modest abode in Andover, the Hampshire town where he'd been born and bred, and to which he'd always returned, no matter how far his wanderings after The Troggs' breakthrough in 1966 with the climactic 'Wild Thing'.

On hearing Wet Wet Wet's 'Love Is All Around', he may have thought that it might buy the family a foreign holiday, a new car or a loft conversion – though Reg, as a former bricklayer, usually carried out such renovations himself. However, after the number leapt out of the cinema screen in the soundtrack of *Four Weddings And A Funeral* – *the* British movie of 1994, it did for Wet Wet Wet what the use of 'I Will Always Love You' in *The Bodyguard* had for Whitney Houston, and 'Everything I Do' in *Robin Hood Prince Of Thieves* for Bryan Adams.

Reg treated himself and his wife, Brenda, to a pub lunch on the summer's day that the new 'Love Is All Around' reached Number 1. There it stayed into autumn, almost breaking Bryan Adams' record for the most weeks at the top. An excited telegram from Reg – 'Thank you, thank you, thank you. Congratulations – and, by the way, thank you' – heralded his attendance at a Wet Wet Wet rehearsal in Glasgow: 'I had a lump in my throat when they were doing "Love Is All Around" – because it was so powerful to hear it on a 20,000 watt PA.'

As the song's creator, more than mere reflected glory put Reg – 'late of The Troggs', according to the *Daily Mail* – back in the news again; on the sofa of breakfast and prime-time chat-shows; on *Top Of The Pops* to introduce Wet Wet Wet, and as a wanted celebrity guest at local charity events like the Winchester and Eastleigh NHS Trust's summer fete at the Royal Hampshire County Hospital where The Troggs' most famous drummer, Ronnie Bond, had passed away at the age of 51 two years earlier.

To paraphrase a line from 'The Ballad Of Jed Clampett', the next thing you know, old Reg's a millionaire – or he would be before tax, a lesson hard-won during a episode in 1977 when fiscal lightning had struck from a clear sky. A country lad who'd climbed to the top of the heap, who could begrudge Reg Presley regaining his fortune?

To many of The Troggs' beat group contemporaries, it was regarded as a triumph for the lost value of composing a song as opposed to producing a production, despite Wet Wet Wet's state-of-the-art over-embroidered lead vocal. Suddenly, 1960s groups still in exile on the nostalgia circuit were making 'Love Is All Around' the token ballad to stress a shadowy affinity with the restored Troggs who, through renewed interest, were a name to drop by the young and hip as exemplified by Pulp, intellectuals of the 'Britpop' movement, performing 'Little Girl' on French television, and The Troggs themselves turning up on Channel Four's *The White Room*, holding their own amid the programme's usual array of Britpop and rap.

In a wider forum, The Troggs rounded off a Solid Silver Sixties package tour at the London Palladium by hiring a string quartet to fairy-dust 'Love Is All Around'. During this trek, they had climbed up the album chart with a TV-advertised CD compilation of their biggest vinyl moments, hammering it home on ITV's *Pebble Mill At One* with a smashed-out 'Wild Thing' and – you guessed it – the contrasting 'Love Is All Around' with guitarist Chris Britton stroking an acoustic six-string. The same numbers were to win the day for them at an all-star Variety Club Of Great Britain bash at Wembley on Wednesday, 11 September 1996.

Chris, bass player Peter Lucas and drummer Dave Maggs had been there to lend moral support at London's Grosvenor House Hotel for the £200-a-head luncheon that climaxed with the Ivor Novello award ceremony for a cast of winners that included futurist egghead Brian Eno, monosyllabic Van Morrison and the 65-year-old King of Skiffle, Lonnie Donegan.

On receiving his three – Best Song of 1994, International Hit of the Year, Most Performed Work of the Year – from Lionel Bart, Reg Presley's acceptance speech contained the sentence 'I've hardly had time to get my runner beans in this year'. Having glided for so long on pop's strongest winds, he'd become a past master at both playing up to the public image of homely old Reg with his bucolic metaphors, and pulling unexpected strokes – often just when critics were about to write off The Troggs. Nevertheless, the group hadn't had all that much going for them when they'd formed in the early 1960s. While they could find his way around their instruments, Reg – a singer by default – had aroused little enthusiasm for his first attempts at songwriting. In truth, The Troggs weren't that brilliant at anything then – but within them, as the world was to discover, they had an intangible something else.

'I remember one gig in Norfolk, Virginia, July 23 1967. We're still owed $2,000 from that evening. I'd write and ask for it, plus interest, but I don't know where the buggers live.'
Reg Presley

To everyone who was ever in the Troggs (or thought they were)

Chapter 1

'That'll Be The Day'

'The groups, some of which sing what I consider to be dubious lyrics, are often recruited from the larger towns.'
Mr RF Knight

The country town of Andover in north-west Hampshire spawned a surprisingly generous litter of hit parade contenders – by affinity at least – during the Swinging Sixties. While drummer Mike Hugg of Manfred Mann and Peter Bartholemew, singer with the Overlanders – UK one-hit-wonders with 1965's chart-topping 'Michelle' – are connected by simple accident of birth, The Troggs will be eternally Andover's as The Beatles are Liverpool's. Indeed, there are middle-aged folk who still boast of having sat next to Ronnie Bond at infant school or served in the same Boy Scout Troop as Chris Britton or danced with a man who danced with a girl who danced with Pete Staples, the bass player.

In 1966, a fellow who'd cadged a cigarette off you the previous month, was the cynosure of unseen millions of eyes on *Top Of The Pops*. Once, Reg Presley – or Reginald Ball as he was then – had been, to outward appearances, an expressionless youth mooching along the pavement, and it had been impossible to deduce that, within his shell, he was an epitome of JB Priestley's assertion in a critique of Colin Wilson's *The Outsider*, 'that butchers cutting off chops may be touched by intimations of immortality, that the grocer, even as he hesitates over the sugar, may yet see the world in a grain of sand.'

Like the other three awaiting destinies as pop stars, Reg had been a semi-professional musician with too few bookings to stay the chill of workaday reality with its school-like sub-flavours of apprenticeships

13

and secondments to colleges as far away as Farnborough – still in Hampshire, but halfway to London, storm-centre of the British music industry, even if it was well outside the geographical limit of the pool where the kingdom's four major record labels were prepared to fish for talent. The mountains had to come to Mohammed, and back-of-beyond entertainers in Andover and its environs, who didn't head east, had to be content with recurrent weekend evenings in musty halls, pub functions rooms and, especially, youth clubs where soft drinks, with-it vicars, a solitary light bulb as *son et lumière*, and a wholesome, self-improving reek were the norm.

Always, it was never too late to give up 'music' – if that's what you called it – and try for a raise and even promotion, instead of just waiting for Friday to roll around – but who wanted to keep his nose clean and slip into a 'cushy' position and henceforth into dull and respectable old age when there remained even the possibility of a more glamorous alternative, no matter how remote?

Andover was remote enough, even after the war, for the distance to the capital to be measured in years rather than miles. Londoners still assumed that the further towards Land's End you travelled, the more primitive the natives. Yet Andover had thrived in its isolation and built-in resilience as an agricultural settlement from the pre-Christian era; its very name derived from the Celtic 'an dwfr' meaning 'spring water' – and that flowed inexhaustibly from Salisbury Plain into the Test and its Bourne and Anton tributaries and, since 1792, the Andover-Redbridge canal. Even in the 1950s, all were aswarm with coarse fish.

Since it was a mere prehistoric hillfort, Andover has also been a confluence of trackways that became Roman and then turnpike roads on the trade route from London to the West by the time the defeated Viking warlord Olaf Tryggvason was baptised by St Alphege, Bishop of Winchester in 994 with Aethelred II as godfather. Yet it is not the chapel dedicated to St Alphege, but the Norman church of St Mary's that dominated what was confirmed as a borough in 1135 when Henry II inaugurated a guild of merchants (dealing largely in leather goods). During the next century, Andover became an official 'town' with the authority to hold its own courts, and contain a leper colony.

A hidden blessing of the Great Fire of 1435 was an opportunity for planned rebuilding, evidenced by the Guild Hall, the town gaol; the priory in Marlborough Street (where James II stayed on the evening before losing his throne to William of Orange); coaching inns such as the Angel, the Globe – and the Star-and-Garter (now the Danesbury

14

Hotel) where George III and Lord Nelson were two who'd sought shelter for the night.

That these eminent visitations are among the most told tales of ancient Andover corroborates its standing as just another point between London and Exeter. To outsiders, it seemed no different from any other cross-shaped market town of sufficient inhabitants to warrant a Church of England Primary School and a railway station by the mid-19th century. After the Great War, the names over the shops in the wide High Street continued to change, but hikers still breasted the surrounding downs where sheep nibbled on grassy old Saxon battlegrounds, and the landscape melted into another endless summer day with not a leaf stirring, a touch of mist on the sunset horizon and a bird chirruping somewhere.

Then the seasons changed from gold to marble, and, as they did, log fires subsided to glowing embers, and the harvest moon in its starry canopy would shine as bright as day over the vastness of story-book meadows and woodlands that were about to be buried beneath an urban overspill sprawl of residential hinterland of raw red brick, built by the book amid small-time light industry, tangles of shopping precincts, arteries of droning traffic, rows of lock-up garages and industrial estates like East Portway and Walworth with their engineering, electronics, chemical and printing works. 'Pace Of Development Is Accelerating,' was to be one local journal's front page truism at the beginning of 1965 when everyone else had stopped talking about it.

Moreover, RAF Andover had established itself at Weyhill and, during World War II, at Thruxton. *Post bellum* war games and manoeuvres on Salisbury Plain scrubland had necessitated the building of further barracks round outlying villages like Tidworth and Perham Down, even Enham – renamed Enham-Alamein – on the very edge of Andover, to contain the Parachute Regiment, the Royal Artillery and the Black Watch (recruited largely from Glasgow's rough Gorbals suburb) as the district accommodated a military presence on a par with those in Bordon and Aldershot, the 'home of the British army', both lying less than an hour's clattering bus ride away.

The civilian population of the district hadn't ceased to expand either. Though one grandfather came from Andover, Reg Ball's forebears had appeared in census rolls in London's East End since dray horses had dragged cargoes on to clippers poised to catch the Thames tide. On migrating back to Hampshire, an outing to Bournemouth had precipitated Ernest, Reg's father's, courtship of

Grace Peckham. She married him, and was blessed with first-born Eric in 1935, and a second son, Ronald, nearly three years later.

Four more years passed, and the War Office, concerned about the stalemate the Allies had reached against the Axis powers, sent for Ernie Ball. As an infinitesimal cog in the machine provisioning the bloodshed, Ernie was posted to the Royal Artillery, and was lucky to escape with his life at Dunkirk before his wife's final confinement produced the most robust – twelve and a half pounds – of her children, the remarkable Reginald Maurice, in a bedroom of 17 Belle Vue Road, two minutes dawdle from the High Street, just after midnight on 12 June 1941, a clear but unseasonably chilly Thursday.

As a round-eyed toddler, Reg was to watch the RAF's diamond formations zooming towards the Luftwaffe's bombardment of Southampton docks where the horizon glowed with ton upon booming ton of death and destruction. Andover, however, finished the war in a less shell-shocked state than other key military centres, and Reg's childhood was undramatic and free of major traumas – particularly after Ernie's demobilisation removed one principal impediment to domestic stability.

Another was Mr Ball's anti-social hours as a bus driver for the company centred on the local depot – until he and Grace invested their savings in a cafe, the Criterion, that earned parochial fame, said Reg, for its 'fabulous bacon rolls'. Business was brisk enough, particularly when, as the country paid for its victory, the West Country was pictured in metropolitan breakfast-rooms as a corner of the map where the families of farm labourers eked out rock-bottom wages via perpetual mental arithmetic. Andover's existence was put to the back of the mind except when national newspapers reported drought, flood and like meteorological extremities affecting harvest yield. Otherwise, nothing much was guaranteed to happen there, year in, year out.

Andover's Town Mill – now a pub – was still grinding corn, and you could park without restriction along the High Street where the offices of the *Andover Advertiser* cooked up its weekly diet of whist drives, winter farrowing, the Operatic Society's production of *HMS Pinafore*, gypsies camped illegally on a disused army base, and the more interesting lots at forthcoming house auctions by Alfred Pearson Estate Agents.

This was spiced with less run-of-the-mill news such as the closure of the Romsey Line in 1963 (a small price to pay for the inconvenience of the level crossing on Bridge Street); the consecration of a burial ground extension by the Bishop of Salisbury; the Vintage Motor Cycle Club (Stonehenge Section)'s run to Winchester and back; a local burglar on the run after escaping from Winchester Prison, and *Coronation Street femme fatale* Elsie Tanner opening a new High Street department store. Among the most eye-catching headlines were 'Poltergeist Drove Us Out, Say Couple', 'Ludgershall – Hants Or Wilts?', 'Pedigree Cow Badly Mauled By Dog', 'Andover A Pretty Scruffy Town' Says Wing Commander IE Hill' – and 'Soldiers Kicked Andover Policeman'.

Brawling and vandalism were all too frequent diversions when contingencies of common soldiers on passes descended like a Biblical plague upon the fun palaces of Andover. Though changed out of their itchy dung-coloured uniforms, the peanut-waged 'squaddies' were marked by regulation haircuts, planed halfway up the skull. The natural enemies, therefore, were local gangs of Teddy Boys, the most menacing if narcissistic post-war teenage cult, with their seedy-flash finery and quiffed glaciers of brilliantine. Fists often swung harder than the dance bands who maintained ghastly grins when soundtracking someone being half-killed out there. 'I saw the biggest fight of my life between the Tidworth Boys and the Paras,' Reg Ball would recall. 'It was amazing no-one died – though one soldier was concussed with a metal-framed chair.'

Bored adolescents with hormones raging and wondering what to do until bedtime had been around from time immemorial when Andover Theatre, once in Newbury Street, had acquired the dubious reputation of having 'the noisiest gallery in England'. In the open air, the town's brass ensemble blasted up the Cornish Floral Dance on the bandstand at the Jubilee Recreation Ground on a site where archers had practiced prior to setting off for Agincourt.

As the 1950s got out of neutral, music of increasingly racier persuasion could be sampled within the walls of all manner of village institutes, regimental messes, working men's clubs and sports pavilions. In the town centre, the places to see and be seen were St Ann's Hall, Moore Hall and, both along East Street, the Fiesta and the Territorial Army (TA) Centre where The Melody Makers Dance Orchestra clung on to weekend residencies well into the next decade.

Yet it wasn't The Melody Makers, but a smaller ensemble that accompanied Reg Ball when, at the close of 1955's summer carnival week, he sang in public for the first time. In the privacy of an after-hours Criterion, he and a classmate, Adrian Jones, had enjoyed many hours of informal fun, practicing *a cappella* harmonies in the *shooby-*

doo-wah fashion favoured by The Stargazers, The Crew-Cuts, The Platters and, later, The Diamonds, a Canadian vocal combo whose 'Little Darlin'' – which lived in falsetto wailing, backing *showaddywaddys* and deep bass spoken passage – was to be, claimed Reg, 'the only record I ever bought'.

This purchase lay two years in the future when, carried away by the exuberant atmosphere at the TA Centre, Reg and Adrian had mounted the stage to give 'em 'Unchained Melody', the ballad that, via several simultaneous covers, was Number One in the newly-established *New Musical Express* record and sheet music sales charts. With the hubbub subdued to frozen faces staring up at them, the lads stood motionless, bar trembling knees, before the lowered microphone. A deep breath, and they were into the opening line – 'oh, my love, my darling, I've hungered for your touch...' Glistening with embarrassment as the number died away, Reg blinked at his feet before glancing up with enquiring eyebrow. An exclaimed 'yeah!' broke the silence and a mingling of amused cheers and protracted clapping for their youthful nerve ensued.

The first time was the only time, and the duo quit while they were ahead. Yet the discovery that an audience of adults had actually listened to him singing began Reg Ball's sluggish flight to the very pinnacle of pop, a fact not much appreciated at the time, least of all by young Reg himself.

Wisely, his parents had not goaded him to formalise musical interests inherited from Grace's side of the family. Various of her nephews had constituted what Reg would recognise later as being 'one of the first pop groups in that it contained bass, drums and rhythm and lead guitars', before the members' departure to marriage beds or the starker truths of the Depression. Nevertheless, Reg had been an entranced listener to both them and an uncle's party piece of coaxing a tune from a mouth-organ with his nose. Next, Reg's investigative pounding with his fists on the upright piano in Number 17's living room had prompted seven weeks of lessons from a Mrs Brown in the house opposite, but these were less pleasant a memory for Reg than his and Brian, her son's illicit experiments with the ocarina that gathered dust on top of the piano. Creating a sound akin to whistling, this blowing instrument made of terra-cotta was to loom large in The Troggs' legend.

At Wolverdene Primary School, the recorder was the key to more sophisticated woodwinds like the saxophone an adolescent Reg was to take up for a thankfully short period when 'I squeaked my mother into insanity'. As it was with most baby-boomers, musical theory was taught almost as a kind of mathematics through cross-legged banging of assorted percussion and – quite a new idea then – in *Singing Together* and other BBC Home Service radio broadcasts to schools.

Making steadier progress at art and oral debate – where he developed an ability to nutshell the most complex arguments – Reg did not conform with school dictates about what was and wasn't 'good' music. Infinitely more meaningful to him than, say, *Das Rheingold* or Brahms' *German Requiem* were 'The Ballad Of Davy Crockett', Frankie Laine's quasi-religious 'I Believe' (in the hit parade for so many weeks in 1953 that 'it was almost sad when it dropped out because we sang it round the school') and the previous year's jogalong 'Walking My Baby Back Home' – the first pop lyric Reg ever learned – by Johnnie Ray, North America's 25-year-old 'Prince of Wails', and the wildest act going in an age when popular singers were generally approaching middle life before achieving worthwhile recognition.

You'd have had some search then for anything wilder on the BBC *Light Programme* beyond infrequent spins of Fats Waller, Hoagy Carmichael and gutbucket blues amid the unchained melodies, Mantovanis, Mambo Italianos and doggies in the window on *Two-Way Family Favourites*. On television, there was *The Black And White Minstrel Show*, but this was very much a false dawn as it was as subject to the BBC's old maidish dictates as the string-laden musak on the wireless; Cy Grant's calypsos on topical *Tonight*, and *Quite Contrary*, built round neo-operatic Ronnie Hilton, who for want of anyone better, was cited by the *NME* as 1955's most popular British vocalist. Over on ITV, *Round About Ten* with its inclusion of Humphrey Lyttelton's Jazz Band was as hot as it got.

A passion for pop would bring puffy smiles to the lips of do-gooders in cardigans who presided over sport, purposeful hobbies, charity work, the Great Outdoors and further hearty pastimes intended to distract young minds from nature's baser urges. When not inside Abbotts Ann Memorial Hall Youth Club, the 1st Andover Air Scouts hut or Tidworth YMCA for ping-pong, 'gang show' rehearsals or 'Brains Trusts' on current affairs , you could be out brass-rubbing, Bob-A-Jobbing or booting a soaking-wet piece of leather about.

Falling into line, Peter Lawrence Staples posed for a soccer team photograph at Andover Secondary Modern – that had yet to be built when he came to consciousness in 1944 – while an 11-year-old Reg Ball had surfaced in a leading role in *The Burst Pipe*, a scout play. Unlike Reg – who left after a year – Charles Christopher Britton stuck it out with the troop, and may have become a Queen's Scout had a girlfriend not twisted his pride into a frown by opining that a 16-year-old looked silly in shorts.

Chris (like Ronnie Ball before him) had passed the Eleven-Plus examination and thus gained a place at the Grammar School – where Lord Denning, sometime Master of the Rolls, had studied from 1905 to 1916 – rather than Andover Secondary Modern where 'failures' like his best friend, Pete Staples – and Reg Ball – had gone after going to pieces on that day-of-days that decided your academic future before the advent of the fairer 'education for all' comprehensive system which allowed you, theoretically, to follow what best suited your abilities and inclinations as they evolved.

A lost cause as a schoolboy before even sitting his Eleven-Plus, Ronald James Bullis lived in Dene Road, a forlorn cul-de-sac within sight of the Criterion. Prised into the world on 4 May 1940, he was nine years old when, with deceptive casualness, he entered the life of Reg Ball. 'He was like a human tornado,' gasped Reg, 'very energetic, upfront and hyper. If you walked past his house, he'd fly out of the door, come right up to your face beyond the point of being comfortable, and demand where you were going, what you were doing, when you were coming back.'

Ronnie was one of a brood of four sisters and four brothers. The eldest, Billy, fancied himself as a singer while, if not as serendipitously as Reg Ball, Ronnie messed about on a 'huge green ocarina which we had lying about the house. I never found out who bought it or where it came from.'

He was not to be remembered, however, as a musical *wunderkind*. Indeed, as a scholar, Ronnie was outstanding at nothing, apart from physical training. He read little beyond War Picture Library and US horror comics with titles like *Creepy Worlds* and *Tales Of The Uncanny*, reflective of his taste in films after he caught *The Bride Of Frankenstein* at 13 'with my hands over my ears' at the Savoy, one of Andover's two cinemas.

During his final years at the Secondary Modern, Ronnie slacked in the back row, dumbly insolent and indifferent to logarithms and the Diet of Worms. In reciprocation, he was ignored by the more faint-hearted teachers as long as he didn't disturb other pupils. Relieved when he was absent, they were as anxious for him to leave as he was.

Chris Britton, on the other hand, was a credit to his parents in days when a grammar school place was as desirable a social coup as an academic one. Born on 21 January 1944 beneath cloudy skies in

Watford, he was blessed facially with a classic Viking bone structure, but was bullied at school for being 'skinny, weak and spotty. Whenever they picked a football team, I was always the one left to last.'

Not helping either was his accountant father Edwin switching from job to job, and Chris, therefore, from school to school with time for only the most fleeting friendships. From Watford, the Brittons zigzagged to Andover, Letchworth, Cromer – where a gaberdine-raincoated Chris enrolled at infant school – Kingston and back to Andover where a nine-year-old was confronted in Wolverdene Primary playground by an ugly ruffian, riled by the new boy's 'girly' accent, so alien to his own strong burr. No coward, Chris put up his fists, looked fierce and hoped for the best. To his delighted astonishment, he found that 'the style of fighting over in Kingston was something of an innovation in Hampshire. My new tactics surprised the opposition, and they left me alone after that. That was my last fight – not counting the odd skirmish on the rugby field.'

Britton was conspicuous also for a mechanical turn demonstrated in a fascination for automobiles: how they worked, the differences between them, and the magic of their whizzing springs and pistons. From an early age, Chris could take an engine to bits and put it back together again. If intellectually gifted too, Chris was loathe to bring his exercise book to certain of his teachers' desks for fear of getting into trouble. Being berated for eccentric spelling triggered an aversion to English lessons, but an aptitude for mathematics grew apace with his liking for its teacher, a gentleman of Russian extraction.

Musically, Britton's technical expertise was more noticeable at first than any creative inclinations. One important influence was Elton Hayes who 'sang to a small guitar' in an arrangement of Edward Lear's 'The Owl And The Pussycat', forever on Saturday morning's *Children's Favourites* (record requests aired by 'Uncle Mac') on the Light Programme. An acoustic six-string materialised on his ninth birthday, and, handsomely endowed with the tenacity to try-try again, Chris positioned yet uncalloused fingers on the taut strings as he pored over exercises prescribed by Jack Dacre, a tutor who had so damaged his left hand in a motorcycle accident that he'd been obliged to relearn the guitar left-handed with the same extraordinary spirit that had motivated 'gypsy jazz' exponent Django Reinhardt to carry on playing despite the loss of two fingers.

Reinhardt was a role model for Dacre's waywardly earnest student too – as were the disparate likes of Segovia, Charlie Christian and, later, Chet Atkins, an electric guitarist then with first refusal of virtually all recording sessions in Nashville, the Hollywood of country and western music.

More 'western' than 'country' were 'Home On The Range' and 'Singing Cowboy' Roy Rogers' 'Four Legged Friend', the songs a 12-year-old Chris performed in his slot during an all-styles-served-here extravaganza at Wallop Village Hall. By the end of his second year at the Grammar, his fingertips had hardened with daily practice and his left hand was big enough to shape the more difficult chords – so much so that he was soon to defy all comers in a tussle over the county line for the Wiltshire challenge cup for a guitar instrumental and 'song with guitar'.

Once, the instrument had been associated mainly with Latinate heel-clattering, but, come the mid-1950s, it was what you heard rock'n'rollers playing on the 45 rpm discs that had superseded 78s. As these span their little lives away on the youth club record-player, swingin' curates snapped fingers and – with little idea how teenagers really talked – exclaimed 'too much!', understanding that God would not cast out this new pestilence from across the Atlantic, despite officialdom's malevolent neutrality when Bill Haley and the Comets made landfall in Southampton in 1957, and their movie, *Don't Knock The Rock* was banned throughout Ireland.

Epitomised by Andover teenagers – Reg Ball among them – jiving in the aisles when the previous Haley film, *Rock Around The Clock*, reached the Savoy in 1956, all but the most serious-minded children had been excited by its title song, a US 'sepia' hit covered by Haley and his tubby old troupers who'd have been daft not to have cashed in on it quickly with more of the same. Rock'n'roll next put forward a more suitable champion in a Mr E.A. Presley, who was less a pubescent female's favourite uncle than her big sister's demon lover with his 'common' good looks, lopsided smirk and lavishly whorled cockade. The unhinged go-man-go sorcery of Presley's in-concert frolics involved him carrying on as if he had a wasp within the thighs and crotch of slacks that his sniffier detractors might deem 'crude'. They also abhorred his shout-singing and sulky balladeering. What more did Elvis need to be the toast of teenagers everywhere?

The hunt was up for variations on the theme. The more dim-witted saw Louisiana fireball Jerry Lee Lewis as just an Elvis who substituted piano for guitar. While Gene Vincent – 'The Screaming End' – went off the commercial boil within months of his 'Be-Bop-A-Lula' debut, black Presleys like Little Richard and Chuck Berry; unsexy ones such as Carl Perkins and Buddy Holly, even homegrown ones like Tommy Steele and, next, Cliff Richard, were leaping up the British charts in an abundance inconceivable when 'Rock Around The Clock' had been dismissed by pundits as the apex of a fad as transient as Davy Crockett fake-coonskin caps.

Duplicates of supposed duplicates followed – because copying one of these new rock'n'roll maniacs from the States was how you gave yourself the best possible chance of being elevated from the dusty boards of a provincial palais to small-fry billing on round-Britain 'scream circuit' package tours and a spot on Jack Good's *Oh Boy!*, the ITV pop spectacular in which a parade of mostly male solo turns chased each other so quickly that the screeching studio audience scarcely had pause to draw breath.

With this in mind, Vince Taylor from Houslow put himself forward as a second Gene Vincent, and Cuddley Dudley as the next Fats Domino. Up in Oxford, singing pianist Roy Young attempted to corner the Little Richard market – while Wee Willie Harris was bruited by his manager as London's very own Jerry Lee Lewis. Sporting an enormous bow-tie and hair dyed shocking-pink, Harris wasn't above an orchestrated 'feud' with Larry Page, 'the Teenage Rage' – though, publicity stunts aside, the two rubbed along easily enough when off-duty; Willie presenting his congratulations at Larry's 21st birthday party, along with guests of such magnitude as Jack Good, former heavyweight champion Freddie Mills and chart contenders Don Lang, Laurie London and Joe 'Mr Piano' Henderson.

When plain Leonard Davies, Larry packed records at an EMI factory close to his home in Hayes, Middlesex. By 1957, however, he'd been signed to one of the company's subsidiaries, Columbia, as a singer. He was 'handled' by Croft and Associates of Wardour Street – a most prestigious shop-window for pop talent. In an age when sheet music sales were at least as vital as the *New Musical Express*'s newly-established record charts, Larry (like Wee Willie) relied chiefly on US covers on the understanding that most home buyers were unlikely to have heard the blueprints. Page's go at The Del-Vikings' 'Cool Shake' attracted BBC airplay, but his 'That'll Be The Day' was totally eclipsed by The Crickets' chart-topping original.

After a sixth 45 bit the dust like all the others, Larry, with lost business innocence, accepted that his time in the spotlight was up – and that solid cash was preferable to the applause of the Great British Public. He had the connections now to make a living behind the scenes, and thus he roamed the offices of Denmark Street, London's

Tin Pan Alley, until he was hired by the Mecca leisure corporation – which had belatedly clasped rock'n'roll to its bosom – to run Coventry's Orchid Ballroom, the jackpot of local engagements for the city's own would-be rock stars.

Down in Andover, venues such as the Fiesta and the TA Centre had started booking dyed-in-the-wool rock'n'rollers too, initially via the Southampton agency of Reg Calvert, an entrepreneur notorious for his human xeroxes of teen heroes, short-term or otherwise. Thus Andover hosted shows by Danny Storm – whose act coincided in every detail with that of Cliff Richard – Buddy Britten and the Regents (Calvert's Buddy Holly and the Crickets) and even a Cuddly Dudley copyist in something called Baby Bubbley.

The town's own entertainers of this kidney were only too pleased if asked to be support acts on these occasions, often for as little as a round of fizzy drinks – as did Andover's first rock'n'roll combo, Lee Peters and the Dynamic Electrons, who'd started in 1956 in artistic debt to Lonnie Donegan, ennobled as 'King of Skiffle' during its 1957 prime. In impregnating an impoverished and imitative scene with vigorous alien idioms, Donegan and his Skiffle Group's impact would be carried across aeons of British pop.

While Lonnie was its wellspring, it was possible to perceive vaguely regional hues of skiffle, largely through folk traditions leaving their mark. In the west, groups such as The Avon Cities Skiffle and Salisbury's Satellites betrayed ancestry in Morris Dance sides via their employment of squeeze-boxes. Yet, like punk after it, anyone who'd mastered basic techniques could have a crack at skiffle – and the more ingenuous the sound, the better. Percussion and chords slashed on an acoustic guitar were at the core of its contagious backbeat, and no-one howled with derision at a washboard tapped with thimbles, broomstick bass, dustbin-lid cymbals, biscuit-tin snare drum and further vehicles of musical effect fashioned from everyday implements.

Bitten by the skiffle bug, Chris Britton's first group had mother Monica on bass, and Edwin on washboard. 'It didn't have a name,' said Chris, 'as we only ever played at home for our own amusement, but our repertoire was huge.' Chris was a focal point too in The Hiccups, an outfit formed with school chums – and in a unit containing some of Edwin's younger colleagues from work, who appeared at a skiffle contest at the Fiesta, where they swallowed dust behind The Moonrakers and a combo with a Mrs Collings on lead vocals – whose younger son plucked tea-chest bass in The Hiccups.

Such displays were generally for the benefit of performers rather than onlookers, but the proprietor of the Savoy, one of two cinemas in the High Street, interspersed movies like *Barabbas*, *Summer Holiday*, *Ben Hur*, *Kid Galahad*, *Tarzan Goes To India* and the latest Norman Wisdom with occasional in-person performances by amateurs such as Reg Ball who had swapped his more expensive saxophone for a guitar, and mastered a few pieces, notably Santo and Johnny's careening 'Sleepwalk', a 1959 instrumental in which he plucked rhythm to the lead runs of the more adept Howard 'Ginger' Mansfield, a shock-headed youth from the flat above, who was the Hank B Marvin to singer Bruce Turner's Cliff Richard in a group called The Emeralds.

Ginger was not involved, therefore, when Reg was roped into The Incognitos, a quartet led by a neighbourhood greengrocer who fretted a Hawaiian guitar, for three numbers – 'Sleepwalk', an arrangement of 'Three Blind Mice'(!) and Reg singing Buddy Holly's 'Peggy Sue' – in a talent competition at the Savoy. Attired like the rest in an apposite bandit mask, Ball was the last to amble out beneath the proscenium: 'My foot got caught in the electric guitar lead, the Hawaiian guitar lead…and ripped all the plugs out. Everyone was miming to nothing except me, strumming away. They could have killed me.'

Having inadvertently engineered The Incognitos' ruin, Reg promised himself that he'd never go on the stage again. Like The Hiccups *et al*, The Incognitos was seen as a vocational blind alley, a folly to be cast aside as he resigned himself to dwelling unto the grave in the same socially immobile situation as his older siblings.

Well, where did music get you anyway? No-one lasted very long. Bill Haley was finished in the UK Top 20 by 1958; Lonnie Donegan appeared to be in decline too, and Elvis was square-bashing in Germany. More to the point, Andover's first homogenous rock'n'roll ensembles were already barring themselves from dances at the staider youth clubs as well as the stuffy grown-up dinner-and-dances upon which they might have depended for virtually all paid work had they traded in 'decent' music.

Nearly all of them also differentiated between backing group and singer. Among those front men who clung firmest to the new music's coat-tails was a certain Pete Mystery. Nothing had stopped him from becoming an Andover Cliff Richard – with his accompanying Strangers conforming to the two-guitars-bass-drums stereotype patented by Cliff's Shadows. But for a hit record or two, Mystery had been the equal of anyone who'd been screened on *Oh Boy!*. He was, nevertheless, both too late and too far away to put himself before the powers behind the sub-*Oh Boy!* programmes like *Wham!*, *Dig This!* and *Cool For Cats* that saw British pop into the 1960s.

In the cat-seat by then were the latest batch of what Pete and fellow Andoverians may have described as 'candy-arsed' US pop idols: interchangeably doe-eyed, hair-sprayed and conventionally good-looking. It seemed a prerequisite for them to bear the forename 'Bobby'. While Johnny Kidd and the Pirates, Screaming Lord Sutch and the Savages and too few other British rockers who hadn't gone smooth were assured of plenty of work, with or without hits, pop was now at its most harmless and ephemeral.

This suited those members of The Melody Makers and their kind who did not resent having to kow-tow to the tastes of those for whom the extremes of palatable modern pop were still represented by 'How Much Is That Doggie In The Window' and 'I Believe'. A spirit of appeasement might permit maybe two current smashes and one dip into classic rock per night, but as a rule, they didn't go in for anything too untamed during each TA Centre evening's otherwise polished mixture of across-the-board favourites, *salvo pudore* in-song comedy, and the onstage glamour of braided costumery and neat coiffure. 'Featured popular vocalists' were brought forward to either specialise in areas thought unsuitable for the usual singer or simply to let him knock back a swift Coca-Cola.

Changeless and changed after rock'n'roll, local groups had polarised into ones that stuck to the tried-and-trusted guidelines, and ones that now aspired to be highly proficient, non-stop copyists of whatever pop commotions were stirring up the nation – as the Twist and its many variations did from 1961. Many outfits had been like it from the onset after stampeding bass players into buying one of these new-fangled electric models that radiated inestimably greater depth of sound than any bull fiddle and, certainly, anything constructed from tea-chest, broomstick and string. Indeed, over in Salisbury, Roy Jarvis of Johnny Nicholls and the Dimes had acquired one of the first electric basses in the country.

After making a financial commitment like this, many musicians found a post-skiffle group's Top 20-derived repertoire unsatisfying in substance. Nevertheless, a strong motive for even the most ill-favoured lad to be in one was sex. After the Pill (and before AIDS), there was licence to lock eyes with short-skirted 'birds' with urchin faces and pale lipstick, who ogled with unmaidenly eagerness the enigma of boys-next-door who were untouchable until the interval when a tryst could be sealed with a beatific smile, a flood of libido and an 'All right then: I'll see you later.'

The onset of puberty had found Ronald Bullis looking for an opening in a pop group. Yet his small stature and runtish build did not mark out the 16-year-old as a darling of the ladies – though it was ideal for training as a jockey. Amused by the memory, Bullis would reconjure how 'I joined a riding school, but I grew myself out of a job and shot up to five feet nine inches in about three months.'

A fortnight afterwards, Ronnie was an overalled trainee carpenter with a firm that specialised in carving out the interiors of caravans. His closest encounter with showbusiness was constructing such a dwelling for a trapeze troupe at Chipperfield's Circus, but, possessing an instinctive sense of rhythm that had been unrealised by his teachers, he ceased smiting furniture to music from the radio, and came home one day with a drum kit.

For hours daily, Bullis attacked it with gusto, showing no signs of ever stopping. His crashing about – that irritated the entire terrace – brought forth hand-and-foot co-ordination, accurate time-keeping and the beginnings of a personal style.

Outside London, drummers were so vexingly few and far between that just his ownership of a kit was sufficient for the welling up of overtures for Ronnie's services from groups all over the region, but he pledged himself to a trio named The Fantastic Threeways and then Bruce Turner and the Senators – formerly The Emeralds – joining in their battles against amateur-dramatic acoustics and overloaded amplifiers with naked wires. 'I should think we had the most dangerous set of equipment ever allowed on stage,' sighed Pete Staples, rhythm guitarist in The Senators to Ginger Mansfield's lead. 'Our amps were all skeleton parts and the leads were wedged into the sockets by matchsticks, chewing gum and bits of paper. Occasionally, a spark would fly off the mikes and burn our lips.'

By day, Pete was an electrician. The group, therefore, looked to him to ensure that the gear was rendered less lethal and less likely to fall silent midway through a number. If you wished too, he could air technicalities too about grades of beef and operating a bacon slicer as he'd been taken on by a local butcher on leaving school. The world of work had also fostered in Pete a grasp of national politics that, if opinionated, was less hesitant than most. His roots were socialist because 'I had the old man (his father, Percy) shouting in my ear at home about Labour, and a fellow at work was a fanatical Conservative. I had to learn something about politics to shut them up. I'm only really interested in Home Affairs – something which is going to affect me directly.'

A different Pete, however, was as serious-minded about more orthodox adolescent concerns. Spots exploded on an otherwise presentable countenance, and he was sensitive enough about his curly hair to flatten it with setting lotion when he made his debut with Turner and the Senators at St Ann's Hall in 1959. Soon after a paid engagement at Boscombe Locarno, 'my whole life was taken up with playing in a group at night, working as an electrician by day, and courting.'

The pursuit of romance was on Reg Ball's mind at the Fiesta one Friday night in May 1960 – for it was then that he first clapped eyes on the coltish charms of the woman he was to marry two years later. Her name was Brenda, and she was a Londoner invited down for the weekend by a friend. If not so sure of himself with her as he was with local girls bereft of metropolitan *sang froid*, he was so bewitched by Brenda's svelte profile, avalanche of wavy brown hair and the deceptive command in a timorously pretty face, that – to paraphrase the song – he found a way to say 'Can I dance with you?' before The Melody Makers struck up the last waltz.

He'd almost decided to stay in, having arrived back at the Criterion late in the evening, tired and ravenous after a day in Basingstoke on a college course pertaining to his apprenticeship as a bricklayer alongside Ginger Mansfield. An interviewer at the Youth Employment Centre, you see, had misunderstood Reg's fancy to be an artist: 'I went down the Labour and told the bloke I wanted to be a painter. He looked through his box and said he didn't have anything for a painter. How about a bricklayer? That's much the same thing. Bricklaying could be interesting work, especially when restoring old buildings – but even working on council houses was creative.'

Ball's weekly wage was barely enough for a half-ounce of tobacco, the bus fare to college and, if he was lucky, a couple of hours shuffling about in the gloom beyond the footlights at the Fiesta or, from 1961, Teenbeat night at the TA Centre where there were records and perhaps some group or other, occasionally augmented with a Twist exhibition team utilising time where an intermission skiffle outfit once did. While not yet exploding with pop, more and more vicinities round Andover seemed to have either a group enjoying parochial fame or a weekly venue given over to out-and-out pop. The Astrals held Enham-Alamein, and Pete Mystery and his boys were still going strong as rulers of the Clatford villages. Four shillings (20p) would buy 'a really good swinging night out' at St Mary's Hall in Overton – and there was more of the same at the Queen's Head Skittle Bar in Ludgershall after a boxed 'Small Band Or Groups Required For Saturdays And Sundays, 8-10.30 p.m. Apply Landlord' was printed in the *Advertiser*. There were 'Jive and Twisting' sessions at Porton Village Hall every Thursday, and, in 1962, a 'beat group' – as they were becoming known – was booked for Andover and District Young Farmers Club at St Mary Bourne Institute.

Snippets about local pop reared up in 'Teen Scene', a column that the *Advertiser* ran from 1962. The newspaper noted too that nationally-known pop singers Michael Cox and Jess Conrad pitched in with the usual comedians and television personalities at the Rotary Club's celebrity football match. At the height of his fame with 'Mystery Girl' in the Top 20, Conrad was back in Andover a few months later as judge of the Carnival Twist Contest, a youthful counterpoint to the Carnival Queen's crowning by Sir Donald Wolfit, 'the famous actor'.

The other side of the coin was that Andover was in the heartland of a prudish Britain that had hounded babysnatching Jerry Lee Lewis from its shores in 1958, and, more recently, had obliged Billy Fury to moderate his sub-Elvis gyrations. Closer to home, Gloucester city burghers had barred a combo called The Sapphires from ever defiling its Guild Hall again because of the tightness of the lead vocalist's trousers.

In September 1963, the *Andover Advertiser* splashed its front page with '"Twist" Club Dismayed Over Fiesta Ban'. Scandalised readers learnt that the hall's director Mr RF Knight was irate about damage by stiletto heels to its pinewood floor by girls who'd coughed up the five shilling (25p) membership fee of the so-called Teen and Twenty Disc Club that had convened every Tuesday for several weeks. 'Mr Knight said that the club was getting out of hand now that over 300 young people attend. "The groups, some of which sing what I consider to be dubious lyrics, are often recruited from the larger towns".'

The case for the defence was articulated by club secretary Mrs June Turner who cited only one instance of dubious lyrics, and 'doubted whether the dances would get much support if only local bands were engaged'.

Chapter 2
'No Particular Place To Go'

*'I never knew The Beatles existed until "Twist And Shout",
and then I thought "Wow!", and sat up and took notice of
everything they've done since.'*
Reg Presley

Only in the music press and on the television would the clouds part to allow glimpses of the gods at play. Meanwhile you made the best of a bad job, sprucing up and forking out a florin (10p) for another small death at the TA Centre, dancing to, say, The Concordes from Bournemouth, Swindon's Hubble Fudges, The Statesmen from Gosport or Dave Dee and the Bostons who'd supported Screaming Lord Sutch at Salisbury City Hall 'prior to their Scottish tour – appearing on Grampian TV', it said on the *Advertiser*'s entertainment page, making the most of the pride of Wiltshire's first cache of professional engagements; not so much a tour as a hellish odyssey of one-nighters when Britain's only motorway terminated at Birmingham.

Andover's own Redwoods would pull a similar stroke with 'back from their successful Midlands tour' when they commenced a virtual residency at the TA Centre's 'Shake-Twist-Rock-Jive' evenings in August 1963. During rehearsals in a potting shed over the previous year, guitarists Chris Penfound, Chris Britton and, later Alan Grindley, (who all owned instruments made of red wood) forged a more fixed line-up via the recruitment of drummer John Hayward, pianist Tom Turner and, on a home-made bass, Dave Glover.

Trading principally in guitar-dominated airs from the portfolios of Duane Eddy, The Shadows and The Ventures, the new group began strutting their stuff at wedding receptions, birthday parties and like private functions – including three out-of-town recitals for inmates of Broadmoor mental hospital. Sometimes, they adhered to the 'somebody and the somebodies' dictate – which differentiated between token 'leader' and rank-and-file – as they did one spring Saturday when Chris Britton *and* the Redwoods accompanied the entrants in an all-day charity Twist contest.

John Hayward's successor, Johnny Walker's Chilbolton address was used when 'Established Beat Group Requires Singer. Smart Appearance Essential' appeared in the *Advertiser*'s 'wanted' section. Though a non-instrumentalist, Dave Smith, commandeered the central microphone for a while, The Redwoods favoured ultimately the simpler expedient of continuing without a replacement on the grounds that skulking in grey mediocrity behind a Cliff Richard-esque pretty boy was no longer as plausible as the group alone – with no specially designated front man – sharing lead vocals, and thus operating as a means of both vocal and instrumental expression.

That The Redwoods were becoming as synonymous with the TA Centre in their way as The Melody Makers was symptomatic of a sea-change in British pop in that the beat boom, spearheaded by this 'Merseymania' or whatever it was called, reduced to anachronisms all the old palais bands from which older members of these new guitar outfits may have sprung. Kicking off a TA Centre Saturday in squarely 'professional' manner, an elderly Melody Maker would kid himself that the rubbish to which his children listened would rise like scum to the surface before dissipating, so that the eternal verities of 'decent' music could surface once more.

Like King Canute, however, he'd be unable to hold back the tide as, in the teeth of adolescent complaints voiced in the *Advertiser* about 'mid-week boredom' since the Fiesta's closure – ostensibly, for extensive renovation – the Anton Arms, the Copper Kettle restaurant in the High Street, the Youth and Adult Centre next to the bus station, Tasker's Sports and Social Club and other premises began offering rehearsal facilities for groups and evenings of entertainment by the same in functions rooms that assumed a separate life from the main building. If an outfit had no place to play, it created one – and, now that the swing towards acephalous beat groups was complete, an increasing number of provincial venues were becoming teenage strongholds on off-peak nights as the Olympic torch of Merseybeat was carried to every nook and cranny of the British Isles.

It wasn't restricted by social class either. At Stowe public school in Buckinghamshire, it was OK by the with-it headmaster for four sixth formers to form The Trekkers in the Merseybeat image – while, east to another such establishment in Felixstowe, singing guitarist Pete Lucas graduated from a duo known as The Two Atoms to The Kombats, seduced as he was by the greater dynamic versatility of a group.

Conversely, Pete Mystery's old backing musicians had closed ranks as The Strangers Rhythm Group to re-enter the lists against such as The Druids, The Voyds, The Blackhearts, The Rumours, The Swinging Machine, The Rabble, The Daisies, The Tall Walkers, The Mundanes, The Teenbeats and, representing Tidworth, The Griefs; the majority of them disbanding as quickly as they formed.

Then there were The Classics 'With The Mersey Sound' – in Andover! You didn't have to look far for the main prototype at a time when The Beatles could have topped the charts with the National Anthem. Every other request from teenagers on the dance floor seemed to be for 'Twist And Shout' or, when some idiot's girlfriend wanted it, 'She Loves You', as The Redwoods dropped more and more of last year's instrumentals, and any number of other outfits from Aldershot to Warminster got someone with a sewing machine to approximate the Beatles' collarless stage suits, and grew out their 1950s cowlicks into sheepdog fringes that resembled spun dishmops whenever they shook their heads and went 'oooooo'.

There'd be an unsmiling lead guitarist who, in his own mind anyway, picked a black Rickenbacker through a Marshall amplifier, just like George Harrison. Some of them even went through a phase of putting on tortuous Scouse accents for onstage announcements – though, when billed as coming from Merseyside at a venue in Nuneaton, The Redwoods' decided it was safer to 'keep quiet all night', admitted John Haywood.

As a Liverpool reader might do so from the *Mersey Beat* entertainment guide, so his country cousin could scan venue information in the pages of the Torquay-based *South-West Scene* or more local sources where a flow-chart of recurring group names unfolded; hence the familiar-sounding rings to the likes of The Zombies – once the Nightriders – from Bath, Them down in Liphook, The Four Tunes in Andover itself, Exeter's Gary Kane and the Tornadoes, and Dave Dee and the Deemen in the faraway West Midlands.

Yet, despite these duplications, the overlapping repertoires and propensity of Beatle copyists, nearly every town and shire within these islands was now supposed to have a 'Beat' or a 'Sound'. In the West, The Severnbeats were purported brand-leaders of the Tewkesbury

Sound as Salisbury's Danny and the Detonators were of the 'Sarum Sound'.

As well as their hire-purchase debts, that Danny and Co. bothered to make known their availability for 'Dances, Socials, Cabarets, Wedding Parties' in the *Andover Advertiser* showed that they meant business. There was plenty of work for them and their sort in the beat clubs littering the south now that hard-nosed entrepreneurs were putting inbred dislike of teenage pop on hold, and moving in on the beat craze by overlooking mere pubs and youth clubs, and catering for hundreds rather than dozens of teenagers with money to waste in one go. Even a boarded-over swimming pool could be turned into an ersatz Cavern for the night, now that they'd smelt the money to be made from all these young groups happy just to have somewhere to make their noise for the many daft enough to pay to hear it.

The average turnover per week for a semi-professional beat musician in the provinces was a couple of quid. Of 45 pounds net takings at one of Ludgershall Memorial Hall's Thursday 'Rock and Twist' sessions, only nine were split between two groups. Typical too was The Redwoods cramming in two separate engagements – at Abbots Ann Memorial Hall and Whitchurch Boys Club – in the space of one evening.

Those boys certainly got around as a 'Teen Scene' feature on 13 March 1964 emphasised. By then, there'd been a change of personnel with Dave Glover being superseded by ex-Senator Pete Staples, persuaded to transfer to bass, choosing a £98 model (and paying his final hire-purchase instalment for it four years later). John Hayward still filled the drum stool, and was the four's premier spokesman with his bold 'We are intending to make a go of it or bust!' This statement of intent was bolstered by the reporter's remark that 'so ambitious are this group that, apart from having Tuesday and Thursday nights free, the rest of the time is taken up performing and practicing.' They'd come back from a second 'tour of the Midlands' with a demonstration tape that included 'All Right', an opus by Andover composer, John Porter.

The article made much too of 'ex-classical guitarist' Chris Britton on lead, without stressing his daytime occupation as a lithographic camera operator, converting photographs into the dots that readied them for newspaper use. His income had been supplemented by a recent 50 per cent profit on the sale of a second-hand Austin Seven. This was ploughed back into an old Wolseley, but after its back axle dropped off a week later, the tireless young mechanic started to build a car from scratch.

Britton's main concern, however, was the group – who were relaunched as Ten Feet Five at an Andover Grammar spring dance before a booking as the first pop group to play the Guild Hall on the grounds that they'd 'recently returned from a successful tour of the North with The Rolling Stones'. Who could contradict them when 'the North' was a fastness almost as unreachable and outlandish as Mars to anyone in Andover who was interested?

Those most interested professionally in Ten Feet Five's modest achievements, true or false, were parochial enterprises like Gaytime Promotions and Groups Incorporated. Most of them saw themselves as no more than bookers, and were inclined to sell the services of beat groups like tins of beans – with no money back if they tasted funny. Nevertheless, the Jaimen Syndicate were doing whatever willingness and energy would do to further the cause of The Just Men – self-proclaimed 'Top Group In The South' – and Ten Feet Five had melted into the managerial caress of Lance Barrett Agencies whose nominal head had told Teen Scene that 'Andover people have for years been going to Salisbury, Winchester and Southampton to see the top class groups, and I think it is about time we had top class groups.'

Like everyone else, Mr Barrett had realised that Brian Epstein's chart-topping manipulation of The Beatles was the tip of an iceberg that would make more fortunes than had ever been known in the history of recorded sound. On this understanding too, Roy Simons, a Bournemouth businessman, was to tear chapters from Epstein's book by putting together four pliant youths – including Bruce Turner – as Trendsetters Ltd to be exploited just like any other item of merchandise.

Yet Lance Barrett was unusual in that he was not deprecating about his knowledge and love of pop. Putting action over debate, he sank cash into bringing to Andover acts that, while not always 'top class', tended to be at least competent. Among the more dependable draws were Kent's Bern Elliott and the Fenmen, Cliff Bennett and the Rebel Rousers from Middlesex, The Marauders (who'd put Stoke-on-Trent on the pop map with a Top 50 entry in 1963), The Falling Leaves – 'Brumbeat' finalists in ITV's *Ready Steady Win* contest – and Dean Ford and the Gaylords, all the way from Glasgow. Some local celebrities saw to it that they were noticed nattering familiarly with the headliners if not opening the show for them; the tacit implication being that though the visitors had recording contracts, even hit records, our own lads were giving them sound reason for nervous backward glances.

Tape-recording *Pick Of The Pops* off the *Light Programme* every Sunday in order to figure out Top 20 items to include in the set, The Just Men, Trendsetters Ltd and Ten Feet Five, who all received actual money for playing, began to nurture the *idée fixe* that if they kept at it, they might break free of the Hampshire-Wiltshire orbit like Dave Dee and the Bostons before them. Engagements beyond Andover and its outlying villages were, however, rare indeed for those in lower divisions of local popularity, mutable in state and drawing personnel from the same bagful of faces in hangouts like the Criterion and the Anton Arms where the town's pop musicians congregated to small-talk, borrow equipment, compare notes, betray confidences and boast about imminent record deals, and a surefire certainty of opening for Johnny Kidd and the Pirates when they next came west.

Minus the rose-tinted spectacles, it could be depressing when you were one of an unexpectedly large number of shadowy human shapes clambering stiffly from an overloaded van outside a hall in Basingstoke. You hobbled from the neon of early evening streetlamps towards the venue's front steps. A janitor answers your banging but does not help lug the careworn equipment into the darkened auditorium with its draughty essence of disinfectant and echo of tobacco, food and alcohol intake from that afternoon's wedding reception.

Nevertheless, under the alibi of a stage act, the glory and stupidity of being in a group enabled a mousy youth to look otherworldly to the girls who clustered, tits bouncing, round the lip of the stage. Neither did he have to be a Charles Atlas to stoke up the first scattered screams that ever reverberated for him.

Either active or in formation were so many of them that *Teen Scene* would summarise 1964 with 'The year just ended will for teenagers be known naturally as the year of the groups. The Record Charts were inundated with them and so was Andover!' The column now contained two Top 10s: national and one compiled from discs sold in the High Street record shops. So it was that the previous March, Cilla Black's 'Anyone Who Had A Heart' was at the top generally while Andover's choice was 'Not Fade Away' by The Rolling Stones – whose debut long-player was popular enough to figure in this singles list a month later.

Seers of a similar musical vision to the Rolling Stones were countless UK beat groups who, attracted to the earthier sounds of the blues – or 'rhythm-and-blues' (R&B) as it became – ditched Beatle winsomeness for a gruff onstage taciturnity and looking, sounding and behaving like the belligerently unkempt Stones and later 'hairy monsters', detested by adults, like The Kinks, Yardbirds, Pretty Things, Downliners Sect and Them (Belfast not Liphook). Many contained weekend beatniks who, via complex inner debates, had decided that there was a certain primitive *épater le bourgeoisie* in the abandoned drive of a form so 'uncommercial', and, therefore, an antidote to the raw pleasure of the audibly grinning Beatles.

Fun for all the family, it wouldn't have seemed all that peculiar if John, George, Paul and Ringo had been soft-shoe shuffling next – and Christmas wouldn't be Christmas without the 'Fab Four' at Number One. Years later, Van Morrison of Them would avow that 'the R&B movement was actually an anti-establishment stance against the Beatles.' Their subdued four-song allocation in 1963's Royal Command Performance 'meant that they couldn't be any good' to younger musicians like David Cook, later 1970s pop star David Essex, but then drummer with a London R&B outfit called The Everons.

Consolidation rather than development was the watchword for combos like The Everons – and the likes of Rhythm And Blues Incorporated, Blues By Six, the Rhythm And Blues Group *ad nauseum*. Less prosaic in name were such as The Howling Wolves, The T-Bones, The Boll Weevils, The King Bees, The Dimples and, gawd help us, The Little Boy Blues. With the best of intentions, they'd try to get to grips with the blunt lyrics and stylised chord cycles of the Jimmy Reeds, Slim Harpos, John Lee Hookers and Howlin' Wolves from the juke joints and speakeasies of black America, but the outcome – especially vocal – was, more often than not, nothing like.

Any notion that there'd be a regular and faithful audience for R&B was taken seriously by few until Mick Jagger *et al*'s unforeseen scamper into the Top 30 in 1963. Sniffing the wind, Manfred Mann, The Animals, The Kinks, The Yardbirds and The Pretty Things were all ordained to appear on *Top Of The Pops* within a year by sticking to their erudite musical guns and not much compromising a gauche image. Grabbed by Fontana, a sub-division of the Philips label, The Pretty Things, for example, were projected as wilder, fouler and more curious than the Stones – kind of Terry-Thomas to their David Niven – and, during the autumn of 1964, they'd creep to the edge of the Top 10 with 'Don't Bring Me Down', a stop-start ditty riven with beatnik slang.

By association, even a couple of R&B's genuine US articles were to score Top 50 entries that year too, namely Howlin' Wolf and John Lee Hooker who, with a hypnotic blues-boogie undercurrent as common thread, had planted successful feet in rural and then urban camps on their native soil during respective migrations from the Deep South to Chicago and Detroit. Others like Muddy Waters, BB King, Little Walter and Sonny Boy Williamson also sold records by the ton in Uncle Sam's 'race' forum without figuring at all in the music trade periodical, *Billboard*'s pop *Hot 100* – and needed a potent financial incentive to be worshipped in person by a hitherto unrealised British audience.

Before that, a lot of their records could only be purchased at import prices from specialist shops, mostly in London, with a wide spectrum of vinyl merchandise from black America, whether the rural exorcisms of Lightnin' Hopkins, Robert Johnson or Louisiana Red; Chicago and New Orleans electric R&B or, via such as Chuck Berry and Bo Diddley, its rock'n'roll derivation.

Though there were no such sources in Andover, the town threw down R&B gauntlets with such as The Bunch ('Authentic Rhythm And Blues Group'), The Madhatters R&B Sect, formed in April 1964 by ex-Redwood Alan Grindley, The Smokestacks – and The Troggs who, according to their first mention in 'Teen Scene' on 29 May, held three hour rehearsals every Monday, Tuesday, Thursday and Friday in the upper room of the Copper Kettle.

A few weeks after this exposure, the Stones were at large in the West Country; most of their shows ending in riot within 15 minutes. They were poised for their first chart-topper in 'It's All Over Now' – and The Kinks' turn would come with a vengeance in August when 'You Really Got Me' kicked off a hat-trick of smashes that stuck to the same riff-based formula.

So enraptured was Reg Ball by The Kinks, that nothing would do but he had to organise a crowded car journey far east where the new R&B messiahs were appearing at a ballroom in Basildon, Essex. A squeak of feedback heralded the first number by an unhappy supporting turn, swamped in screams and chants for the headliners, swelling to a pitch where you drowned in noise. Somehow, the ear-stinging decibels climbed higher – as if they'd all sat on tin-tacks – when The Kinks, still outwardly enjoying their work, sauntered on.

The party from Andover tuned into the situation's epic vulgarity: the pulsating bass, the crashing drums, the ranted vocals and the most unsubtle guitar work as the group walked what seemed to be an artistic tightrope without a safety net. Admittedly, the audience was charged up by their hits, but, God, The Kinks were great! When they stumbled off after exacting their customary submission from the few there who hadn't wanted to like them, Reg Ball vanished into the night, lost in wonder and half-formed ambition.

A marginally feasible means of achieving this was through The Troggs. During a tea break when slapping down bricks on a housing estate to the west of Andover in early 1964, Ginger Mansfield had badgered Reg into learning bass for the group planned since '"The Senators" Require Lead Guitarist. Preferably With Own Equipment. All Applicants Considered' had appeared in the *Advertiser* the previous October. Before that, Ronnie Bullis had also left (or been sacked from) Bruce Turner's employ. He'd been chief advocate of the new venture; Mansfield joining him after some heart-searching calculation.

Ronnie's off-stage machinations were at least as crucial as his drumming. His silver-tongued guile was brought into play when approaching Stanley Haydn Phillips, portly and middle-aged founder of a shopfitting and building firm – and proprietor of the Copper Kettle. Another new piece in the jigsaw, rhythm guitarist Dave Wright, averred that 'If there had been no Stan Phillips, there would have been no Troggs' – for, before Mr Philips knew it, he was the yet untitled group's Brian Epstein – or, more specifically, its Lance Barrett – allowing it free use of one of his (Stan's) vans and a storey of the restaurant for loud rehearsals that distracted staff in the adjoining *Andover Advertiser* offices.

There was a time and a place for that kind of row. Even younger employees within earshot caught little that was comfortingly familiar to break up the monotony of work because 'All that Beatles stuff didn't sit right with The Troggs at all,' surmised Reg. 'Rhythm-and-blues was what we decided finally was what it was all about. What's more, why did other local groups go for candy-arsed guitar work from America and stick with that like it was gospel? We wanted it dirty, grungier, more aggressive – and, without devices that were developed later, we had to get that out of equipment that was available. You could get really weird noises from a bass, for instance, by bending its neck right in front of the amp.'

With such experiments audible halfway down the High Street, Dave Wright could have guessed where the group was when he arrived for his audition: 'I was an apprentice at a factory, and I'd only just learned to play the guitar, just the 12-bar blues. One day, somebody said, "Do you want to join a group?" So I went down to the Copper Kettle, and there's a ballroom upstairs, and the first thing I heard was Ronnie singing on a little stage. Reg was leaning against the piano, dark glasses on, with a big Burns bass. I knew him locally to say "Hiya, Reg", not as a personal friend, but I came up and asked how long he'd been playing bass. He said, "All day!"'

Over the next 30-odd years, this would be one of many oft-repeated quips by one who'd got by with a borrowed instrument until the nascent group's trip to London's Shaftesbury Avenue area to help him select a bass. 'That was what made me stick with it no matter what,' said Reg, 'because I had to pay for it on HP.'

En route, a vexing discussion about a suitable name was resolved by two hitch-hiking trainee teachers, picked up on the A30 through Camberley. On noticing the dilapidated state of their hosts' van, one suggested 'The Grotty Troggs'. In preference to Mansfield's 'The Croaks' – and minus the disobliging adjective – this diminutive of 'troglodyte' (meaning 'mythical cave dweller') was emblazoned on the poster outside when the group was unveiled at the Copper Kettle on Tuesday, 2 June 1964 in front of those who'd handed over the four shillings admission.

One of The Troggs' chief selling points was what the 'Teen Scene' reviewer described as the 'Chuck Berry-styled voice' of Dave Wright. Berry's musical celebrations of the pleasures available to US teenagers were prominent in The Troggs' nine-song repertoire that, said Reg, 'We played in reverse, frontwards, sideways, but we managed to do it for three hours.' Vocals were shared between all four on 'Maybelline' – a Berry item from 1955 that owed as much to C&W for all its springing from a blues environment – and, Reg Ball gave 'em 'No Particular Place To Go', that, high in that summer's Top 10, was the only current smash in the set, unless you counted the reissue of John Lee Hooker's ancient 'Dimples' on the edge of the Top 20, and Troggs' retreads of retreads from the Stones album like Bo Diddley's 'Mona', 'Walking The Dog' from Rufus Thomas and Slim Harpo's 'I'm A King Bee'. On their first LP, The Kinks had been the first Britons on vinyl with Harpo's 'Got Love If You Want It' – also appropriated by The Troggs (and still in the show in the 1990s) – as The Animals and Birmingham's Spencer Davis Group had been with 'Dimples'.

'Dimples' was another of Reg Ball's specialities. With concentration on every word lighting his face, he proved capable of taking on Hooker's gutbucket leering without affectation despite the burden that 'it is very difficult to sing and play bass at the same time – and I just about managed it – only just. Besides, I was so nervous that I wore dark glasses: I can't see them, they can't see me.'

A more marginal Ball donation to the proceedings would be one or other of the few self-composed pieces he'd finished by then. Songwriting used to be an eccentric diversion at most to nearly all working British groups until the demarcation line between artist and jobbing tunesmith was eroded for all time when the gift of a number by John Lennon and Paul McCartney had become like a licence to print banknotes. Every track on 1963's *With The Beatles* had been covered by another artist from 'Little Child' by a Billy Fonteyne to an overhaul of 'I Wanna Be Your Man' as a stabilising second single for The Rolling Stones.

That's as maybe, but if a group in the sticks attempted a home-made song, it often served as a background noise, an opportunity for dancers to chat with friends, get in a round of drinks or go to the toilet. This was especially true of R&B exponents when inaugural A-sides by such patron saints as the Stones, Animals, Kinks and Yardbirds were arrangements of non-originals. Members were more prone than not to laugh with affectionate scorn if, say, a bass guitarist chugged a coy introit to one of his own efforts. Where did it get you anyway? You could never beat the Yanks at that game anymore than you could at any other aspect of R&B. Did the group need more than the classics that got the customers on to the floor? If they did, could anyone in The Troggs come up with anything of the necessary standard?

Nevertheless, stirred in particular by The Kinks' continued run of hits from the pen of their own endlessly inventive Ray Davies, Reg had tinkered with fragments of melody and rhyme until the ghost of maybe an opening verse or a sketchy chorus smouldered into form. Initially, he was dependant upon basic structures that recurred throughout pop: the 12-bar blues and, later, 'the three-chord trick' as epitomised by Richard Berry-via-The Kingsmen's 'Louie Louie' (and featured by hundreds of beat groups including The Kinks) and 'Hang On Sloopy', 'the first three-chorded thing I heard,' believed Reg – that shifted a million in 1965 for The McCoys. 'I wrote about four for that line-up of The Troggs,' he'd remember. 'The first thing I did was a very easy blues tune entitled "You're Bad". Another was "That's What You Get Girl".' It was not unreasonable for Reg to hold in his heart the hope that, however derivative they were, the insertion of one or two of these in the performance might be considered by the other Troggs.

However, Wright's erudite record collection provided some material that didn't put them up against simultaneous versions by others – for, though the intention was to make 'Dimples', 'Route 66', 'My Babe' and all the rest of them *not* sound like any other group's arrangement, they were heard no more than a mariner hears the sea by most self-respecting R&B aficionados. Indeed, all but one of seven competitors had a go at 'Walkin' The Dog' when The Troggs took part in the *Hampshire Beat* Contest in Southsea's Savoy Ballroom with its grand prize of £70, a recording contract and a month's tour of Germany.

The Troggs had spiced up their 'Walkin' The Dog', apparently, with an introductory quote from the Bridal March (!), but there was only so much you could do to avoid lapsing into stylistic cliché of rote-learnt set-works. 'Dave used to get most of the albums: Slim Harpo, Muddy Waters and so on,' recalled Reg, 'but we discovered that The Stones, Kinks and other groups were beating us to it. So then we wondered if we could write our own R&B. Our manager reckoned we wouldn't get anywhere unless we did.'

As for stage dialogue, Stan Phillips agreed that it might be better if they dispensed with it altogether, bar 'Thanks very much' and 'Goodnight'. Their dialect didn't have the ear-catching extraneousness of either Scouse or the beefcake Welsh of Tom Jones, the proverbial 'pop singer who can really sing', who'd just broken through with 'It's Not Unusual'. Neither did The Troggs talk in tones sufficiently bland to not trigger sniggers from those Londoners who viewed 'Hampshire hogs' as ignorant, good-for-nothing oiks.

'Teen Scene' passed this off as 'giving value for money without wasting valuable time by speaking and cracking jokes' when reviewing The Troggs debut at Salisbury City Hall (supporting an Essex group, The Fairies) after they were compelled, upon pain of legal action from the council, to remove the posters they'd pasted up all over the city the previous night. This was mitigated vaguely when someone was spotted cavorting on *Top Of The Pops* in a T-shirt with the legend 'TROGGS' emblazoned on it by means comparable in mystery to those that brought a particular brand of footwear to St Kilda, the most remote Hebridean island, barely a year after its appearance in Victorian London.

Those viewers not in the know assumed that a 'trogg' was similar to a 'gonk', the soft toy embodiment of the Swinging Sixties, but the group bearing the name, if not too hot for Andover to hold yet, were no longer fermenting in Copper Kettle security, but had extended a tentacle into Basingstoke when second-billed to The Pretty Things in another one of these venues that had sprung up along with the Swinging London-type boutiques now operational in provincial town centres.

Another early out-of-town expedition was to the Bure club in Muddiford, further than John Lee Hooker's younger self would have ever imagined before he rolled up, guitar case in hand, to preside over John Mayall's Bluesbreakers and The Troggs. With infinitely more awe in the wizened Hooker's presence than that of Mayall – then 'excellent but little-known', according to *South-West Scene* – Ball, behind his sunshades, exercised an inadvertent disrespect towards one of the founding fathers of the British blues movement when 'all of a sudden, John Mayall came up round the side of the stage and asked to have a go on my bass. I told him to get lost, although I was to realise later that he could do it ten times better than me.'

The Troggs were nowhere as out of their depths when back hosting the Copper Kettle every Tuesday night – and, less regularly, Wednesdays and Saturdays too. It came to be known locally as 'The R&B Club' – and why not? While London boasted by far the highest accumulation of 'live' R&B outlets, an increasing number of provincial buildings were being transformed likewise by devotees beyond the pale of the capital. Off-the-cuff examples are the R&B Cellar in Swansea, Bluesville in a Sheffield pub, the Downbeat in Newcastle docklands, the Gamp in Edinburgh and, beneath the shadow of Birmingham Town Hall, Rhythm Unlimited where The Spencer Davis Group were resident as The Troggs were at the Copper Kettle.

Saying much about the clientele at its R&B Club was the infrequency of the violence that marred (or supplemented) pop evenings elsewhere in Andover where the music and character of the group were secondary to punch-ups and the pursuit of romance. Instead, the place was inclined to attract 'young adults', more certain than the TA Centre's 'youths' to accept graciously both The Troggs' apology in the *Advertiser* for the non-appearance of The Classics the previous week, and sixpence concession next time for anyone producing a ticket stub for that particular evening. Afterwards, indulgent parents might collect Copper Kettle music-lovers in Morris Minor 'woody' estate cars.

From further afield than the errant Classics came Portsmouth's J Crow Combo and, both from Southampton, The Double-O-Sevens and The Soul Agents – then fronted by a Rod Stewart yet to trouble mainstream pop – but more typical R&B Club fare were The Mundanes, Men Friday – 'the fab new group' with Mick Matthews, an organist who was to boast later of 'sitting in' with The Troggs sometimes – The Other Versions, and The Meddy-Evils ('It's A Sin Not

To Hear Them').

Only two months old, The Troggs had been running faster than nearly all of them. The wheels had been oiled by means such as a letter to 'Teen Scene' in October, purportedly from four female fans: 'Hearing so much about The Troggs in the last few months, we are still in the dark about this "Fab Group". We have been arguing for weeks about who is the leader of The Troggs, and how they started playing together.'

Doubtful strategies aside, The Troggs had triumphed in a Battle of the Bands in Oxford – winning the price of petrol back to Andover – before losing by just two points to The J Crow Combo in the Runner-Up finals of the beat tournament in Southsea, with 15 minutes that embraced what a contemporary music critic might term a 'rockaballad' in 'Tell Me' – one of the young Rolling Stones rare originals – and an instrumental, 'Green Onions' that, like The Downliners Sect, did without the reptilian organ at the core of the Booker T and the MGs' template.

The groups were judged by Lancastrian comedienne Dora Bryan who'd put a yuk-for-a-buck entitled 'All I Want For Christmas Is A Beatle' in 1963's Yuletide chart, but one better qualified to do so was *Pick Of The Pops* presenter Alan Freeman who pontificated that Ten Feet Five 'obviously have the right idea' when they dashed off 'Route 66', 'My Babe' and Buddy Holly's 'Think It Over' in June 1964 at Salisbury City Hall where 47 groups had endured seven months of eliminating rounds in Wiltshire's *Battle of the Beat*.

Meanwhile, Dave Wright's complexion poured sweat as his fellow Troggs drove him through a savage 'Mona' in a contest devoted only to R&B in Basingstoke. Yet they weren't so purist that Wright couldn't think about applying on the group's behalf for compere Hughie Green's attention in an audition for his *Opportunity Knocks* search for talent on ITV – 'and they might have been in the running for the *Ready Steady Win* contest,' sympathised 'Teen Scene', 'had they been able to make a demonstration disc.'

Taking this to heart, the fellows pulled cash from their own pockets for the earliest extant musical archive of The Troggs. When few *bona fide* studios outside London were more than customised garages, sheds and living rooms, an Aladdin's cave of tape recorders, editing blocks and jack-to-jack leads down in Southampton was the location for recording two of Reg's creations plus 'You Really Got Me' and the Stones' latest hit, '(I Can't Get No) Satisfaction', for a purpose that was then non-specific – though Dave, the most willing to picket on the group's behalf, started ringing London numbers he'd noted from the classified section of *Melody Maker*.

If you didn't have the clout to enchant an agency, publisher or record label to send even one of its underlings west of London to hear you in your natural habitat, immortalising yourself on tape or acetate seemed the only way forward. Nonetheless, through dogged pursuit, The Just Men had landed supports to The Yardbirds, Moody Blues, Pretty Things and Nashville Teens, and dates in their own right over the hills in Bognor Regis, Birmingham and Cheltenham.

They, The Troggs, Ten Feet Five and, when they deigned to appear in Andover nowadays, Trendsetters Ltd were on terms of fluctuating equality as elder statesman of local pop. Yet being enormous in Andover was no longer enormous enough. Sodden with bitter fulminations in the Anton Arms, none of them would ever concede that groups that could take chart strikes for granted were any better than they.

What else could they do? So inward-looking were group scenes in the provinces that there seemed to be few realistic halfway points between obscurity and the Big Time – and a policy of territorial defence was epitomised by a closed shop of venues in England's westward regions where, visitors of hit parade eminence notwithstanding, work tended to be given only to acts from the area such as The Betterdays, a quintet who were to Plymouth's Guildhall what Ten Feet Five were to the TA Centre. Why bring Ten Feet Five over when our own lads can do the job just as well for a fraction of the cost?

The combination of a demo tape and grassroots petitioning had forced a Fontana recording manager to at least listen to The Betterdays. Moreover, a power at the same company had alighted likewise on Ten Feet Five. The Troggs drew up level when two London publishers each fell for Dave Wright's spiel, and wanted to meet them. One of them, however, was merely after a marginally proficient group to record Jimmy Reed's 'Bright Lights Big City', but the other, a Pat Sherlock, was so enthused by The Troggs' piledriving 'You Really Got Me' that, there and then, he rang The Kinks' manager with the information that 'I've got a group here who do your boys' number better than your boys do.'

At the other end of the telephone was Larry Page who had left the Coventry ballroom on beginning a more lucrative career by procuring recording contracts for Johnny B Great, The Orchids and Shel Naylor – all local talent – before The Kinks became his main focus to the extent that he was to use his own Larry Page Orchestra for his self-explanatory *Kinky Music* instrumental album, just as George Martin had done the year before for his studio charges on 1964's *Off The Beatles Track*.

Further syndication on The Kinks' behalf would include a version of Ray Davies' 'I Go To Sleep' by Cher who, with her other half Sonny, came to Britain that same year to promote their 'I Got You Babe' chartbuster; a visit that was arranged by Page – as was that of Baltimore folk singer Bob Lind after his big moment with 'Elusive Butterfly'.

The Kinks and his dealings with these US attractions had enabled Larry to maintain an exclusive property – christened 'The Book' (because it had Pages in it) – in Surrey's wooded stockbroker belt from where he commuted to London in a Daimler. He was also in the process of establishing a new production company-*cum*-record label with Dick James, another former pop singer of the 1950s, but now full steam ahead for his first million as the Beatles publisher. Nonetheless, it was to be another two years before 'Page One' was able to declare its independence of a lease deal with Fontana.

All the same, Larry could permit himself to be blasé, even condescending, about Pat Sherlock's excited summons to hear this Troggs tape. Settling his cinemascope spectacles on his nose and leaning back cosily in his chair, he was not extravagant with praise. They weren't obvious no-hopers, he said, definitely more promising than some of the other groups who'd supplicated him recently. The sub-text of this verdict was that Page didn't want to alienate the increasingly more volcanic Kinks by taking on any other group just then, least of all one that he felt, with some justification, could be potential rivals. 'It's as clear as day now what Larry was thinking,' sighed Reg. 'He thought we might present a threat to The Kinks, who'd just broken through, and he wanted them to have a clear run – which meant that he wasn't going to take on anything that sounded like them.'

Thus the Troggs re-entered the trivial round of local bookings, always, it seemed, one week ahead of Ten Feet Five and one week after The Just Men – or else in revenue-draining clashes like, say, engagements in Newbury – Ten Feet Five at the Corn Exchange, The Troggs at the Plaza – on the same night. They tussled too over support spots whenever any of Lance Barrett's 'top class groups' came within spitting distance. While The Troggs were on hand when Lance brought Liverpool's Tommy Quickly and the Riot Squad to the TA Centre in

45

April 1965, Ten Feet Five snared the task a month later of warming up for the trendier Birds – on the wings of their solitary week in the Top 50 – and, also from Greater London, Les Fleurs De Lys.

Through their manager too, Ten Feet Five checkmated The Troggs again via supports to Wayne Fontana, Dave Berry and Brian Poole in Swindon – though Newbury's own Reverbs did the job when The Who played the Plaza. However disappointing this was, Ten Feet Five were more than compensated by Lance Barrett's crowing congratulations in the *Advertiser* on Fontana's release of their single – the first by an all-Andover outfit – of John Porter's 'Baby's Back In Town' coupled with the faster 'Send Me No Loving' from Claydon and King, another local songwriting team. The following week, readers were drawn by a footprint trademark to the address – down Suffolk Road near St Ann's Hall – and annual membership subscription of the Ten Feet Five fan club.

There was talk too of their lip-synching 'Baby's Back In Town' on ITV's *Thank Your Lucky Stars*, and the group behaved as if this was still a possibility when honoured with a civic reception at the Mayor's parlour on 11 June 1965. His Worship's good lady, Mrs Horne, went as far as fishing in her purse for two half-crowns (25p) to join the fan club after Ten Feet Five presented her with flowers – while a speech from Councillor Horne himself concluded with 'Pop music is not everyone's cup of tea, but I think it has a place in the community, and I wish you every success.'

For what it signified rather than its sound, 'Baby's Back In Town' was a yardstick of achievement in Andover. Nevertheless, cracks appeared within a month. That it didn't reach even the local Top 10 was the final straw for Johnny Walker after Tony Taylor from The Daisies became first his deputy and then his successor. Rallying, the group abbreviated its name, hence the poster reading 'Dance To *The Feet* At St Luke's, Overton on 2 September' – and muddling along with temporary personnel because, chuckled Lance Barrett, 'I don't expect the replacements to be from Andover.'

While believing in his boys as a good manager should, Lance was deluding himself that capable semi-professionals of their ilk couldn't be found in virtually any other area of the country. Few could gripe about any falling off in onstage quality, but there were signs that, unless The Feet pulled another stroke, they'd be overtaken as Andover's boss beat merchants by fresher sensations like Jon Bates, a Secondary Modern contemporary of Pete Staples, who'd quit Men Friday on sniffing fame with the issue in August of his solo 45, 'Where

Were You Last Night', B-sided by Claydon and King's 'If Nothing Goes Wrong'.

Further exemplifying the passing of the old order was Howard Mansfield and, surprisingly, Dave Wright's resignations from The Troggs; upsets worth no more than a snippet in a increasingly less frequent 'Teen Scene' column, now more interested in the Grammar's *Youth Activity Day* or the archaeological dig at Walworth Industrial Estate than the trials and tribulations of the town's key pop personalities.

These paled anyway besides the summer's big showbusiness news of camouflage nets sparkling with dew over Centurion tanks guarding The Beatles as they mimed 'I Need You' up on Salisbury Plain for a sequence in their second movie, *Help!*. Closer to home was the broadcasting of an edition of Southern TV's *Pop The Question* quiz from the TA Centre with a celebrity panel that included Jonathan King, a Cambridge undergraduate with pop star aspirations, who'd just scored in the Top 10 with wordy 'Everyone's Gone To The Moon.'

During the subsequent autumn, Andover at large forgot the existence of Ten Feet Five and The Troggs until a hybrid of the two materialised – with both Stan Philips and Lance Barrett taking care of business. This Hampshire precursor of a 'supergroup' contained Chris Britton, Pete Staples, Ronnie Bullis – and Reg Ball, who had been coaxed centre-stage on the understanding that 'Pete had better command of the bass then...though I would have been as good in about a year's time. Rhythm guitar seemed to get in the way. Ronnie was very laid-back, and it consolidated our sound with Chris doing simultaneous rhythm and lead.'

If a timid songbird at first, Reg proved equal to the task, taking on Slim Harpo *et al* without losing any of the overriding fervour. That TA Centre onlookers noticed this too afforded him quiet pride, and drew from him an underlying humour and an ability to slip comfortably from suppressed lust through lazy insinuation to intimate anguish, sometimes mingling ecstasy and gloom in the same line.

By European *bel canto* standards, Ball's nasal baritone was devoid of vowel purity, plummy eloquence or nicety of intonation. Instead, you got both slurred diction and stentorian vehemence as he strained his two middle octaves through a muffled public address system. In context, it was not unattractive, even gruffly charming. It was also the ace up the sleeves of Mick Jagger and The Animals' Eric Burdon who likewise reinforced an idiosyncratic appeal by warping a limited range and quirky delivery to their own devices. Other personable vocalists in this oligarchy included wobbly Ray Davies, frail Phil May of the Pretty Things, laconic Dave Berry and mesmerically ugly Bob Dylan.

Unburdened by a bass hanging round his neck, Reg broke sweat, never sacrificing impassioned content for stilted expertise, and delivered the show when, from scanty run-throughs and simple structures that required little instruction, stylistic outlines dissolved between the two factions within the group. While the more clean-cut Ten Feet Five had stopped trying to catch that chartbusting Beatle lightning, and had cottoned on to the earthier sounds of R&B of late, Ronnie and Reg found Chris a very quiet guitarist. Moreover, he could be a little precious about arrangement as demonstrated during the routining of 'With A Girl Like You', a newly-concocted Ball original. 'Chris came up with call-and-response vocal harmonies that were interesting,' allowed Reg, 'but they took too much away from the song.'

Such aberrant smooth edges were still being roughed up when the quartet chanced its arm – as The Troggs – at the Moore Hall on Boxing Day Monday with seven songs from Reg, and the rest sung by either Pete, Ronnie or Chris while he tapped a tambourine. Just as far too many would profess to have been at Woodstock or to have seen The Sex Pistols' early fiascos, so there would be in microcosm a profound lack of retrospective honesty about this first manifestation of the classic Troggs line-up.

Hundreds more than can have actually been there were to conjure affectionate memories of that wild evening at the Moore Hall when the prickly heat grew by the minute as The Troggs earned 15 quid with a sweaty intensity rarely experienced on an Andover stage before. Seizing songs by the scruff of the neck and wringing the life out of them, the new combination was a howling success – but it seemed fanciful for them to look very far into the future when there were so many others battling likewise for chart placings, record contracts, even mere encores. Yet with the mutating of 1965 into 1966, the slow pageant of sunrise was soon to begin.

Chapter 3
'The Greatest Group Since The Beatles'

'Important people suddenly realised that pop groups were
not a silly game, but big business.'
Reg Presley

In The Troggs' neck of the woods, Newbury, Swindon, Basingstoke
and Aldershot were where-it's-at as far as working outfits within
hailing distance of the charts were concerned these days. None of
them would bother with below-the-salt Andover for less than a king's
ransom, which was why Newbury Plaza had had The Who; Aldershot
ABC was about to get a package tour headed by Herman's Hermits –
and the re-opened Fiesta put up with Gogs and the Reefers (no, I'd
never heard of them either) on 6 May 1966.

By then, the town was under the sway of what the *Advertiser* called
'Our "Mod" Mayoress', *i.e.* his newly-elected Worship's daughter
instead of his disinclined wife. On the basis of appearance *per se*,
Mods wouldn't necessarily be turned away from the parish dance.
They'd even earn praise from the vicar for their smart turnout. You
could be a bank clerk and, long hair or mini-skirt aside, look the part
without inviting the sack while boys could be only half-a-step behind
Swinging London, with gear from Bradley's in the High Street, whose
'Teen Appeal' advertisement in mid-1964 had pictured a young man
with a velvet-collared 'Teener' suit 'for those who are completely
"with it"'.

These days, however, there was a male Mod conformity hinging approximately on Cuban-heeled boots with elastic gussets, hipster flares in Billy Bunter check, a corduroy jacket with narrow lapels and faint faecal odour, and ties ranging from knitted plain to op-art slim-jim to eye-torturing kipper. You could also cultivate the slouch, the Brooding Intensity, the lips pooched out like Mick Jagger's.

Lambrettas with a dozen mirrors each would phut occasionally in Parka-ed cavalcades up the A30 to get a piece of the action in one of the bigger towns – as would the greasier mechanical steeds of Andover's Rockers in their less mutable gang costumery of real or imitation leather windsheeters, blue jeans, motorbike boots and T-shirts. Their oiled duck-tailed coiffeur was in direct line of descent from that of the Teddy Boys, and so was their taste in music.

Yet enmity between Rockers and Mods had never been as virulent in Andover as newspapers made out it was at set-piece clashes in holiday resorts during bank holidays, *circa* 1964. With army 'squaddies' more the common foe than each other, differences between the sects usually went no further than congregating at opposite ends of a cafe. Both extremes were represented in the Troggs in leather boy Ronnie Bullis and Reg Ball, the local Mod fashion leader, thanks to visits to his London in-laws via Carnaby Street.

Chris Britton's shaggy bohemianism and Pete Staples' non-commitment to any specific sartorial tribe meant they were a motley crew visually but this hadn't affected the widening of The Troggs' work spectrum. During a month dotted with local engagements, there were now side-trips to maybe the Agincourt in Camberley or an atmospheric evening at the end of Southampton pier with Dave Dee, Dozy, Beaky, Mick and Tich – the former Dave Dee and the Bostons – still slogging their way to stardom after their third single, 'You Make It Move', had inched into the Top 20 at the beginning of 1966.

Whereas the customers tended to dance to Dave Dee's mob – despite an element of stylised clowning – they were spellbound into immobility by the rough-and-ready Troggs. Chris's guitar was now brutally loud, while Reg leapt into an onslaught of caperings, bucking and shimmying like a composite of every rock'n'roller he'd ever admired, from the first apocalyptic seconds of the opening number until the thunderous final coda. Then came a long moment of thunderstruck hush as the musicians met an unnerving stare from what looked like a gigantic photograph, silent and unresponsive, until a spatter of clapping crescendoed to a whistling, cheering, stamping tumult.

The Troggs were a hard act to follow now, in spite – or because – of their carrying on as if they couldn't care less about the audience, and were just having fun up there among themselves, seemingly unaware of the more-than-passive interest of the girls near the front. Other combos were copying their repertoire and off-hand stagecraft, and had envied the multitude of fans that had arrived ridiculously early for The Troggs' return to the Moore Hall on Saturday, 26 March. It was becoming clear that some sort of crunch was coming, and that The Troggs – like other outfits in the first division of local popularity – would either be overtaken by younger heroes or else they'd fly the nest, leaving long-time partisans to grouse about how the group had betrayed them by defecting to London.

How did you get up to that next level? Where did you go if you dared to remove yourselves from the treadmill of cyclical engagements on the old, old circuit? True enough, the group was now working the bigger provincial ballrooms which provided a link from Fiesta-type engagements to small-fry billing on round-Britain 'scream circuit' package tours, but, even as far east as the Agincourt, no London big shot was ever likely to check out The Troggs.

All signposts pointed the same way – back to Larry Page. He had kept the Troggs on ice, but was no longer as indifferent towards them as they may have perceived him to be, even after the structural tampering. The Kinks had slipped from his grasp amid a blizzard of high court writs, but, with his mettle hardened by their perfidy, he remained game enough to try any viable means of climbing back on his perch as one of about half-a-dozen pop svengalis in Britain that really counted for anything.

Like everyone else, he'd made a few blunders while learning his craft, but he was respected universally as a shrewd administrator with hard-won knowledge of the sly quagmires and downright thuggery of the music industry, not to mention the tenacity and cautious confidence to strike as bellicose a stance in negotiation as the best of them. He'd proved no slouch either when he chose to get involved in the creative activities of his charges. Like Andrew Loog Oldham, the Stones' flamboyant man-of-affairs, he presumed, for instance, to produce records and be more than an *eminence grise* behind publicity and further merchandising ballyhoo. If he'd graduated from the old school of British showbusiness management, he was not inclined to work according to the lodged conventions of his kind.

Convinced of something incredible taking place in Andover, Larry understood what it actually was better than his 1970s counterpart would be when looking for a New Sex Pistols. One of his reservations, however, was, after The Kinks had exploded in his face, 'I was determined not to manage another group unless I could get 100 percent co-operation. The only one I could see me having trouble with was Chris – he is the deep thinker in the group – so I called him into the office and told him so, and we straightened things out.'

Because of past disappointments, Britton – and, to a lesser degree, Staples – had been bemused by Bullis and Ball's eager championship of Page, but 'the first time I saw Larry, he wasn't at all like I expected. Coming from the country as I did, I had the traditional image on my mind, and expected a bloke of about 60 with a cigar in his mouth. He was more with-it than I expected him to be. The thing that impressed me most was that he sat and listened through the audition and then just said: "This is it. We'll go into the studio and record it".'

'It' was 'Lost Girl', a Ball composition in a tidier state of completion than 'With A Girl Like You'. To Larry, 'Lost Girl' was not an unmistakable smash hit, but was still worthy of him persuading a record company to cast it adrift on the vinyl oceans after The Troggs puffed apprehensive cigarettes, tuned up and acquitted themselves well enough for first-timers.

CBS, a US label probing the European market gingerly, knew Page as a supplier of sturdy commodities, and issued 'Lost Girl' in February 1966 as a one-shot A-side, just after Larry had drawn up a provisional five-year contract with The Troggs. In one crucial clause, the Page organisation was awarded 20 percent commission (twice the amount received from The Kinks) with an additional five percent to be split between Lance Barrett and Stan Phillips – for, as with his previous clients The Kinks, Page had been obliged to lumber himself with two incumbent and comparatively small-time managers. There was as much similarity between their operation and his as there was between low-fat margarine and dairy butter.

It was early days, but there was nothing much to indicate that Larry had struck lucky with The Troggs. Yet, now that they were 'CBS Recording Artists', embargos by local agencies were relaxed, and they were becoming bigger than Gogs and the Reefers, despite 'Lost Girl' missing the Top 50 after a solitary airing crackled from Radio Luxembourg so late at night that even its writer couldn't keep awake to hear it.

Sleep was a precious commodity when you were burning the candle at both ends with a double life as a bricklayer and singer with a hitless group in the midst of a staggered procession of one-nighters. A telephone call would have Reg and the others shoulder-to-shoulder in a van within an hour, driving, driving, driving to another strange backwater. 'We used to set off for a gig with a telephone number and a contact scrawled on a scrap of paper,' groaned Chris. 'When we got to the town, we would look out for posters advertising the gig to see what time and where we were on.'

Somehow, they found time to record an intended follow-up to deleted 'Lost Girl' in 'From Home', another RM Ball opus, despite being informed by post that CBS was not going to take up its option on a second 45. Yet Larry didn't mind. In fact, he'd actively encouraged the company to erase the group from its books – because prospects were looking rosier with the then more prestigious Fontana whose parent company, Philips, was harrying that year's Top 20s with one funereal-paced *lied* after another from The Walker Brothers, three unrelated Californians who had become leading pin-ups in schoolgirls' periodicals, and mainstays of ITV's epoch-making *Ready Steady Go!* pop magazine.

Fontana itself had had the tardy foresight to sign The Merseybeats in 1963, and were milking the group still three years later via a Top 5 strike with 'Sorrow' (a revamp of a McCoys B-side) by a connected entity, The Merseys. Wayne Fontana and his Mindbenders, Millie, The Pretty Things, The Spencer Davis Group and Dave Dee, Dozy, Beaky, Mick and Tich were further acquisitions. Yet, for every chartbuster, there were a dozen Ten Feet Fives. It was like a lottery: all these bloody bands are the same; let's snap up as many as we can, see which racket catches on and cash in quick. None of them last long anyway so why waste resources endeavouring to prove otherwise.

Larry Page's new clients were as likely to do the trick as anyone else, but, contemplating the group's immediate future, it was thought best not to chance another Reg Ball song. One tried-and-tested strategy to lift a new act off the runway was to get its cover of a US hit into the shops before the original. On a recent expedition to North America, Page had come upon 'Did You Ever Have To Make Up Your Mind' by New York's Lovin' Spoonful, which was about to peak at Number Two in the *Hot 100*.

Back in London, Dick James was one who thought 'Did You Ever Have To Make Up Your Mind' had more going for it than a second possibility from Larry – a piece that walked a tightrope between inspiration and rubbish. First recorded as a novelty by US comedian Jerry Branigan, 'Wild Thing' had dripped from the pen of James Voight, alias 'Chip Taylor', brother of Hollywood actor Jon Voight, and one of a supplicatory influx of North Americans who, after The

Beatles' conquest of the continent in 1964, had anticipated correctly further demand for Limey pop.

Chip had staked his most lucrative claims in the musical diggings in the UK itself with 1965's 'On My Word' for Cliff Richard and, most spectacularly thus far, by co-writing the Hollies' 'I Can't Let Go', almost a Number One the following spring, aided by a chugging backing track and, the asinine words notwithstanding, vocal harmonies that were every bit as breathtaking as any of the Beach Boys choral intricacies. Such achievements obscured memories of other Taylor ditties that had fallen on stony ground such as 'Don't Do It Baby' by Linda Laine and the Sinners and Chip Fisher's quite dreadful 'An Ordinary Guy', which swiped at multi-purpose 'protest' songs like Barry McGuire's 'Eve Of Destruction' – and 'It's Good News Week', written by Jonathan King for Hedgehoppers Anonymous, an outfit from an RAF aerodrome in Bedfordshire.

These one-hit-wonders had already made a recording of 'Wild Thing' in a vaguely Hollies-like fashion after much hard listening to a version by Jordan Christopher and his Wild Ones, itself an edited arrangement of the lengthy Branigan reading, and a regional chart strike in the States – particularly around the participants' native New York where they'd been omnipresent in Arthur's, a discotheque part-owned by Sybilla, Richard Burton's ex- and Christopher's present wife.

Of all the treatments of 'Wild Thing', The Troggs were most impressed by Chip Taylor's demo with its whistled interlude – though at first Reg wasn't entirely at ease with the elementally simplistic and rather dated lyrics that were as devotional in their sensual way as a hymn. The story goes that it was he who broke the news to Page about the final choice: 'I rang Larry to tell him the number was great. He asked how we got on with the vocal harmonies. Harmonies? There's no harmonies on "Wild Thing".'

Indeed, there weren't – apart from the unison chorus. Brenda Ball – another who preferred The Lovin' Spoonful number – was to weep when she heard her husband's monotonous snarls and mutterings over the stop-start three-chord thrash. It wasn't all smiles domestically, either, because Reg's Trogging was frequently to the detriment of an otherwise regular £19 a week as a bricklayer. Not only was he absenting himself and turning down jobs too frequently, but, delivered from the treadmill of the road as the graveyard hours chimed, he'd grab what rest he could before struggling through daily travail with budgerigar eyes, barely able to think straight.

In turn, Brenda was a handy peg on which to hang his frustrations when he slammed in from work, bolted down a meal, bathed and washed his hair, and waited for the overloaded van, an hour late, to transport him and the others to some dancehall two counties away. It was hard enough already to find the rent for their cramped flat now that Brenda had given up her job as a secretary in the later months of a pregnancy that had produced a daughter, Karen, and subsequent months of disturbed nights and the close stench of soiled nappies.

Newly-wed Ronnie's situation was similar, and gazing at him tunnelling into egg-and-chips across a wayside cafe's formica table with the jukebox playing the Stones' most recent 45, 'Nineteenth Nervous Breakdown', Reg wondered whether 24 wasn't a suitable age for both of them to settle down like Ginger and Dave had done. Such a decision, however, could be suspended until 'Wild Thing' had run its course.

The Troggs had recorded it one cold February morning at London's Olympic Studios at the tail-end of a Larry Page Orchestra session for its second album, *Executive Suite*: an easy-listening *mélange* that was to include its 'Waltzing To Jazz' spin-off single and recent hits like 'Everyone's Gone To The Moon' and The Beatles-via-The Overlanders' 'Michelle'.

Precisely how long they'd have was uncertain as, huddled in the van outside, The Troggs had sunk into a languid daze induced by the fixity of gazing at the complex's door until the Orchestra began filing out. With necessary speed, the amplifiers and instruments were lugged in and assembled, and 'Wild Thing' punched out – with an ocarina solo replacing Chip Taylor's whistling. This was blown by Colin Frechter, one of Larry's musical associates, for Reg to duplicate parrot-fashion on stage where it would be drowned in any case beneath the sound of screaming fans if all went to plan.

The rest of the seven pounds-worth of studio time was filled with a 'With A Girl Like You' that was nearly up to the fighting weight of 'Wild Thing' but, with his producer's hat on, Page shook his head: 'We wouldn't have got the plugs. Great song as it was, there was no immediate impact in the introduction: nothing to make you sit up and take interest.'

'From Home' might have been solid enough to rate as an A-side too had it not been coupled with stunning 'Wild Thing'. Yet 'I don't know – what do you think?' was the attitude within the industry that pervaded its release on 22 April 1966 and, a few days later, the first published photograph of the misspelt 'Trogs' in the national pop press. It loomed above a paragraph about their 'weird sounds and crazy musical ideas' in *Record Mirror*'s 'Names And Faces' newcomers section that also brought to the populace a Petula Clark lookalike, Episode Six – with future members of Deep Purple within lens range – and a Kim Davis.

For another week, nothing happened. Glancing over his shoulder for the nosier members of staff, Chris made illicit use of the dark-room telephone during lunch hours to contact Larry for progress reports. Cautiously, no Trogg had yet burnt the boats of his humdrum day job. 'There wasn't much we could do apart from bother Larry,' said Reg, 'and even with our jobs, we kept ringing him every few hours to see if we had any TV shows, radio dates or bookings coming up.'

While it forgot to print the group's name, a gushing *NME* review of 'Wild Thing' correlated with a rise in booking fees to two hundred pounds, and a sprinkling of spins on the crowded wavelengths of the pirate radio stations burst a dam on a river of exposure that floated the Troggs to Number 44 in *Melody Maker*'s 'Pop 50'. Avid surveyors of the hit parade, the chaps were a-twitter with excitement when 'Wild Thing' also entered the *New Musical Express* chart at 27.

From a site opposite the Balls' flat, it blasted from a pocket-transistor when Reg was finishing off a gable. On another scaffold, a workmate painting the eaves shouted 'Have you heard this "Wild Thing"? If it isn't Number One next week, I'll eat my brush!' Chasing the fade, the disc-jockey announced its climb to Number 11. As if acting out a dream, an enraged Reg hurled down his trowel, clambered down the ladder and left his tools to be shared out among the rest of the lads, just starting a tea break.

After telling Brenda of this drastic step, he ran to the nearby telephone box to call his manager. With a note of urgency in his voice too, Page directed Ball to round up the other three and drive post-haste to London so that together they could try to solve what was a good problem to have.

Breaking the journey only to pick bluebells for Larry's secretary, the four returned a few hours later with a weekly wage of £25 as fully professional musicians, and much to think about. As he'd tried to do with The Kinks, Page's first task was to make The Troggs altogether smoother pop 'entertainers' without diluting their raw musical power. At the meeting, he'd re-emphasised the importance of making themselves pleasant to media folk; playing to a fixed programme, and back-projection rather than focusing on the front rows.

While offering promoters more in the way of 'professional'

behaviour, the group weren't to tolerate, say, being paid in loose
change anymore or frowzy dressing rooms like the one Ronnie had just
mentioned 'where there wasn't even a toilet door.' Artistes of The
Troggs' calibre were above that sort of treatment now. 'In fact, there
are four places they've appeared at during the last month where
they'll never play again,' Larry would be informing one agent,
'because the conditions were so bad.'

He intended also to compel The Troggs to wear a stage uniform. For
the first important TV plug of 'Wild Thing' – on *Thank Your Lucky
Stars* – it was suits – black jackets, white trousers *à la* Dave Clark
Five – and not too way-out accessories other than slightly oversized
shirt collars. This, however, was a holding operation while Larry
concluded a deal with Carnaby Street's Take Six boutique for the
striped suits – 'We felt as if we were dressed in pyjamas,' moaned Reg
– that would define the public image of the group for the rest of the
decade.

More enduring than this – as well as the expected years subtracted
from certain Troggs' ages by publicist Keith Altham, and the bouffant
Mod haircuts that all members had had sculpted on their scalps – were
the new surnames foisted on Ronnie and Reg. Both Page and Altham
have claimed responsibility for suggesting that neither 'Ball' nor
'Bullis' had the same rings to them as, say, 'Jagger', 'Starr' or even
'Britton', and coming up with 'Bond' (after Ian Fleming's immortal
007) for Ronnie, and giving Reg an affiliation with the most famous
pop star of all time.

Anyone with the unmitigated audacity to let himself be renamed
'Presley' deserved attention – and the organisation needed to attract
as much as it could to give 'Wild Thing' the best possible chance. A
harder nut to crack than *Thank You Lucky Stars* was the more
discerning – and now completely 'live' – *Ready Steady Go!* that the
previous year had cancelled Twinkle's slot to promote her 'Terry'
death-disc, not so much for its morbid content as its non-conformity
to the Mod specifications of the programme. 'Their production team
had initially regarded "Wild Thing" as a joke,' sneered Larry, 'but
after I ran into its producer down Bond Street, and pitched it to him,
Saturday Club was the first to accept the record, and with this and the
pirates we were away with the public. *RSG* came back on the phone
and said: "That 'Wild Thing' certainly grows on you."' Even so, in
case they weren't capable of reproducing it in person, its makers had
to audition in front of an abashed audience of two in a corridor as the
usual Wembley studio wasn't available.

Nevertheless, further wounding of their dignity when handed chihuahuas ('wild things': get it?) to stroke on ITV's *Scene At 6.30* – just like Elvis had been made to holler to a bored hound dog on US television ten years earlier – was flattery of a kind in that they were at least considered to be in the same league as established hitmakers such as Manfred Mann, Tom Jones, Sandie Shaw and others whose paths The Troggs were crossing in backstage corridors and dressing rooms that had mirrors bordered by light-bulbs.

While they could now realise a conceit in referring to older luminaries by familiar forenames, the men-of-the-moment soon found themselves frequenting metropolitan clubs where pop conquistadors could hold court with only their equals contradicting them. The Bag O' Nails, the Speakeasy, the Pickwick and the Cromwellian and maybe four other hangouts were attractive for strict membership controls; no photographers admitted; tariffs too high for the Average Joe; a clientele up too late to pester anyone for autographs, and the grooviest sounds in deafening disco areas either as black as pitch or flickering with visual projections that were already being described as 'psychedelic'.

'I'd never been in these so-called swinging, with-it clubs before,' confessed Reg Ball-Presley. 'Now I've been to see what they're all about. Frankly, I don't see what most of the customers find worthwhile. They're just dance and drink places yet they cost pounds! I don't see why I should have to pay for a lot of fancy lighting. Well, I don't mind paying a bit extra – but not that much!'

That was the price of admission to the pop elite with its informal sense of solidarity that dissolved competitiveness into much the same camaraderie in its way that there was back in the jive-hives of Andover. 'See you at the top, fellows,' grinned John Maus of the Walker Brothers at a *Ready Steady Go!* rehearsal, just as The Just Men (now 'the Top *Semi-Pro* Group In The South') shelled out for a boxed salute to the Troggs in one July edition of the *Advertiser*. Then a cover of 'Wild Thing' by a resident vocalist (who imagined that holding your nose was all you had to do to sing like Reg Presley) on *Workers' Playtime*, Wednesday's lunchtime show on the BBC Light Programme, had set the seal on the real thing sweeping in at Number 3 in a Top 10 where it nestled amongst 'Sorrow', Roy C's 'Shotgun Wedding' and a most mixed stylistic bag in the latest from Manfred Mann, The Beach Boys, Bob Dylan, Dusty Springfield. The Lovin' Spoonful, Frank Sinatra, Dave Dee's lot and, straight in at 6, The Rolling Stones with 'Paint It Black'.

Could anyone not empathise with the newcomers' mortification when, before 'Wild Thing' fell from its high of Number 2, only 'Paint It Black' stopped them from lording it on *Top Of The Pops*? Yet, if it didn't reach the top on aggregate, a fraternal telegram from Andrew Loog Oldham to Larry Page praised The Troggs for knocking the Stones off the top in the *NME* list.

Mick Jagger felt secure enough to be magnanimous in print about how 'interesting' he found the Troggs, even as the same periodical – noting Reg's cobra-like habit then of moving his head from side to side on-camera – touted their lead singer briefly as Jagger's rustic rival. 'Not even my mother could see that,' smiled the one they'd dubbed 'Sexy Trogg', 'but it was nice while it lasted.'

He was, nonetheless, to be a teenage Michelle Pfeiffer's first pop idol – and before this film star's native North America had even heard of The Troggs, Reg looked every atom a pop star on the group's first national tour in September 1966 with ten minutes just before the headlining Walker Brothers – backed by Johnny B Great and the Quotations – after Dave Dee, Dozy, Beaky, Mick and Tich closed the first half.

Although the Brothers' most recent single had been a relative flop; Dozy *et al* hadn't yet dropped their comic capers, and The Troggs weren't – and never would be – ones for any wonderful-to-be-here vapourings, the predominantly female audience went indiscriminately crazy over all three outfits as autumn leaves fell on the beat boom. The music drowned in tidal waves of screams that hurled rampaging girls towards crash barriers where they'd be flung back again by exultant bouncers, shirt-sleeved in the heat, and aggravatingly nearer to Scott Walker, Dave Dee and, yes, Reg Presley than those who'd give their souls to be. In the boiling *melée* further back, unluckier ticket-holders burst into tears, rocked foetally, flapped programmes and scarves, hoisted inexpertly-daubed placards, tore at their hair, wet themselves and fainted with the thrill of it all.

Seeming oblivious to the commotion, the Troggs soldiered on unheard as the circle seats buckled and the walls trembled. If not the Surprise Hit of the tour, the Hampshire lads gave a workmanlike account of themselves then and, after a maiden aeroplane flight to Ireland, for 20-minute ballroom spots, conspicuous for both Sexy Trogg and Chris Britton being dragged off-stage at the Belfast stop as speaker columns toppled and the colleens conducted themselves as if totally deaf to warnings from the compere about rushing the stage.

More of the same awaited The Troggs in Germany where the record had also reached the Top 10 – as it had in France, Sweden, Italy and Australasia. In the most important market of all, appetites had been whetted by a promotional film of the Troggs miming 'Wild Thing' on an underground railway platform as promenading commuters looked on. Thus 'Wild Thing' jumped from 71 to 22 in the US Hot 100, but, sniffing a perishable commodity, Fontana stampeded the group into Olympic for an LP to be padded, so it was presumed, with the Hit and standbys from the stage act, thus serving the Troggs as Decca had the Zombies (St Alban's, not Bath) after their 'She's Not There' had captivated North America.

To be titled *From Nowhere*, the collection's front cover portrait of the quartet was snapped in the Cheddar Caves one Sunday in May. It was witnessed by a class of Bristol schoolchildren on an educational visit. One of them, Alan Burridge (later, fan club secretary to 1980s rebel rockers, Motorhead), was to recall that Reg needed reminding what his new stage alias was.

Bewildered by their abrupt rise to fame, and not yet at ease as London clubmen, The Troggs gravitated back to the west whenever they could. On the afternoon streets of even Bath or Salisbury, they might be mobbed, and the serenity of the Balls' short holiday in the Channel Islands was overturned by the pestering of fans and reporters, but back in Andover, Chris, Pete, Reg and Ronnie could still frequent pubs without having to listen with heavy patience to starstruck drivellings.

The local-boys-made-good took celebrity in their stride, and, while heads turned when Chris Britton's old Wolseley halted at the zebra crossing along Weyhill Road, it didn't attract the beginnings of a crowd, and there was merriment rather than annoyance if a teenager, bold with bravado, shouted 'Hey, wild thing!' at Pete Staples as he ambled from the newsagents near his parents' normally sleepy street where a few children swooped from nowhere to see the smile and wave that was diffused generally as the bass player who'd been on *Top Of The Pops* hurried indoors.

Exhausted but exhilarated by the speed of events, Pete had had 'no time to stop and think about what we have achieved. Every now and then it hits you that we've made the top, but to me it seems like a dream, like it was happening to someone else.' A Trogg's leisure time was brief these days, but sundown might bring on an onset of high spirits, and it was sad to sink them into a sofa when they cried out to be shared with more than Anton Arms drinkers, ready to take him down a peg or two if he got too full of himself just because the group had sold a million gramophone records.

Chief among those alighting with nit-picking hope on the remotest indication of The Troggs' fall were those *Advertiser* employees who had been disturbed by the startling and distorted noises from next door when the first edition of the group rehearsed. I may have got the journal all wrong, but it gave the illusion of getting its duty to the Troggs out of the way by shoving the impressive showing of 'Wild Thing' in the charts into a small paragraph on page eight below the latest doings of The Melody Makers. Even Ten Feet Five's little 'Baby's Back In Town' had had far more than that.

When 'Wild Thing' seemed on target for Number One by the end of May, the *Advertiser* was forced into a headline, 'The Troggs Are On The Up And Up', and a lengthy quote from Reg Presley that included a civil 'I remember when the *Advertiser* predicted our success. It looks as if you are going to be right.' Either flaunting this triumph for all it was worth or substantiating a safety net of local connections in case 'Wild Thing' was all there would ever be, Lance Barrett placed an advertisement on the entertainments page, howling the Troggs' trip to Germany from the rooftops while adding a cautionary 'Never mind about saving Mr Wilson's £s, don't forget to save your own!' (a reference to the Prime Minister's fight against a formidable balance-of-payments deficit).

Lance paid likewise to brag when 'Andover's Own Top Ten Group' was about to fill Salisbury's capacious City Hall to overflowing on 14 July. You could argue that this was the event that divided The Troggs' Dark Ages from the buoyant optimism of their mediaeval era. With the last chord of 'Wild Thing' yet reverberating in the pandemonium, they'd dashed pell-mell to a ticking-over getaway car in a back alley, and were halfway down the road before the crowd realised that there wasn't to be an encore. It was hardly The Troggs' fault that, governed by fire regulations as much as a prohibitive fee of five thousand pounds, it was impractical (and unsafe) for them to play in Andover anymore. Even the Guild Hall was as off-limits as the Cavern had long been to the Beatles – and it wasn't possible to honour local contracts settled when they'd been only semi-famous.

However, it was still tenable for old pals to worm their way into bustling backstage alcoves in Bournemouth, Southampton or Bristol for coded hilarity and selective reminiscences about The Redwoods and what Bruce Turner had said to Ginger Mansfield at the Fiesta in 1962. Mick Matthews had 'never doubted that they would finally make it at one time or another,' and, with observed good humour, Dave

Wright assured the *Advertiser* that 'I am not really sorry I left. I'm quite happy with everything, and I still enjoy going out with them whenever they are home.'

If a protective bubble within the holocaust of pop, Andover was becoming suffocating in its country quiet, particularly to Reg and Chris who were debating whether to uproot to the capital like The Beatles, Animals, Moody Blues, Hollies and other far-sighted provincials before them. Until then, the group would have to continue attending to recording and broadcasting necessities by commuting from wherever their booking itinerary had placed them. If benighted in the capital, they'd bed down in hotels or avail themselves of the hospitality of new acquaintances.

In August 1966, Reg began his London domicile by renting a *pied à terre*: 'It was getting very difficult, rising at dawn to come into town. So I've moved, and the other boys are flat hunting now. I can't say I like being in the middle of London all that much. I'd prefer to have a house on the outskirts. Still, it's convenient – and I've been taking a look round the London scene.'

In a professional capacity, The Troggs were to be sighted less often in Andover than the Monster in Loch Ness. For many years, such instances could be counted on the fingers of one offensive gesture: they posed outside a High Street shop in 1966's late summer for a scene in a documentary for Southern television, and much later, they actually performed to an invitations-only audience at the TA Centre for an edition of *Radio One Club*, an updated *Workers' Playtime* for one of the BBC's two new national pop radio stations.

As a beehive can function for a while after losing its progenitive queen, so did the scene in Andover. The tenacious Just Men, for example, had reinvented themselves as, first, The J Men and then, more fundamentally, as The Rage, just as the St Ann's Hall pop evening was now the Dee-Jay Club. New outfits such as Four Hits And A Miss still shook exasperated fists in the direction of London, and did their set as the Fiesta filled for The Soul Society, The Ugly's (sic) or something else from outside.

Yet a unit like Four Hits And A Miss could be all-powerful and perhaps immortal if it merged itself by affinity of geography with The Troggs, and thought of itself as much an embodiment of the Andover Sound – if there was such a thing – as they. Who hadn't glowed with civic pride when, after Stan Phillips rang in the wee, small hours on Tuesday 2 August with the news that 'Wild Thing' was Number One in the States, 'TROGGS ON TOP OF THE WORLD!' had blazed from the *Advertiser*'s very front page? My God, it *was* the front page! And on it, Stan spoke for both his boys and everyone else: 'It is now a proven fact that the youth of Andover have produced something great. All over the world, The Troggs are hailed as the greatest group since The Beatles!'

Chapter 4
'I Just Sing'

'Songs started flowing from Reggie, and he started singing them. That was the turning point.'
Stan Phillips

Neither Stan, Lance, Larry nor The Troggs themselves were so dazzled to think that pop stardom lasted forever – or that they could retire on 'Wild Thing', regarded by some pundits as the commercial zenith for yet another classic local group who'd got lucky and would probably be back on the buses by this time next year. Fast comes the hour when fades the fairest flower. Where were The Marauders now – and The Birds? While Hedgehoppers Anonymous were picking the bones of 'It's Good News Week', The Overlanders had been booted off the top by Nancy Sinatra in February 1966, and couldn't get so much as another week in the Top 50 to save their lives.

In 1966, you were still only as popular as your latest 45. 'If you didn't have a hit single,' elucidated Jim McCarty of The Yardbirds, 'you were a fading band.' As 'Wild Thing' lost its grip on the Top 20, whatever came next had to sell at least as well.

It wasn't easy for The Troggs to grasp that another number smashed out at the same session could be as potent as 'Wild Thing'. Larry had agreed to a remake of 'With A Girl Like You' in April, but a great light dawned and The Troggs realised that he had been right all along in that the better version was the earlier one that they had committed to tape instinctively.

Vigour not subtlety was the name of the game. In any case, subtlety was a quality The Troggs could ill-afford as they were propelled into even more of what the economist would call a 'full life'. Too busy in the bread-and-butter ballrooms to rehearse properly, The Troggs' methodology at Olympic during the taping of *From Nowhere* seemed slapdash and crude to outsiders, but a more complicated approach may have emasculated the overall drive of this ragbag of tried-and-tested stand-bys from the stage act – and a cache of originals, nearly all by Reg Presley.

Like a painter coming to dab at a hanging canvas minutes before the gallery opens, he had walked into the Baker Street studio with what were less songs than perhaps just chord sequences, odds and ends of lyrics or half-formulated ideas computed in his mind. While the engineer was occupied with some tedious mechanical process of spools, switches and faders, Presley might be on the other side of the glass-fronted booth, surrounded by cigarette butts and smeared coffee cups, collating the rest of the words or hunched over a guitar or Pete's bass, teasing a melody from nothing more than a riff. 'Larry kept going up to him,' remembered Ronnie, 'and saying, "Reg, have you finished it yet?".'

Under the managerial lash, a structure would shine through with increasing clarity as the studio clock dictated short cuts and the ditching of more and more clutter. After the backing track and lead vocal had been organised, all that remained to be done was the fairy-dusting – such as the apposite harpsichord on 'Jingle Jangle' or the breath of the Orient in Chris's 'I Just Sing' solo – any editing needed, and the mixing. 'We really struggled to be different,' insisted Reg, 'if there was another way of doing anything...like putting ADT (automatic double-tracking) for the voice on the bass drum. People accept the way things have always been done – and I hate that.'

There wasn't much room for innovation in the few hours allocated. When Reg's songwriting well ran dry, the fellows turned to current crowd-pleasers like 'Louie Louie' and Chuck Berry's 'Jaguar And The Thunderbird', sung by Ronnie. Yet *From Nowhere* was freighted as heavily with riflings from the vaults of a progressive form of R&B known as 'soul'. Along with 'classical', 'soul' is the most abused expression in music. Does it mean someone who sounds as if he needs to clear his throat? Is it the West Indian next door lilting a never-ending 'Baby Love' as he creosotes the tool shed – or it it the hammy ritualism of most soul revues in the mid-1960s predominated by black artists signed to pioneering US labels like Atlantic, Tamla-Motown and Stax/Volt?

Whatever it was, it had infiltrated the repertoires of groups all over Britain, especially after 45s by exponents like James Brown, The

Supremes, Dobie Gray, Lee Dorsey, The Four Tops and Nina Simone
had been saturation-plugged into the charts by pirate radio. While it
was hip to say you preferred these black US blueprints, all manner of
British recording acts, famous and obscure, were trying on soul for
size. Brown's 'I'll Go Crazy', for instance, had been a pot-shot at the
Top 50 by The Untamed – while First Gear had a go at Gray's 'The In
Crowd', and The Four Tops were robbed of a UK hit by the
Fourmost's heist of 'Baby I Need Your Loving'. The Hollies would be
planning to release the Tops' 'Reach Out I'll Be There' purely for the
European market if the original missed – as Cliff Bennett and the
Rebel Rousers were to do with Sam and Dave's 'Hold On I'm Coming'.

The jettisoned version of 'With A Girl Like You' had been a try at
a Tamla-Motown feel, while 'Ride Your Pony' and 'The Kitty Cat
Song', were the respective A- and B-sides of a Lee Dorsey single from
1965, and, also selected for *From Nowhere*, 'Hi Hi Hazel', a more
recent release (and minor hit) for Geno Washington, a US ex-
serviceman who'd carved a niche as a *gen-u-ine* let-me-hear-you-say-
'yeah' soul shouter in Britain.

Another seam of mid-1960s pop was mined less explicitly. 'I like
Bob Dylan's anti-war songs,' said Reg, 'as they express a basic hatred
of war and killing which everyone can understand.' Though Dylan
had moved on after setting in motion a 'golden age' of protest, *circa*
1965, constant replay of his early albums had resulted in creations
such as The Beatles' attempt at a Dylan-like opus in 1964's 'I'm A
Loser', and vinyl ballast like 'It's Good News Week' and The
Downliners Sect's 'Bad Storm Coming', a euphemism for impending
nuclear holocaust. Though not so war-is-wrong, '(I Can't Get No)
Satisfaction', Chip Taylor's 'An Ordinary Guy', 'Shapes Of Things'
by The Yardbirds and The Pretty Things' 'Death Of A Socialite' could
be seen too as searing indictments of the Society In Which We Live.

Because they expose a point of view, all songs are political by
definition – even 'From Nowhere's 'Our Love Will Still Be There'. 'I
don't rate my own songs as having great social significance,' agreed
Presley in the *NME*, 'but when I wrote "Our Love Will Still be There,"
I felt it and thought maybe I was capturing some of the magic Lennon
and McCartney manage.'

With a more pragmatic end in mind, Larry Page, sometimes in
collaboration with Colin Frechter, was putting forward his own songs,
among them 'I Want You' on the flip of 'With A Girl Like You', and
'Your Love', a royalty-earning makeweight for The Troggs' first US
album. Such a practice was by no means uncommon. Ken Jones, The

Zombies' recording manager, had squeezed an instrumental he'd written on to their debut LP – as Page had on to that of The Kinks – and, though she had not only sung but written 'Terry', all a resentful Twinkle's Decca B-sides were by her producer, Tommy Scott – who was to benefit too from an almost Twinkle-like monopoly on all Them B-sides as he foisted his songs on a young group still too much in awe perhaps of the condescending voice calling them to order via the control-room intercom to splutter, 'We'd rather not, sir.'

Larry's efforts were, as he'd tell you himself, not hit material, but the choice for one A-side by The Searchers had come about through the recommendation of producer Tony Hatch – 'and it wasn't till later,' disclosed bass guitarist Tony Jackson, 'that we found out that he'd written it himself under a pseudonym.'

A recording dredged up from one of The Searchers' Hamburg visits intruded upon the UK Top 50 entry in 1963, just as CBS's re-issue of 'Lost Girl' did on the Dutch Top 10 in the aftershock of 'Wild Thing'. This foreseeable occupational hazard of Making It was outweighed by advantages such as other acts investigating *From Nowhere* with a view to covering one or more of Reg's compositions, starting with 'Jingle Jangle' from The Truth, quite a feather in Presley's cap as this twosome had left the Top 30 only in May with no less than 'Girl' from The Beatles' latest album.

Monetary rewards from The Truth's 'Jingle Jangle' would be meagre, but, sent on its way by a partisan track-by-track review in the *NME* by Keith Altham, *From Nowhere* scrambled to Number 6 in the album list, and 'With A Girl Like You' proved as enormous as its predecessor across Europe and throughout the Empire, even wrenching Mick Jagger's production of Chris Farlowe's 'Out Of Time' from the top in Britain. There it remained an unarguable Number One for a fortnight, following an initial entry at Number 19 and the celebratory knees-up at Larry's Surrey mansion where the framed photograph on the cocktail cabinet of him embracing Dean Martin prompted enquiries about when The Troggs were off to America where stadium managers in frantic offices were on the line to Page, yelling 'Klondike!' at the prospect of a carnival of Beatle-sized magnitude.

A coy Page said that he was negotiating a US tour for the autumn. If that didn't happen, there was always next year. America could wait as there was plenty to do at home. Pop's meritocratic structure based on chart seniority may have enabled The Walker Brothers to take the stage at the optimum moment on the summer tour, but Larry cancelled a show in Nottingham because of a dispute over billing with Georgie

Fame, whose star was on the wane then. No-one was permitted to pull rank now that 'With A Girl Like You' and the lingering 'Wild Thing' bracketed the Top 50, and Fontana was wringing additional financial blood from both with a four-track *Troggs Tops* EP.

On paper, The Troggs were coining it too through net income from concerts as they zigzagged from the Bird Cage in Plymouth to Southport Floral Hall to the Rock Garden Pavilion in Llandrindod Wells to Margate's Dreamland to the Palace Ballroom on the Isle of Man via a matinee somewhere in between. Often they'd have to drop everything to fit in *Saturday Club* or a trip to the deconsecrated church in Manchester where *Top Of The Pops* was shot. Pondering that fat year, it appeared to Reg that 'We were never out of the charts. It was, like, "Oh no, it's *Top Of The Pops* again. Those kids must be fed up with our faces by now, surely." Mind you, I'm not knocking it. It really made us. That TV exposure broke us wide open.'

Supposed 'days off' were packed with interviews, shopping excursions for new equipment, and photo calls like the one in which The Troggs, armed with balloons, succumbed to The Beatles' much-copied mid-air leap. After Dick James created a publishing receptacle for compositions by Reg and, hopefully, others in the group, there were also closetings with accountants and solicitors where eyes glazed over during circular mumbo-jumbo about franchises, merchandising and estimates, containing phrases like 'tax concession', 'capital expenditure' and 'convertible debenture'.

The simplicity of mapping out a deal on a serviette over lunch – as had been Brian Epstein's contract with Billy J Kramer – was vanishing in ratio to the upgrading of pop from ephemera to Holy Writ after a prosy *Times* article in 1963 had discussed The Beatles' 'pandiatonic clusters' and 'Aeolian cadences'. Believing that they were really 'the greatest composers since Schubert', Lennon and McCartney's conscious artistic progression had taken them thus far from 'She Loves You' to 'Tomorrow Never Knows', the eerie omega of *Revolver*, their 1966 album with its sitars, backwards tapes and quotes from *The Tibetan Book Of The Dead*. Even old Tich from the Dave Dee mob had picked at a balalaika on their 'Bend It' that autumn, and The Yardbirds with near enough the same instrumental line-up as The Troggs, were now far more than the 12-bar blues band they once were.

Across the Atlantic, Bob Dylan had stopped going on about war being wrong, fairer shares for all and so on, and was singing through his nostrils about myriad less wistful topics, revealing greater possibilities beyond protest and boy-girl relationships. Indeed, an edition of the 'underground' magazine, *Oz* was to embrace a mind-boggling word-by-word analysis of his 12-minute 'Desolation Row', a 1966 album track, by an obsessive who, in order to prove one pet theory, had placed a wanted ad in an *Oz*-like outlet in New York for a Dylan urine sample.

You'd have had some search to find a corresponding Trogg-ologist. True enough, Reg Presley had thought the French 'so way behind it's laughable. Last week, we did a TV show in Paris with their biggest pop name, Johnny Hallyday. Basing his act on old British hits, he sounded like an early Marty Wilde. They're more hip behind the Iron Curtain.' Nevertheless, Presley also articulated the view of an English-speaking majority not in complete agreement about shifts in parameters of musical consciousness as the watershed year of 1967 loomed: 'Pop lately has got bogged down with cleverness. We have reverted to an elementary lyric and three elementary chords. "Wild Thing" was like a breath of fresh air to ordinary listeners. Pop music should be progressive, but it shouldn't wander too far ahead of the public.'

The Troggs certainly hadn't. 'They're so far behind, they're in front!' laughed Graham Nash of The Hollies. Sounding as if Chip Taylor had scribbled it on a scrap of cardboard with a leaky biro while sitting in the launderette, 'Wild Thing' was as wondrously dim as 'Hound Dog', 'Louie Louie' and, from 1965, Sam the Sham's 'Wooly Bully' and 'She's About A Mover' from The Sir Douglas Quintet. Even as 'Wild Thing' was yet to touch the Top 20, there'd been mumblings about the depth to which pop had sunk from those for whom 'culture' – watching a film by Cocteau or Warhol, listening to some minimalist composer, guffawing knowingly during a Shakespeare 'comedy' – was second nature (and 'pop music', therefore, beneath contempt). Magnifying the gap between themselves and the common herd, such snobs believed that the more arduous the effort needed to 'appreciate' something, the more 'artistic' it is.

What chance did Reg Presley have when 'You must be joking' was his riposte to an *NME* query about his musical education. As he'd never learnt to sight-read or write musical script, Reg was untroubled by the do's and don'ts that traditionally control creative flow. There were only those which had been ingrained since he'd first shaped that E chord on the guitar when he was a teenager.

Now he was the linchpin of the Unthinking Man's Pop Group in the light of Jonathan King – via his weekly column in *Disc* – rubbishing

'With A Girl Like You' for 'lowering the bottom boundary of pop', echoing a Tory Member of Parliament's bleating about The Beatles in 1963 – that 'we must offer our pop kids something better': something as good as 'Everyone's Gone To The Moon'? On *Juke Box Jury* already, King had hammered home his opinion that if you liked 'With A Girl Like You', you may consider yourself 'the very lowest common denominator in the pop audience'. Thus spake the four-eyed exquisite predestined to deliver 'Johnny Reggae' to the world.

The first Trogg to round on King was Chris Britton: 'He can make as many stupid remarks as he likes, but he can leave our fans alone. We never pretended that our discs were educational or musically improving. In fact, we stressed that the numbers were simple, uncluttered pieces of entertainment. If anyone considers that by providing dance music which people seem to enjoy, we are catering to the "lowest common denominator", then I am happy to be considered one of those. We have neither the desire nor conceit to set ourselves up as improvers of others.'

In tacit support, the discriminating Manfred Mann included jazzed-up readings of 'Wild Thing' and 'With A Girl Like You' on *Instrumental Assassination*, an EP out in December 1966 – and this from a unit that exuded a Powerful Intellectual Aura by pop standards. After all, they were led by a bloke with a beatnik beard and glasses, and had been fronted by Paul Jones, a singer who sported a CND badge and had been to university – and if that isn't Intellectual, then I don't know what is.

Lines were drawn, but the burning issue was resolved when Jonathan King honoured a pledge to stand The Troggs a champagne meal in a posh London restaurant if 'With A Girl Like You' reached the top. 'I was delighted to foot the bill,' he beamed, 'One can't help being pleased when a destructive prediction doesn't come true.' Drawing on a cigarette and nodding in agreement, Reg was to cap this with 'Feuds are ridiculous. They can't carry on if you don't join in. Before we made it, I used to look on pop stars as if they came from another planet. Then I met them and found they were ordinary nice people, mostly.'

Reminding Larry of his younger self's contrived conflict with Wee Willie Harris, it was all grist to the publicity mill. More insidious was Page's projection of The Troggs far beyond the Nice Lads When You Get To Know Them angle. Not for them was the surly, slump-shouldered introspection of the Stones, Pretty Things and Them. More natural to a Trogg was coming on like a farmer's boy disorientated in the metropolis. A role model might have been rural blacksmith Joe Gargery in his new suit, looking up city slicker Pip and trying hard not to put his foot in it in Dickens' *Great Expectations*.

With *Record Mirror*'s HERE'S THE STORY OF THE COUNTRY BOYS AND THE WICKED CITY a prototypical headline, the media rendered 'I' as 'oi', 'were' as 'was' and 'was' as 'were' when quoting a Trogg. The only stroke they missed was 'we' as 'us' and vice-versa. Give them credit, the group went along with it, answering the most arrogant hack's pedestrian and ill-informed enquiries with 'good copy': plain speaking laced with quirky wit and a naivety that was not entirely assumed, uttered in larger-than-life *ooo-arrr* West Country.

Gilding the image further were the biting back on even admissible expletives like cr*p and bl***y – as Ronnie had to after two souvenir hunters sneaked backstage and fled with his hi-hats – standing up whenever a woman entered the room, and liberal application of expressions like 'sir', 'madam', 'please' and 'thank you'. For all the Long John Silver-isms in their speech, The Troggs were encouraged by Page to keep their cool and be politely dignified when folk made unkind remarks about them – though they weren't above generalised *bon mots* like Reg's 'I think we get two sheep and a camel for every hundred copies sold' on hearing that 'Wild Thing' was high in the charts in Amboina (somewhere in Indonesia, I believe).

The Troggs, if not his marionettes, were much more trusting of Page and willing to follow his instructions than The Kinks had been. It was hats off to Larry when, thanks to him, the plug had been pulled and they'd been sucked from Andover into a vortex of events, places and situations that hadn't belonged even to speculation once upon a time. Had Larry confirmed an engagement at a ballroom on Venus, they'd have asked what time they had to be there for the soundcheck as they let themselves be pushed in whatever direction fate and their svengali dictated.

If a Trogg lost a sense of acting on his own free will sometimes, there were no thoughts yet of resisting the force that, effectively, had finished off his old life. In the studio, Presley's hackles would not rise when, in front of a reporter, Page snapped 'Well, find an unbruised bit' to his 'I've been bouncing this tambourine on my thigh every night for the past week, and it's a mass of bruises.' Back on *Ready Steady Go!* in August, there was amusement rather than offence when, at the very second presenter Cathy McGowan announced The Troggs, Larry seized Reg (whose voice was overworked after a three week stint in Germany) by the lapels: 'Right, go out there and if you don't give a good performance, I'll murder you.'

He could have cited the example of The Dave Clark Five a year earlier who, caught off-guard by a rise in British sales for 'Catch Us If You Can' in the middle of a US tour, had boarded the next jet to England to mime it on *Top Of The Pops*; big smiles masking their jet-lagged weariness.

Since racking up heftier achievements abroad, the Five considered themselves past demeaning publicity stunts these days, but it was still part of a day's work for The Troggs as exemplified by a December press conference – with Pete in full-length fur coat against the cold – in Berlin Zoo which concluded with all four shut in a cage, and a keeper poking raw meat at them through the bars.

The pace *sur le continent* was, if anything, more hectic than at home. Among recreational high points was a frolic round a hotel swimming pool with the local Playboy Club's dancing *frauleins* when unwinding after the wry shallowness at the zoo, and what was more a tribal gathering than a musical recital before 10,000 at the Wembley-sized Deutschlanerhaller with the Hollies.

Reg's growing misgivings about flying were bolstered by some of the paint-peeling antiquities that flew them from here to there. Haunted perhaps by the ghosts of Buddy Holly and Jim Reeves, he'd slip into an easier slumber with the road buzzing in his ears in the group's ageing Ford Transit, maybe one oil change from the breaker's yard. Along some twisting, pot-holed trackway in Finland *en route* to the ferry terminal in Helsinki, a rueful but light-hearted mood persisted after a tyre burst until 'we found that we didn't have a wheel brace,' lamented Chris Britton, who, with his mechanical skills, had assumed command of the calamity.

'Eventually, after hammering it with rocks, we changed the wheel. During the long drive, we had an endless stream of punctures, and we ended up with a six-wheeled transit with only three roadworthy tyres. As well as that, we had a fuel pump problem and the choke had to be left out permanently, so we were using a lot of fuel, and at junctions and crossroads, it tended to cut out and had to be restarted every time. Eventually, we made it to Helsinki where customs informed us that we were too late for the boat. We had to catch that ferry to Sweden as we were playing that night, so we totally ignored the customs guys and drove straight on to the boat as they were pulling up the gangplank.'

Hot and bothered, the peacocks showed their feathers on time, but went the distance in a blizzard of electronic crackles, ear-splitting feedback, and a malfunctioning house sound system. 'Whoops!' cried Reg as Pete's amplifier exploded and, from the disasters of the past 24 hours, came a sudden meshing of the customers' gaiety and the fiery-eyed frenzy of a group alert with hunger and beyond sleep. The crowd almost took over – almost but not quite – as Reg pulled out every attention-grabbing trick in the book for a crowd prevented from mauling him by a burly cordon of bouncers laid on by the auditorium director.

A lot of impresarios, however, couldn't give a damn about what happened to a pop group as long as the teenagers handed over the admission money. Take care of the pennies and the lads can take care of themselves. 'When we left a gig in Dublin,' recounted Reg, 'we ran to the car from the dressing room. The alley was full of kids. The road manager went to drive away, and the car did not move because there was such a weight of kids on the car. He put it into first gear, then second gear. It wouldn't move. We gradually got away as every time the kids jumped on to the car we could creep forward a little bit at a time.

'Another incident I remember was when I was on stage and there was evidently a little nick in my trousers at the bottom, and the seam had started to come undone and there was a thread hanging down. Some girl in the front spotted it and gave it a yank, and the stitches went straight up one leg and down the other – so I exited stage right with my trousers in a state. It was lucky I had underpants on that night. After a change of trousers off stage, it was on with the show.'

Such a shy-making occurrence was shrugged off as part of the index of possibilities. At least it was a sign that The Troggs were satisfying the primary requirement of any pop entity, *i.e.* simply to be liked.

Not everyone adored them. Girls shrieked at The Troggs in defiance of their jealous boyfriends' sporadic heckling, central to a flow chart of barracking, the hurling of decayed fruit and more odious projectiles, and lying in mob-handed wait for the group at the stage door or outside the hotel to settle vendettas born from their watching like lynxes for the slightest excuse for one – a grimace from a soloing Britton; Staples catching the eye of some such ruffian's 'bird'; homophobic irritation at hip-shakin' Presley, or Bond lashing out verbally at some catcall or other.

Hooliganism had been a sub-flavour of pop since before Bill Haley, and much of the time, The Troggs were able to defuse such instances of menace, even win over those determined to hate them.

Nevertheless, the ever-present danger of assault on the principals was sufficient reason for the hiring of bodyguards by Liverpudlian tour manager Hal Carter, a music industry shellback who Larry Page had employed to instil into The Kinks the 'professionalism' displayed by Billy Fury, Marty Wilde and other stars with whom he'd worked.

The Troggs may have giggled indulgently at name-dropping Hal's bottomless pit of anecdotes about the old days, but it wasn't all smiles with Larry Page just then. Already, they'd applied a brake to alarming if press-friendly proposals like Reg attempting to swim the Channel, and everyone parachute-jumping on to Thruxton airfield. They'd turned their noses up too at exposure in January 1967's San Remo Song Festival – in which Reg would have been required to sing phonetically in Italian – but, with bad grace, had stopped off at a trade fair in Cannes, a semi-private function where live music was incidental to networking, and the wheeling and dealing of promenading moguls.

There were rumblings too about plans that had gone awry such as an EP – to be titled *Trogg-A-Track* – which, in a similar fashion to 1966's *Solo Scott Solo John* by two Walker Brothers, was to divide needle time into lead vocal showcases by all four members. Then there was Larry's prediction of a future in a new medium altogether for Britton: 'Chris has always been the "face" of the group. He has the intelligence and the looks to progress into films.'

Of more direct concern, however, was that, with most of their earnings tied up, The Troggs' wallets held little tangible cash. Road managers and other menials took care of minor purchases, and only had to ring the office whenever larger amounts were needed, such as that for a portable television to switch on when time hung heavy between arrival at a venue and performance. Nonetheless, real or imagined anxieties about finances had necessitated the appointment of Ronnie Bond as group treasurer: 'The others dare not order so much as a round of sandwiches without obtaining a receipt for me. We were running up incredible bills for cokes, taxis and late night meals. Someone had to get a grip on it. We were losing hundreds of pounds.'

Yet how could that matter much when, in the States, the *Wild Thing* LP was hovering round the middle of the album *Hot 100*? What's more, 'With A Girl Like You' had sneaked into the Union's Top 30. This, however, was a remarkable climb considering that it had already B-sided 'Wild Thing'. Impetus in North America, see, had slackened through legal wrangles that had reared up following Larry's negotiations – via Walter Hofer, Brian Epstein's US attorney – with

74

Atco, an Atlantic subsidiary, who were appearing to turn down The Troggs' British hits. Therefore, Page settled instead for Mercury, Fontana's US outlet. So began the great Atco-Fontana debacle.

Mercury had also been one of two labels that had released Eileen Barton's million-selling 'If I Knew You Were Coming I'd Have Baked A Cake' simultaneously in 1950 – and now history was repeating itself with another mix-up whereby a coupling of the two British hits was issued by Atco, and separately by Fontana with their UK flip-sides, 'From Home' and 'I Want You' – both acceptable enough, but nothing more than flip-sides. On the basis of economics alone, two smashes for the price of one – albeit released after the Mercury 'Wild Thing' had entered the Hot 100 – from this latest sensation from England, was the soundest investment for the overwhelming majority of the continent's music lovers, *i.e.* those for whom the concept of collecting-every-record-The-Troggs-ever-made was too new to grasp. 'No-one buys a hit twice,' sighed Reg. 'This meant the follow-up suffered, and it broke the chain. We've been trying to repair that damage ever since.'

Chapter 5
'Last Summer'

'None of us were drug-mad.
We had enough trouble with beer and scotch.'
Chris Britton

Fontana won against the opportunist Atco, but it was a Pyrrhic victory as the Troggs turned out to be good for one more Top 10 placing in the *Hot 100*. While they did not disappear from the US scene with the same indecent haste as recent nine-day-wonders from Britain like Cilla Black, The Nashville Teens and Adam Faith, the general feeling was that Atco had been fortunate in bleeding the group when they did.

Against this glum inference, Reg Presley immersed himself in one of his most prolific periods as a songwriter, a quickening creative rush commensurate with increases in both booking fees and record sales outside Uncle Sam's fair land. There were so many ideas chasing through his head that it was all he could do to write them down as he grappled with his muse, ploughing a similar furrow as Ray Davies had before the Kink Komposer began forging a more intrinsically English pop form with the likes of 'Sunny Afternoon', 'Dead End Street' and 'Waterloo Sunset'.

The old R&B enthusiast peeped out on The Troggs' fourth 45, 'I Can't Control Myself'. Into the bargain, his singing was compared to that of Steve Winwood, whose gravelly, elastic tenor was The Spencer Davis Group's principal asset. This was a fair comparison for, however much the Group's typically knotted-browed *aficionado* refuted the suggestion, both they and The Troggs were pop entertainers. After amassing the strongest possible local reputations with R&B, each had been signed to a Fontana lease contract. 1966 yielded two fast UK Number Ones each and the leaving of a wound in the USA before going off the commercial boil there almost instantly.

The Davis quartet's 'Keep On Running' sounded as American as 'With A Girl Like You'. The main difference lay in the image that attracted fans of either entity. Like Manfred Mann, Spencer – the first Bachelor of Arts to top the charts – got by on the 'intellectual' ticket, but there was nothing intellectual about 'I Can't Control Myself' unless it was in a middle eight suspended over an unchanging minor chord that nodded towards the salient points of 'Paint It Black' and The Kinks' 'See My Friends', perhaps the first try at integrating Indian music into Western pop, and its 'first reasonable use of the drone', estimated The Who's Pete Townshend.

The Troggs had spent three days in a house outside Andover routining 'I Can't Control Myself' for a two-hour session at Olympic – where blue smoke curled from a compressor connected to Ronnie's drums. Very much a bass player's meat musically, the result sounded like a hit as big as the two before, but with the added piquancy of what was almost said in the lewd bridge passage. Indeed, the general atmosphere was, noted Keith Altham, 'a bit near the knuckle.' Reg himself granted that 'It's a bit saucy, but I don't think there's any question of it being banned.'

He had another thing coming. With the business about 'authentic queers and phoney virgins' on Scott Walker's 'Jackie' over a year away, and the likes of heavy-breathing 'Je T'Aime...Moi Non Plus' and Max Romeo's 'Wet Dream' on a more distant horizon, 'Bend It', The Rolling Stones' 'Let's Spend The Night Together' and 'I Can't Make It' from The Small Faces were excluded from priggish airwaves for sexual innuendo, and the word 'hips' in its first verse was enough for an injunction preventing dealers from selling 'I Can't Control Myself' throughout Australia in tandem with the first complete censoring of a disc in the country's history. When disc-jockeys began spinning its 'Gonna Make You' coupling instead, 'I Can't Control Myself' was relegated to a B-side.

Such an adjustment of emphasis was unnecessary in Britain, though an appearance by the group on *Crackerjack* in BBC television's 'Children's Hour' was vetoed. 'Someone is trying to make "sex" a dirty word,' glowered Ronnie Bond. 'Who are they trying to kid? The youngsters of today know what's going on in the world. Who do these small-minded people think they are protecting?'

Yet the controversy did no harm whatsoever as 'I Can't Control Myself' beat a well-tramped path into the UK's autumn Top 20, and went flaccid at a tantalising Number 2. Striking while the iron was hot, The Troggs waded in next with downbeat and placatory 'Anyway That You Want Me'. Layered with ersatz-Mozart cellos, it exposed both the group's and composer Chip Taylor's soft underbellies in that it was as unlike 'I Can't Control Myself' as it could be.

Though 'Anyway That You Want Me' didn't bound either as quickly into or rise as highly up the Top 10, The Troggs warranted a full half-hour to close a *Ready Steady Go!* special on 16 December 1966, the penultimate edition of a show that had honoured The Rolling Stones, The Walker Brothers, James Brown and The Who in the same way. It had forgiven The Troggs for siding with The Hollies a few weeks earlier, joining them in walking out on the programme when it was discovered that the headliners were to be The Dave Clark Five, in the throes of a still-successful campaign to take the USA for every cent they could get but undergoing a long, slow **descent** in the domestic charts.

With some justification, The Troggs could argue that their lead vocalist was now one of Britain's most commercial songwriters. While the ambience and space restrictions of travel arrangements circumscribed serious composition, his flashes of inspiration could be revised and developed in hotel room seclusion. Like Brenda and his children back home, Reg's colleagues learned to leave him alone and field all outside interference when he was in a creative mood – though sometimes, 'I get a commercial noise first, and leave it to the rest of the group to create the complete number.' This might occasion Chris, Pete and Ronnie – and Larry and Colin – slinging in rhymes, chord changes and twists to the plot as Reg paced up and down the carpet, guitar and notebook within reach, and bedevilled with an impulse that might have manifested itself at an inconvenient moment in, say, a lift, backstage corridor or during an airline lunch.

In between discursive proselytising about Einstein and the relationship between time and space ('The train that never leaves the station') to an interviewer from *Beat Instrumental*, Presley revealed that 'normally, I have a song in my head for three or four weeks to more or less sort it out before we record it, but "Give It To Me" was completed in just three days from the time of writing to the finished disc.' He didn't consider this new A-side the group's best, 'but it has the one important feature which has remained a constant commercial success through all these booms – skiffle, rock'n'roll, rhythm and blues, twist and trad – a driving beat. Beat music is the only trend which has kept in the charts since the advent of pop as we understand it. It's an essential part of nearly every composition I write, either pushed back in the sound or brought forward. It's always there.'

Still intrigued by The Troggs, Mick Jagger popped his head round the door at Pye's Marble Arch complex where a careering riff was pulsating beneath a trenchant vocal: punk or what? A week later, 'Give It To Me' fell one place after its initial chart incursion, but sufficient momentum was regained for it to struggle to Number 12. While this was a comedown by previous standards, the piece was adapted to permeate folklore as an *omnes fortissimo* football terrace chant, *e.g.* 'Give us a go-o-al!/Give us a go-o-al!/Aldershot F.C.!/Aldershot F.C.!' (or whatever).

None of the recent singles were given a look-in on a second album, *Trogglodynamite*, but their contrasting emotional dynamics were embraced comprehensively with the restraint of 'Last Summer' and Larry Page's 'Cousin Jane' the most extreme contrasts to such as 'Mona' – Pete's lead vocal debut on vinyl – and Chuck Berry's 'Little Queenie', sung by Chris and issued as a single in the Netherlands. *Trogglodynamite* also marked Ronnie's debut as a composer (with 'It's Too Late'), and the Troggs' purloining of a number hitherto exclusive to another group. Co-written by the ubiquitous Tommy Scott, 'I Can Only Give You Everything' had been a Them album track and US-only 45. With the Ulster outfit's year-old treatment as a helpful demo, The Troggs would think highly enough of this rousing thrash to be encoring with it 20 years later.

Over as UK chart entrants since 1965, Them had been hanging on in North America via crucial grassroots support and their influence on Anglophile 'garage bands' – some trying to pass themselves off as genuine Britons – that had crawled from the sub-cultural woodwork throughout the continent after they'd been able to grow out their crew-cuts and seize upon whatever aspect of the new Limey idioms they felt most comfortable. For The Byrds, it had been The Searchers' fusion of Merseybeat and contemporary folk, while The Yardbirds outfitted San Jose's Count Five with the vestments of musical personality that had just propelled 'Psychotic Reaction' into the US Top 20. Them's 'Gloria' (like 'With A Girl Like You') had started as a B-side before a moderate showing in the *Hot 100* – and then a Top 10 reawakening in 1966 by Chicago's Shadows Of Knight.

Within months, 'Wild Thing' would be on a par with 'Gloria' – and 'Louie Louie' and 'Hey Joe' – as a baluster of hundreds of minor US

79

outfits as a confirmation that Them was very much last year's model
of three-chord instrumental directness and oddly attractive stentorian
drawl. Indeed, a combo led by Jimi Hendrix had been demolishing
'Wild Thing' when this journeyman guitarist from Seattle was
'discovered' in autumn 1966 by Chas Chandler, bass player with The
Animals, in a half-empty New York cafe, and had been brought over
to England as a pop Wild Man of Borneo, to become almost the last
major icon to come in from the outside of the British beat boom.

With Hendrix and so many others borrowing from the Troggian
dialectic, no time seemed to be better for a second coming, but Page
cited too many examples – including that of The Kinks in 1965 – of
artists and investors losing their shirts with premature and ill-
conceived treks to the USA: 'Well, here we are with a hit single in
America. Jolly good! What are we going to do about it then? Better fix
up a tour and get on television over there, eh? Er...big place, isn't it?'

While they may have regarded such caution as a lost opportunity,
The Troggs had had a good run. Pop music was and is a commodity to
be bought, sold and replaced when worn out, and, no matter how
much their luck continued to hold as other acts came and went, always
The Troggs expected it to fizzle out at any second. Nevertheless, if it
was important to them, they could die easy in the knowledge that,
without exception, every parochial rival had never even been on *Top
Of The Pops* in the first place.

Never more than semi-professional at most, a lot of them could be
visualised in some fixed pose, doing what they did *circa* 1963 – and,
sure enough, still playing the TA Centre, the Fiesta and St Ann's Hall
were Bruce Turner, Jon Bates and Dave Wright who, beset with
conflicting emotions when their friends had topped the charts, were
back in the fray as mainstays of what became The Loot – whose self-
image, like that of other rising local units, had been cast with The
Troggs lurking in the background. Indeed, it was a strange week if one
of them didn't pile into 'Wild Thing' as a rueful salaam to four heroes
seen but seldom these days.

Old or new, most Andover groups were in it for beer money and a
laugh, but a few, believing that they had Troggs-sized potential, were
drawn like iron-filings to the magnet of Stan Phillips as Larry Page's
representative in Hampshire. Even Rod Stewart, now *sans* The Soul
Agents, pursued that connection in hope that, after his third flop 45,
a move to Page One would lift him off the runway.

The label's inaugural single was 'I Can't Control Myself' by its
flagship act – and the only one to enjoy any measure of chart

longevity. Groomed for pastures as green, however, were The Loot who'd been advantaged by direct associations with the brand-leaders of the 'Andover Sound'. 'It's like a tree with two branches,' pontificated Reg Presley, 'We are both of the same tree, but only in the way that The Beatles helped sprout groups like The Searchers.'

The Troggs' drummer was head-to-head with Larry Page in the control room as The Loot's producer, now that his comprehensive logging of Larry's technological donkey-work since 'Lost Girl' had ripened in him the self-assertion to issue jargon-ridden instructions through the talkback, and make learned recommendations to the engineer about equalisation, vari-speeding, bounce-downs, spatial separation and mixing.

Ronnie Bond's first mark on The Loot's output was made after the failure of three self-penned singles. Nevertheless, his coming for 1968's 'She's A Winner' still defied Larry Page's 'before 1967 is out, The Loot will be in the charts', an assertion reiterated by a feature-writer in *FAB 208* – a widely-circulated pop magazine sponsored by Radio Luxembourg – which touched too on the group's outing to Coombe Gallows, five miles from Andover, to watch for UFOs after Dave Wright had digested a book about cosmic communication.

This tome was lent to Reg Presley who was also keeping a benevolent eye on The Loot (who were to cover 'Meet Jacqueline' from *Troglodynamite* on a French EP) and another Page One act, The Nerve. After a first single 'Magic Spectacles' and its follow-up went the way of The Loot's efforts, Reg lent a hand as overseer of The Nerve's 'It Is' and then 'Piece By Piece' but was unable to work any commercial magic as he held trepidations about hitherto untried skills as a producer in check.

Neither he nor Ronnie had been out on a longer limb in the studio, but, once they'd taken on the job, they'd ascertain what they could *in situ* and, as they'd done on Troggs sessions, banish unknowingly many preconceptions and invent new ones. They'd apportion trackage, short-list devices and effects, and furrow their brows over, say, stereo panning and degree of reverberation on the rhythm guitar as if it was the most natural thing in the world.

Reg's interest in The Nerve extended to management, albeit via a sub-contraction to Larry Page who was overloading himself too with further non-Andover clients like Svenske, a promising blond duo with Viking good looks from Bournemouth. They sustained an undeserved miss with 1967's 'Dream Magazine', as pleasant an evocation of pop's gingerbread castle hour as The Rolling Stones' 'Dandelion' or

Traffic's 'Hole In My Shoe'.

Earlier, Larry had been as keen on Lee Drummond, a solo singer in an age of groups, who'd put one of his compositions the way of The Troggs. 'His voice – and the song – were so good,' said Larry, 'that I decided to sign him up. He'll be very big.' Page was wrong too about Los Brincos, who were brought to London after 'Black Is Black' by another big Spanish group, Los Bravos, had been kept from Number One only by 'With A Girl Like You'. He also looked beyond the Pyrenees for Massiel, a chanteuse whose 'La La La' was to crush Cliff Richard's 'Congratulations' as winner of 1968's Eurovision Song Contest, but swallow dust in the British Top 40 behind the chart-topping Bachelor Boy.

Apart from Troggs' singles, the label's most enduring chart strike in the 1960s was with ponderous 'Everything I Am' by Plastic Penny. Given to adventurous attempts at 'Strawberry Fields Forever' and 'MacArthur Park' – grandiloquent relics of pop's fleeting 'classical' period that less assured groups would shun – Plastic Penny shone with 'Any Way You Want Me'-like strings as 'Everything I Am' processed to Number 6. However, the outfit's many remaining releases fell on stony ground, owing to its *dramatis personae*'s comparative facelessness and dearth of outlaw chic like that which adhered to The Rolling Stones after their famous drug bust in February 1967.

The consequent hoo-hah had gained the Stones further approbation from the blossoming hippie sub-culture, but this type of publicity, however unsought, was not Larry Page's way. 'I Can't Control Myself' was all very well; it was to do with business, but if his Troggs had been indiscreet with drugs or anything remotely scandalous, he – with Dick James' like-minded assistance – would have called in favours, twisted arms, turned screws and done everything in his power to ensure that no nicotine-stained fingers would type out lurid coverage of it for next week's *News Of The World*. It was Larry's judgement that any public besmirching of The Troggs and other of his ostensibly wholesome clients by the scum press was damaging in the long run.

If nothing else, it could signal ceaseless harassment by customs officials who'd clocked in for work after disparaging Mick Jagger over breakfast, tarring all these long-haired scruffs with the same brush. 'If you were a pop group in the 1960s,' said Reg, 'they assumed you had to be taking drugs. Ronnie had a body search once. If you'd got up early and you'd had a gutful of beer the night before, you could look like a junkie.'

Such assumptions had substance in many instances for, though admirable young men in many ways, roving minstrels in the Swinging Sixties had their quota of young men's vices. I know it's distasteful to mention such things, but, alas, it's true: The Stones weren't the only 1960s pop entertainers to partake of illegal drugs. Nevertheless, most of them, if all too aware of 'purple hearts', 'black bombers' and like amphetamine-based pep-pills, regarded marijuana ('pot') initially as a bit too cloak-and-dagger. It was a herb, see, that was packed into a large cigarette called a 'reefer', and smoked communally. It was flattery of a kind if a musician looked sufficiently disreputable to be asked – as a gesture of free-spirited urbanity – if he'd care to sample its short-lived kicks in an equipment van or like hidey-hole.

More sinister were the mind-warping effects of the lately-outlawed lysergic acid diethymalide – LSD – that possessed cavorting berserkers in London's 'underground' clubs with their flickering strobes, ectoplasmic light projections and further audio-visual aids that simulated the chemically-induced glimpses of the eternal that were part-and-parcel of psychedelic experience during 1967's Summer of Love. 'Dropping acid' had become so prevalent that Dave Dee was driven to insist to *Melody Maker* that, as far as his clean-minded lads were concerned, LSD still stood for pounds shillings and pence.

Those 'flower children' and the rest of a perpetual small-change of hangers-on that were able to contrive access to The Troggs expressed hipper-than-thou surprise too at the Hampshire boys' refusal of the ingratiating tabs of LSD and 'tokes' of marijuana that passed as common currency among those whose links to the outer world were being severed by the dealers who'd got them 'into' drugs in the first place. 'The goody-goody tag is a bit sick-making,' scowled Pete Staples, 'especially as we know that other pop musicians call us country bumpkins.' The same faddish cabal were also talking openly about their LSD-addled escapades to even the 'straight' press even as Reg Presley went beyond mere repudiation of drugs in support of the common belief that 'pop favourites do have a duty to their fans. I'd rather not be photographed smoking or drinking.'

Larry Page took it a step further with an announcement in April 1967 that he was confining his groups to provincial engagements to minimise the chances of big-city corruption sticking to them. 'What's so colourful about spending all night in a smoky club,' demanded a supportive Pete, 'and all day in bed like a lot of them? If that's what you've got to do to qualify for the In Crowd, then we'd sooner stay out. We've got an old-fashioned notion that it's how you play and not how much you play around.'

That The Troggs were in such total agreement with his strategy gave Larry Page another idea almost immediately. Chris Britton was as bothered by the drugs issue as the next Trogg. As the most hirsute member, he'd long grown tired of being frisked and interrogated about his migraine tablets as he and the others threaded through customs areas resounding with jack-in-office unpleasantness and every fibre of red tape bureaucracy could muster. What if, thought Larry, there was a 'security leak' that Chris had had his fill of the glamorisation of narcotics within the record business, and was intending to retire as a professional musician.

The plot could thicken with Dave Wright rehearsing with The Troggs for the forthcoming foreign tour as a contingency measure if Page's ultimatum to sue Britton for breach of contract was ignored. Then Chris would materialise at Heathrow with seconds to spare before the flight. He couldn't let his old pals down, but would be quoted as saying: 'As far as I am concerned, the position is exactly the same: I want to leave the group. I am unhappy with the long-haired, drug-taking image of the business. Larry is within his rights, but I am hoping he will release me when he finds a suitable replacement.'

As it had been with Ronnie and Reg's stage surnames, the group only became aware of the opening stages of the scam when they read about it in the music papers. From the same source came revelations about a scheme for a Troggs probe behind the Iron Curtain, but arranged already was The Troggs' immovable round-Britain trek second-billed to Gene Pitney, the balladeer who, barring Roy Orbison and the remote Elvis, had come to command the most devoted British following of any US pop star.

For his dentist's-drill tenor, defiantly short hair, smart attire and artistic consistency – 'squareness' some might say – Gene was idolised by older consumers who'd been disenfranchised by beat groups and their psychedelic heirs. It was his corny habit to feign delighted amazement when aides wheeled on a huge birthday cake before an audience cued up to chorus 'Happy Birthday To You' as he blew out the candles. It was to happen every night on this particular tour, ageing Pitney – not quite 30 – by 20 years in as many days.

Genuine celebrations of Pete's birthday on 3 May and that of Ronnie a day later took place with far less fuss in the jovial surroundings of licensed premises with attendance from a something-for-everybody cast completed by The Loot (at Page's insistence) plus David Garrick – an elegant Merseysider who'd twice almost-but-not-quite slipped into the Top 20 in 1966 – and Normie Rowe, a big name in Australia testing the British waters. Both were backed by Kent's robust Sounds Incorporated with their sensational horn section.

It was standing-room-only most of the way despite competition from a rival all-styles-served-here touring party showcasing The Walker Brothers, Cat Stevens, The Jimi Hendrix Experience and ex-palais crooner Engelbert Humperdinck – who'd end the year as the UK Top 50's prize exhibit – with Johnny B Great and the Quotations mirroring Sounds Incorporated.

At the Aldershot stop, Noel Redding and Mitch Mitchell of the Experience had paraded along the main street – just as girls from the High School were going home – with Noel in the trousers and Mitch in the jacket of the same bright orange suit. A week later, The Troggs were on the pop page of the *Aldershot News And Military Gazette* through a mid-afternoon excursion from the same ABC cinema to Trader's, a backstreet junk shop that was thriving during that spring's craze for Victorian military uniforms.

Now that the ancient Transit had given up the ghost, the group had arrived early in a Humber Snipe with Alex, a new road manager, at the wheel. While the rest of the supporting fare had been flattered but not quite comfortable when Gene Pitney chose to slum it in the coach now and then rather than be chauffeured separately like the star he was, nobody felt intimidated if any of The Troggs did the same. Indeed, one of The Loot had handed his camera to Ronnie Bond to take a souvenir photograph of him with Pitney, not thinking to ask the American to snap one of him with Ronnie. 'Playing with some familiar faces from home is like travelling with a local football team,' was Reg's explanation. 'We've been having a great time.'

To amuse those watching from the wings at Bournemouth Winter Gardens, The Loot tormented Normie Rowe during his on-stage patter by squirting him with water pistols. Another diversion from the daily grind of road, dressing room, stage and hotel was the kidnapping of The Troggs in Dublin by students for a rag week stunt.

Not so funny, however, was Bruce Turner's dislocated shoulder when pinned in a doorway by libidinous females. Mistimed falling curtains weren't in the script either for David Garrick – nor the malfunctioning of the microphones whenever The Troggs were on the boards, causing embarrassing delay as a road manager blundered on with a replacement. So persistent was it that many suspected sabotage by the Pitney camp, disconcerted by sustained cheering that invariably followed the group's big finish. 'Everything was going wrong,' recalled Reg. 'We'd had night after night of somebody unplugging the mikes during the first or second number because we were too potent for the main act. It ruined our impact. It didn't happen to anyone else.'

The sound crew wriggled and pleaded that it was unfortunate but nothing untoward was going on. However, after three evenings of containing his fury, Reg shook them into a shocked gasp by dashing an apparently dead microphone to the floor, and complaining openly to the audience. Fearful that he'd do the same again, a cash-conscious chief engineer ensured that The Troggs at least would always go the distance without interruption.

Before the tour wound down, Reg was seeking the particular company of Sounds Incorporated with a view to producing them, and considering one of their originals for inclusion on the next Troggs album. Pete Staples benefited too from Reg's professional solicitude when he demonstrated 'Oh No', a composition that he felt might also fit on the successor to *Trogglodynamite*. 'It's very good, Pete,' reckoned a benevolent Reg, 'but you've said one or two things which you can't say, and you play the same way.'

'Oh No' was to be a highlight of the album, even eliciting a cover by another Larry Page production client, Bobby Solo, an Italian seemingly omnipresent at every mid-European song festival on the calendar. This personal triumph by Staples was, however, checkmated as usual by Presley, now recognised as The Troggs' X-factor by the most indifferent of Alan Freeman's Sunday afternoon pop-pickers.

It had been, indeed, a Sunday afternoon when the words and melody of what the world would come to know as 'Love Is All Around' had come to Reg. His ears had caught the televised cantillating of The Joystrings, a Salvation Army 'beat group' whose prayers had been answered with two Top 50 ascents in 1964. 'They were singing a song about love,' remembered Reg, 'and that gave me the idea. I turned the TV down, and in 15 minutes, I had written the whole song.'

Chapter 6
Night Of The Long Knives

'They weren't talking to Larry, and they'd asked for their
contracts back from Dick.'
Colin Frechter

There would be one important counter-offensive during the
routing of The Troggs from the domestic charts, and hefty
achievements in foreign climes would hold this dispiriting
demise back home at bay. In November 1967, for instance, the group
was acclaimed as 'the new interpreters of youthful rhythm in
international dancing music' at the Mar Del Plata international
record festival in Argentina, and finished sixth – between The Rolling
Stones and Sonny and Cher – in the readers' popularity poll in *Bravo*,
the German equivalent of the *NME*. Its 'Golden Otto' award,
incidentally, was won by Dave Dee, Dozy, Beaky, Mick and Tich, who
beat The Beatles by over 3,000 votes.

Back in Britain, The Troggs would be out of the frame altogether in
the 'World Vocal Group' section of the corresponding *NME*
tabulation, and would scrape in at 18 as 'British Vocal Group', three
positions behind Dave Dee *et al* (at 13 in 1966, The Troggs had been
slightly ahead of their West Country blood brothers). This comedown
had resulted in part from an influx of new chart contenders like The
Casuals, Love Affair and Plastic Penny, harmless purveyors of
popular song attuned to the cautious programming of the BBC's
middle-of-the-road Radio One, now in the cat-seat because of the
fading of pirate radio after the Marine Offences Act became law in
August 1967.

Reg Presley cited another reason: 'We may have overdone things a bit in England. That is, I think some kids in towns where there are two other big names billed regularly, say to themselves: "Oh, it's The Troggs. We'll go to see group X because we can always see The Troggs when they come again next month.' Like a London tube train, if you missed one Troggs concert, there'd be another along if you waited.

There was anxiety, too, about the next single. Since losing their grip on the UK Top 10 with 'Give It To Me', a restorative ploy was in order, and there was much hand-wringing about what form it ought to take. 'Our next release was going to be "My Lady",' said Reg, 'but after it was recorded, we decided that there was something wrong with it. We couldn't pinpoint it, but there was just something. Then we did a session, and thought "Night Of The Long Grass" was much better, so we released that instead. We felt that the song needed an outdoor feeling, and we wanted that to be immediately apparent – so we used this sound effects record on it. Then we added the girls' voices in the background, and it was just right.'

While ex-Shadow Jet Harris's version of 'My Lady' did not repair his broken fortunes, the rush-released 'Night Of The Long Grass' – all wuthering heights, trees clawing the moon, and wraithful choral headwind – made the Top 20...just. The fact that it hadn't proved to be a 'Ghost Riders In The Sky' or 'Johnny Remember Me' for the later 1960s rather undermined the group's bickerings with Larry Page about the material he foisted on them – like the 'pile of crap' that was 'Number 10 Downing Street' and, though all the Troggs were composing now, still-regular B-sides penned by himself, most recently with 'You're Lying' on the back of 'Give It To Me'.

Gone were the days of open-handed conviviality round Larry's desk now that they had accrued sufficient record-industry experience for glibness to defer to probing suspicions about fiscal wool being pulled over their eyes – and no wool was so white that a dyer couldn't blacken it. *L'affaire* Atco-Fontana rankled still – as did the procrastination about touring the USA. The four musicians – with Britton and Staples the principal advocates – began taking an earnest and unwelcome interest in Larry Page's management.

Discontent had never been expressed so nakedly since The Kinks as Larry fielded circular and sometimes half-understood cross-examinations – usually conducted by the tenacious Ten Feet Five pair – about where this percentage had gone or why so-and-so had been paid that much. As legal forces were mustered by The Troggs and Messrs Phillips and Barrett, Page was victim to intensifying character assassinations over venomous pints in a pub's murkiest corner.

After solicitors' letters fluttered on to his and Dick James' doormats, Larry turned a thoughtful steering wheel *en route* to Andover to sort out what must be surely some mistake. Who'd poisoned their minds against him? Sadness turned to shocked dignity and, back in London, rage that was terrible to hear on his discovery that The Troggs were thousands of miles away, ensconced in some record executive's air-conditioned flat in Greenwich Village, New York's vibrant bohemian district. God knows what avaricious leeches, hustlers and lawyers were queuing to submit their bids, and coming on to his boys like over-attentive if friendly wolves.

Looking for a new record company was as chancy as looking for a new girlfriend. 'We were getting mixed up with people in New York,' explained Presley, 'meeting label representatives and receiving offers. We couldn't say yea or nay, but they were pressurising us into making a decision. We were too young, too nervous about making the wrong move. We shifted hotels, but they found us. Stan flew over and suggested that we gave ourselves time to think – so we got a Dutch liner that took nine days to get back to England. We were almost the only ones in first class. We had the time of our lives – fantastic food and as much of it as you wanted. I was a big eater in those days, and I thought nothing of having two Sunday lunches, one after the other.'

With disembarkation in Southampton came the information that an understandably self-protecting Larry Page had issued counter-writs and had started cashing in what chips were left by issuing the antique 'Hi Hi Hazel' as a single – and it became the group's first serious miss since 'Lost Girl', lingering in the lower reaches of the Top 50 a week less than Geno Washington's arrangement of the same mediocrity had managed exactly a year earlier.

Yet, if no longer able to take chart placings for granted, The Troggs were to leave a final wound in the UK Top 10 with Reg's Sunday-afternoon special, recorded with Page as executive producer but Colin Frechter calling the shots: 'A friend of Dick James's had been sent to the studio to supervise the Troggs, and that all foundered. So I got a call to go in. They weren't talking to Larry, and they'd asked for their contracts back from Dick. I was a bit edgy about this, but "Love Is All Around" had something that's absolute magic.'

It was sent on its way with a superimposed string quartet – and a publicity junket fixed up at the Marquee club in Wardour Street. Similar in concept to the nonsense at Berlin Zoo, it involved a circus *grande dame* bringing along a full-grown lion on a chain. That the lady had two fingers missing wasn't conducive to relaxation, even as she attached the beast to heavy wooden pallets. 'For God's sake, hurry!' seethed an assistant sound engineer when thrusting forward a microphone to catch a growl. He got more than expected when, its sensitive nose tickled by static, a roaring half-ton of heaving muscle ran amok as far as it was able. Before calming down, the goaded brute had so frightened one female journalist that she dug her fingernails into a pegboard wall in an attempt to climb to safety.

For all the ferocity of its promotion, 'Love Is All Around' came to be regarded as a flower-power anthem like The Beatles' 'All You Need Is Love', as it revitalised The Troggs' flagging career with hit parade strikes across Europe – and boosted further the group's unlooked-for credibility with US hippies after 'Night Of The Long Grass' suffered airplay restrictions on the ridiculous premise that it referred to drugs.

Following a year in which schmaltz was represented in the charts as much as psychedelia, 'Love Is All Around' was so different from The Troggs' last big US smash that it might have been by a different group. As such, it brought much of the aura of a fresh sensation to the squirming ether of the USA, and, after months of dogged plugging, 'Love Is All Around' slinked into the *Billboard* list, gathered pace and came to rest high in the Top 20, and orchestral versions entered the supermarket muzak repertoire among other future easy-listening standards like 'Light My Fire', 'Up Up And Away' and Van Morrison's 'Brown-Eyed Girl'.

Though 'Love Is All Around' was also The Troggs' *Hot 100* swansong, its makers' name had been kept before the public through such as an 'Anyway That You Want Me' by Chicago's HP Lovecraft – after The Troggs' original wasn't released in the States – and The Mothers of Invention quoting 'Wild Thing' as a *leitmotiv* in their *We're Only In It For The Money magnum opus*. 'Wild Thing' was also the vehicle for a Top 20 send-up of presidential candidate Robert Kennedy – soon to die at the trigger-jerk of a lunatic – by Senator Bobby (TV funnyman Bill Minkin) and his Hardly Worth It Players. Finally, it was during 'Wild Thing' that Jimi Hendrix had sacrificed his guitar in a famous *woomph* of petrol at the International Pop Music Festival in Monterey, a few miles down the coast from San Francisco, at the height of the city's psychedelic summer.

It was now a false economy for the Troggs not to rake in the dollars in the baseball parks and concrete colosseums across the Atlantic – though, before they did – on a tour with The Who – there'd come a request for them to approach North America by stealth by entertaining the troops in Vietnam during the hottest period of the war. Ultimately, this proposition came to naught because the State Department in Washington couldn't offer protection to non-Americans as they hadn't even been able to prevent injury to the nation's own Timi Yuro, a singer direct from Hollywood, when the Vietcong had marched on Saigon.

'We didn't want VIP treatment,' protested Reg. 'We just felt that the soldiers and refugees were having a bad time, and needed some sort of entertainment. Naturally, we didn't expect to be flung into the front line. We just felt that, as we're playing in America, it seemed a shame to leave out Vietnam. Also, we were rather inquisitive to know what exactly is happening out there – to see if the newspapers give you the full story. A pop artiste usually only sees the bright side of life. People should see the bad things too.'

After this trail went cold, the Great Adventure began finally in March 1968 with disembarkation at Kennedy airport and long corridors of light and shadow; cameras clicking like typewriters, and stick-mikes thrust towards their mouths in hopes that one of the last unreconstructed British beat groups would crack back at the now stock questions about long hair, mini-skirts and all that, with a Beatle-esque combination of zaniness, unsentimentality, unblinking self-assurance and the poker-faced *what-are-you-laughing-at* way they told 'em. Yet nothing notably droll or even significant came from the lips of an overwhelmed and most unbrash Troggs during this press conference and other episodes of wry shallowness on pop radio conducted by yapping disc-jockeys with lurid *noms de turntable*.

The days when The Troggs might have headlined were past – and, as it was The Who who were going to sell tickets, The Who got top billing. Nevertheless, the ice broke and the two groups became pally in their common confinement in this torpid bandroom or that chartered flight. Moreover, the high point of the day wasn't always your spell on the boards, but the building-up, the winding-down and roguish pranks while other acts were on. Somewhere in America, Keith Moon, The Who's madcap drummer, sawed halfway through Ronnie Bond's drumsticks and wrapped tape around the cuts so that Ronnie ended up with only one stick with which to play three-quarters of The Troggs' set – not that the effect was noticed much as Reg virtually gulped the microphone when squaring up to a public address system constructed for sports commentators. His continuity and the 'Love Is All Around' *pianissimo* was undercut by a ceaseless barrage of stomping, whistling and bawled requests for the good old good ones.

After The Troggs were accorded a standing ovation in Birmingham, Alabama, reaction to The Who was a little more subdued than usual. At other venues too, the customers were on their feet and rippling spontaneously stagewards during the opening bars of The Troggs' casually cataclysmic performance. Afterwards, members of US garage bands might troop backstage to pay their respects to these distinguished living artefacts of the 'British Invasion' – who were becoming used to even the most garrulous fans suddenly falling silent in an awe-stricken sense of *deja vu* – as if The Troggs weren't quite real.

Box-office takings were astronomical, and what with 'Love Is All Around' and *The Who Sell Out* lingering in their respective Top 20s, the tour was extended to six weeks and into Canada where Reg would recall a confusing few minutes onstage in Montreal: 'Halfway through the act, everyone started applauding – and I thought that's good because we weren't actually playing at the time. Then we discovered the news of the president's resignation had just reached the auditorium.'

When the troupe crossed the frontier into New York state, they encountered The Yardbirds on their last legs after immortalising themselves on a lacklustre in-concert album in the Big Apple at the same 'funny gig where a lot of hippies turned up,' noted Reg, 'and they put a light show on before us'. This epitome of change was food for thought for individual Troggs as they wrestled with occupational as well as personal stock-taking in the anti-climax that followed those astounding moments on the US stages.

With a kind of despairing triumph came the realisation that these hadn't been an accurate barometer of market standing. That the writing seemed to be on the wall for the group was evinced by 'Little Girl' – 'I thought of that one in a lift in the Piccadilly Hotel in Manchester,' said Reg – released just before the North American expedition to elude the UK Top 30 as surely as the hated 'Hi Hi Hazel'. Apart from the most snowblinded fans, potential buyers tended to listen to Troggs records before purchase these days.

Another single, 'Surprise Surprise', was the subject of a promotional film short shot in New York to keep *Top Of The Pops* happy until its makers were available – if required – to plug it in the flesh. With Colin Fretcher pounding the eighty-eights *à la* Jerry Lee Lewis, 'Surprise Surprise' coincided with 1968's rock'n'roll revival as Bill Haley and Buddy Holly reissues crept into the charts, and medleys of classic rock closed the shows of post-psychedelic 'nice little bands' like Andromeda, Bethany (which contained a future Trogg in Pete Lucas), Tea And Symphony and Puce-Exploding Butterfly: names that implied musical insights less immediately graspable. Not so obviously 'regressive' were contemporary smashes such as The Move's 'Fire Brigade' with its Duane Eddy twang, and, reminiscent of Fats Domino, The Beatles' 'Lady Madonna'.

Under the circumstances, 'Surprise Surprise' should have scored more than a solitary week in the *NME* Top 30, but lukewarm reviews were the tip of an iceberg that had holed the metaphorical hulls of other old heroes too. On a downward spiral in the States, both The Dave Clark Five and Herman's Hermits were trying to recover lost ground at home. The latest Manfred Mann 45 had been their first to falter outside the charts, and the *NME*'s 'Alley Cat' tittle-tattler was crowing that 'this year, Yardbirds absent from Top 30'. On the slide too were The Kinks whose 'Wonderboy', released in the same week as 'Surprise Surprise', was the first indication that their sojourn in the UK chart was nearly spent.

Through amused or po-faced *Top Of The Pops* excursions, certain of these ailing 'bands' (not groups) indicated that they were past caring about the chart performances of fiddly two-minute singles that were marginal to a main body of work on 'albums' (not LPs). In this, they were abetted by the press offices of record labels now committing more of their budgets to 'concept' albums, rock operas *et al* by groups entering realms far distant from their R&B bedrock.

A borderline case, The Troggs had taken more trouble over their last album, *Cellophane*, than its predecessors. Though few tracks leapt out of the album grooves as potential smashes for others, never had each of the group worked so fully according to his capacity. A spirit of co-operation also exuded in such as 'Little Red Donkey', written by all four Troggs, and a Number One in South Africa for 17 weeks as a spin-off single.

There were also respective flying visits to the US *Hot 100* with 'You Can Cry If You Want To' at Number 93, and to the German Top 30 with 'Hip Hip Hooray', but otherwise The Troggs were in such desperate straits that knives had been withdrawn from Larry Page's back *pro tempore*, and he'd been back in the control booth for *Cellophane* and some of the A- and B-sides that were to fatten up 1968's *Mixed Bag*, The Troggs' final album before the Sixties stopped Swinging.

Treasured by most only in retrospect, *Mixed Bag* was a culmination of the group's attempts at adjustment to the slings and arrows of fashion via investigations into psychedelia that didn't quite get the point. Notable among these were Chris Britton's self-explanatory 'Maybe The Madman' (flip-side of 'Little Girl') and, with old Reg going on about 'the bamboo butterflies of yer mind', 'Purple Shades' – a number that he'd own up to being 'not really us. It's difficult if you weren't on drugs to write lyrics like that.'

Mixed Bag marked another stage in the initially imperceptible isolation of Pete Staples from his colleagues, telegraphed perhaps by the absence of his image in the 'live' photograph that graced the front cover of *Trogglodynamite*. Of less tangible significance, however, was when Plastic Penny and, more profoundly, The Loot found themselves running out of credit, and various members left to try again in another incarnation – three of The Loot re-formed as Hookfoot – while keeping the wolf from the door with session work that ranged from pot-boilers for comparative unknowns like Issac Guillory, Cochise and White Horse to better-paid jobs for Kevin Ayers, John Kongos, Lou Reed, Al Stewart and Mike Hugg. They were most extensively employed, however, by a cabal attached to Dick James' DJM label. This included Long John Baldry, Kiki Dee, Ann O'Dell and, most prestigiously, singing pianist Elton John.

Nevertheless, Plastic Penny's newest recruit, 24-year-old bass player Tony Murray's most important session – though it didn't seem so at the time – was helping out on a couple of *Mixed Bag* tracks while Pete, the last Trogg to marry, was honeymooning with his bride, Hilary. By now, he, Presley and Bond were living in Andover. Actually, Pete and Ronnie had never left; the former remaining with his parents until the nuptials, and the latter staying on in a council flat with his wife and two sons.

It might have been folly to hanker for a more upmarket abode before The Troggs had disassociated themselves formally from Larry Page. The writ had been served, and irreversible legal wheels set in motion. Indeed, High Court mud-slinging had dragged on for nigh on a year since the preliminary hearing, but soon the grey-wigged judge was to declare in Page's favour.

Groups, eh? Who needed them? It may have crossed Larry's mind fleetingly to follow Larry Parnes' example and quit pop management altogether, fling all of it back in their faces, so that there'd be one less poor sod to be used as a scapegoat by some silly little shower when its first serious flop came. To hell, anyway, with the record industry's short-sightedness, its mental sluggishness, its cloth-eared ignorance! Who needed the time-serving incompetence, the fake sincerity, the backstabbing and the contradiction of excessive thrift and heedless expenditure?

For a Trogg, getting shot of it would be like completing National Service in the sense that your old job might be waiting for you when you got back. An ostensibly uninviting prospect it might seem, but it wasn't too late for Reg to resume his bricklaying or, via supplicatory letter or application form, Chris to snare some cushy office job like Colin Blunstone had done when his group, The Zombies, had packed it in. Back on the lathe, Ronnie would be ribbed by workmates for having had ideas above his station, but they'd be less inclined to tease him about the aberrations of a flaming youth after they'd seen him perform at weekends or in support whenever a big name came to Andover. Then the years would fall away as they glimpsed a profile once defined by a *Top Of The Pops* arc-light.

Chapter 7
The Big Pranny

'It's the way I place the lyric on the beat; Ronnie hits a fraction behind it, and Chris's guitar is somewhere between the two. There's such a closeness in how that happens - a matter of a split second. Sometimes, we can do a whole show and it doesn't happen.'
Reg Presley

The old firm was back in business with Stan Phillips gripping the reins of management, albeit advised by a new agent in Danny Betesh, whose operational hub was in Manchester. Once enrolled into the chain of social clubs, civic halls, welfare institutes and citadels of 'quality' entertainment that fanned out from this 'Entertainment Capital of the North', a faded pop group could feed off it for years, often on the same bill as stand-up comedians, corny variety acts, thunder-thighed dancing girls and third-rate Sinatras. They'd be a 'forthcoming attraction', spoken of in the same breath as Freddy 'Parrot Face' Davis, George Formby impersonator Alan Randall and honky-tonk pianist Mrs. Mills – all diverting entertainers in their own fields.

The Troggs had completed their first northern cabaret engagement as early as March 1968. Current chart status had less meaning for the group than than the maintenance of the good humour of smartly-dressed audiences, rotten with money, who'd punished pricey liquor and guzzled their supper while a sunken orchestra sight-read discreet muzak as showtime crept closer. Then The Troggs, disinterested in the wings, would be subjected to a facetious build-up by some buffoon of an MC with only the foggiest notion about the music the customers were about to hear.

Less than five years after the frenzy of their first hit, there were no more screams as they walked on. Yet The Troggs were resilient. That they were still thought worthy of the odd mention in the music press put them above most other 1960s veterans in the same boat, and there was a sense of marking time on the understanding that, sooner or later, another song as good as 'Wild Thing' would come their way or that Reg would rediscover his knack for turning out 'I Can't Control Myself'-sized smashes.

After two years in London, Reg was now Andover's most renowned addressee, but, mooching drowsily to the nearby garage for cigarettes – and he was getting through two 20-packs of Rothmans per day now – Reg pondered that some stretches on the boards nowadays went by as blurs like some run-of-the-mill job you'd done since leaving school. Now and then, the group could be bought for more than they'd ever realised as chart-toppers – as they'd been recently for a week in cabaret at Birmingham's Dolce Vita – but usually it was one-nighters that were yielding perceptibly dwindling fees.

He felt sometimes as if he'd never made those hit records, won that acclaim, seen America or done any of the other things spoken of in orgies of maudlin reminiscence about the group that had had everything it took back in 1965 when the world was young. Dejecting too was the curtness of old music industry associates 'in a meeting', 'on another line', 'out to lunch' and 'too busy' to call him back. Time was when they were falling over themselves for The Troggs.

Pop obeys no law of natural justice, does it? How else could you explain why chart victories belonged to today's bland lookalike, soundalike acts – Edison Lighthouse, White Plains, Pickettywitch, Blue Mink, Brotherhood Of Man, Arrival *ad nauseum*, while The Troggs had tramped a well-beaten path from nearly overtaking The Beatles to making the most of every chance that came their way during the downfall that followed; their very name a millstone round their necks? No hit record for over a year meant that no member could be trusted not to stray now time seemed to be running out. It seemed silly to be anything but pessimistic.

About once a month from around the middle of 1966, the music press had reported a schism in some group or other – or a key member setting himself apart from those with whom he'd been in earshot for every working day since God knows when. Lead guitarist Dave Davies had had a Top 10 strike, 'Death Of A Clown', in 1967 without his fellow Kinks, and Wayne Fontana had cast aside his Mindbenders. It was Eric Burdon *and* The Animals now – just as it was Don Craine's *New* Downliners Sect. Drawn from his exile as an insurance clerk, Colin Blunstone had reappeared in the UK Top 30 as 'Neil McArthur' with 1969's orchestral revamp of his Zombies hit 'She's Not There', while Dave Dee pursued a middle-of-the-road path after parting from Dozy, Beaky, Mick and Tich – who, as 'DBMT', were attempting to woo the 'progressive' market.

Though The Troggs would never split so decisively, all four inaugurated parallel solo careers, one way or another, as the decade turned. Ronnie Bond's first A-side in his own right had come about, allegedly, by accident after he volunteered to enter the vocal booth when Reg proved unable to get to grips with 'Anything For You', a number intended for the group until it was decided to chance releasing it under the drummer's own name.

'Anything For You' was no 'Death Of A Clown' – and neither was Reg's 'Lucinda Lee'. Lost to the archives of oblivion too was *As I Am*, a Chris Britton solo LP. These commercial plummetings were to fuel Pete Staples' sour retrospection that 'When everybody started to release their own thing, it just disintegrated. We were fragmented, and that's when it broke down.'

Physically at least, Ronnie had been none too hale when he was prostrated – with 'nervous exhaustion' so it was put about – during the season in Birmingham. The Troggs had finished the week with Roger Pope from The Loot, as glad of the work as Plastic Penny's Tony Murray had been when filling in for Pete on *Mixed Bag*.

From merely deputising for Staples, Murray was to become his successor. Later, Pete was to cite family commitments as his reason for leaving. However, Reg Presley insisted that 'We were always considered basic and simple but Peter was one step behind us. He had to go, but it's a shame because he's such a nice guy.' Presley was long enough in the tooth as The Troggs' front man to detect the most subtle negative reaction from even those who lapped up any deficiencies as the prerogative of glamour, and 'it was becoming clear that Pete wasn't getting the live shows together.

'One night, his bass packed up – as it did regularly – and he went off to find the dressing room to get his spare lead. He plugged it into the guitar, and on the way back, it got wrapped round a pipe. Even if he'd come out and just given them something to see, it'd have been better than nothing. Another night, we came to do "With A Girl Like You", and he insisted that we'd already played it. It brought the whole band down, and it started to fester.'

Chris in particular was emitting an almost palpable aura of self-loathing as he slouched on with a face like an Aldershot winter. Yet, despite everything, he and Pete had been bound for longer than the other two by common ordeal and jubilation. Finally, Britton dared the speech that he'd been agonising over in bed. Though Ronnie and Reg had run out of patience too, 'we hadn't liked to say anything because we were from The Troggs and they were from Ten Feet Five.'

The cards were on the table, and, within a week, an announcement was made to any interested press that Tony Murray was the new Trogg. Just as The Animals, eternal Geordies, had brought in a southerner to replace their departing organist, Alan Price, so The Troggs now had a Irishman – and a player as technically accomplished and versatile as Chris Britton. After studying piano at Dublin's London School of Music for three years, the adolescent Tony had been gainfully employed in a showband, that eclectic institution as peculiar to the Emerald Isle as mock-yokel bands were to the West Country.

Weary of yellow-keyed, out-of-tune palais pianos, he underwent a crash course in the rudiments of bass guitar, and, on forging a lithely contrapuntal style, set sail for England as one of Bob Ormsby's All-Stars, who'd found a niche in Midlands clubs for expatriate Irish such as Birmingham's Hope and Shamrock and like oases of draught Guinness, altercations between Loyalists and Republicans, and the juke-box balm of 'Delaney's Donkey', 'The Rose Of Tralee' and Jim Reeves.

With this the ceiling of the All-Stars' ambition, Murray sought studio work in London. From session circles, Plastic Penny took shape, had its hit and petered out, and its personnel returned to studio security. As providers of rhythmic backbone, Tony and Roger Pope became the Tweedledum and Tweedledee of DJM sessions, notably ghosting current smashes on the 'Hot Hits' series of budget albums and applying their touch to 1969's *Empty Sky*, the debut LP of one yet to be a mainstay of 'contemporary' rock's ruling class. 'At that time, Elton John was a tea boy on fifteen pounds a week at DJM records,' recalled Tony, 'and Bernie Taupin, his lyricist, was on a ten pound a week retainer from Dick James. They asked me to do the album – which went to Number One in the States. I actually got paid the session money when I needed it, but it would have been nice if he had sent me a cheque for ten grand.'

Murray entered The Troggs' orbit via *Mixed Bag*, Chris Britton's *As I Am*, taped in Regent Sound, and the two Page Orchestra albums that saw the decade out, lushly-arranged *From Larry With Love* and an eponymous 1969 offering of more of the same. 'After an Orchestra session, Larry approached me and asked if I'd be interested in actually joining The Troggs,' said Tony. 'I'd had my first son; I needed some regular money, and they offered a wage. For me, this was something new, so I said OK. Then I had to go to see Larry at Page One offices. There was this reception area where I had to sit and wait for Larry to finish with someone else – when who should walk in but Pete Staples. It was very embarrassing. I was living in London at the time, and Reg said to come down to Andover for a weekend which ended with a permanent move.'

As Chris Britton had been on his first day at Wolverdene Primary, Tony began as just a satellite in his new workmates' established firmament as, not purposely snubbing him, they spoke of venues he'd never played, people he didn't know. Logging the characteristics of the longer-serving Troggs, Murray noted that, as well as self-immolatory tendencies, Ronnie was as fond of practical jokes as Keith Moon. Sharing a Swedish hotel suite with Bond much later, the prematurely white-haired Tony asked if the drummer, about to go shopping, to bring back some auburn hair dye. However, the colour that the devil in Ronnie purchased was the brightest red available – so red-hot, in fact, that after it dried, Murray's shocked eyes widened in the mirror, and, apart from the necessary delivery of the show, he remained hidden in the room, contemplating revenge and how long the muck would take to grow out.

Eventually, he saw the funny side of this particular diversion from the monotony of relentless touring – for, with singing and playing instruments their only saleable trade, The Troggs seemed to be in the same endless-highway dilemma as the olde-tyme rockers or black bluesmen of a pre-Beatle age – as records had become adjuncts to earnings on the road.

'Evil Woman', 'Easy Livin'', 'Lover' and, gawd help us, 'The Raver' had each made a heart-sinkingly familiar journey into the bargain bin before the parting of the ways for Page One's principal shareholders; Dick James to concentrate on DJM Records, Larry Page taking The Nerve, The Loot, Plastic Penny and his latest finds, Vanity Fair, Kincaid and Craig (containing drummer Carl Palmer, later with ELP).

Apart from Vanity Fair with their hat-trick of Top 20 entries, none of these acts prospered, even when on the roster of Larry's new Penny Farthing label – which stayed afloat, nonetheless, with an early 1970s chart bonanza of country-pop persuasion by Birmingham's grizzled

Daniel Boone, alias Peter Lee Sterling, failed 1960s pop star, successful jobbing songwriter – and Dave Dee's musical director. Penny Farthing scored too with Shocking Blue, The Johnny Pearson Orchestra, Billy Howard and even Chelsea Football Club (with 1972's jingoist 'Blue Is The Colour').

Caught between the devil and the deep blue sea, The Troggs had gone to DJM, on the crest of a wave now that Elton's John's second album was the first of his seven consecutive US million-sellers. For a while, DJM did not deny hearsay about Reg Presley composing the main title theme for a Hollywood movie, and The Troggs being offered acting roles in one. None of this was actually true, and it was an *au naturel* incident that was to bring them their only enduring taste of fame – or, more appropriately, notoriety – during this period.

On *Mixed Bag*, they'd consumed needle-time with a dialogue track, 'Off The Record', but an unscripted and illicitly recorded studio discussion was to be the group's best-remembered – and most inadvertent – artistic statement from the early 1970s. According to 'The Raver', *Melody Maker*'s gossip-monger, the first recipients of run-off cassettes of this bootleg 'Troggs Tape' were Elton John and Jon Hiseman, drummer-leader of Colosseum. Apparently, it was priceless in every sense of the word – and word circulated quickly that it was on a par with the Rolling Stones' X-certificate 'Cocksucker Blues', and the original version of 'Je T'Aime...Moi Non Plus' – recounted by those who hadn't heard it as being nothing less than four minutes 35 seconds of Brigitte Bardot and Serge Gainsbourg in actual sexual congress.

This was not correct, but the essence of both 'Cocksucker Blues' and 'Je T'Aime...' was such that you can readily understand why the artists involved were opposed to official release. Yet the master tapes of both were not destroyed, but locked away to lie unforgotten for years as erroneous legends persisted – just as they did about the Troggs Tape.

The group's own eyes were opened to its existence nine months after the event when they entered a bar frequented by London showbusiness folk. The landlord and his cronies spoke in low voices and exchanged knowing smirks as The Troggs settled at a table with their drinks. Then from the small speakers of the pub's sound system came Ronnie's prelusive '...get into it! It's a fuckin' Number One! If that bastard don't go, I fuckin' retire...' By the time this idea of a joke stretched into its 20th unforgiving minute, it had occasioned titters that became a subdued laugh and then a delirium of appalled joy with sly glances at The Troggs who had stiffened, stared hard at each other and looked as if they were about to do something before chuckling along too, especially when a squabble exploded like shrapnel over a one-bar percussion fill a child could do; Bond – 'the cunt who's doin' it' – almost coming to blows with Presley, addressed as 'you big pranny!' However, the reviling of each other had an underlying if brusque affection to it that ensured that the drummer's pent-up rage did not overflow into violence.

Though such florid dissension was not untypical of many other groups, a tabloid newspaper editor, on learning about it one day from his pop columnist, was to authorise the pungent disclosure that exactly 137 cuss-words – some of them (eg 'pranny') peculiar to Hampshire – had emerged from the lips of those of whom so much had been made for their politeness and ingenuous decency. During the 'I Can't Control Myself' furore, hadn't Larry Page swooped to its composer's defence with 'I doubt whether Reg Presley is capable of an obscene remark. He and his mind do not work that way'? Presley himself would agree that 'I never used to swear much. The strongest word I used was "bloody" or the occasional "bugger". I didn't like to hear people swear.' Furthermore, as recently as June 1968, Ronnie had been asked by Lynda, the fan-club secretary, if the group ever swore. 'Yes,' he replied, 'but only when pressed.'

Now brutalised by five years in the music business, The Troggs thought nothing of plunging into toilet-talk that would shock a drunken marine, despite Larry's continued assurance that they were still as pure as the driven snow when conducting a rather haughty US impresario to the group's dressing room. The visitor's own observations were to bely this impression until four shame-smitten musicians became aware of his presence after excruciating moments that had lasted forever for Page while they were marinating the air with the vilest curses. 'Because Pete had done something wrong during the show,' explained Reg, 'we were calling him all the names under the sun!'

The language was generally as strong during rehearsals in garage or village hall back in Andover – and had the group foreseen what was going to happen, they may have insisted on more time to iron out disagreements in this usual way when Dick James rang one Friday afternoon in 1971 to say he wanted them in an Oxford Street studio the following Monday to record the remaining single they had to make for DJM before the contract's expiry date.

At such short notice, nobody had either the time or inclination to routine anything that weekend, and so it was that the Troggs hoped that form would overall the content of 'Tranquillity', an umbrella term for particles of a would-be Presley song from which only traces of pattern were discernible after interminable centuries of false starts and scrapped takes, punctuated by the musicians and their entourage – with no Larry Page figure in charge – arguing about hiring an independent producer before trying to sort out the mess themselves.

Nothing from the session was seen as salvageable – or was it? As if watching a tennis match, the engineer – whose name no-one has hitherto recalled – blinked from one corner to the other of an increasingly more agitated debate as flare-ups, simmering huffs and murmured intrigues, all riddled with swearing, scaled a height of vexation and cross-purpose that was beyond his experience. It made him want to collapse, screaming with hilarity, onto the floor, but he suppressed the howl of laughter that was nearly hurtling out of his mouth to switch on the tape machine and keep it running. What else could he do but preserve the fiasco as cultural history, a comforting 'bad example' for nervous studio novices – and perhaps a little profit for himself?

Chapter 8
'Everything's Funny'

**'I knew how to accept that our records weren't selling
without getting bitter about it.'**
Reg Presley

For most of the 1970s, the post-Staples Troggs would be waiting, like Mr Micawber, for something to turn up as the seasons of pop revolved in time-honoured growth, death and rebirth, and the group stood still in hope of a fertile spring when they'd bloom again. While so marking time, The Troggs were to reach out in the first half of the decade to headbangers rather than introverted adolescent diarists who preferred becoming pleasantly melancholy with the acoustic solemnities of singer-songwriter James Taylor (a sort of Woodstock Generation Pat Boone) and, if in sentimental mood, to 'Love Is All Around' on the bedsit stereo – to getting out of their brains on Black Sabbath's blues-plagiarised sound-pictures of Genghis Khan carnage after limbering up with 'Wild Thing'.

What with a recent revival of 'I Want You' by Michigan's uncompromisingly violent MC5, The Troggs were well-placed to pander to the assumed desires of the heavy-metal consumer – as they did with 'Feels Like A Woman' with its affinity to Free's 'All Right Now', *the* hit song of 1970. 'Power trios' were the thing then; most of them harking back to the one guitar-bass-drums test cases of such as Johnny Kidd and the Pirates, The Tony Sheridan Trio, Liverpool's Big Three and, when honest enough to admit it, The Troggs. That said, any 'Shakin' All Over'-type muted subtleties or 'Any Way That You Want Me'-esque restraint that Led Zeppelin, Free, the après-'Tommy' Who, Rory Gallagher's Taste and even Black Sabbath might

Above: The Senators, 1960. Left to right: Pete Staples, Arthur Smart, Johnny Walker and Bruce Turner.
Below: Ten Feet Five, '63. Left to right: Dave Smith, Chris Britton, John Hayward, Chris Penfound & Pete Staples.

Above: Ex-brickie Reg revisits his old stamping ground.

Below: Backstage on tour with David Garrick (centre) and Stan Phillips (first manager of The Troggs) with a member of Sounds Incorporated just in shot.

Mean and moody (**above**) gives way to flowered shirts in '67 (**below**).

Left: Reg suited and booted.

Left: Jurassic Park foretold? Pete, Ronnie, Chris and (foreground) Reg have monster success in Germany.

Above: Behind bars in Berlin as zookeepers and group ham it up for the camera.

Above: Bringing it all back home. The Troggs pose in November 1966 outside a music shop in their native Andover.

Right: Pete in full flight on *Ready Steady Go!*

Above: Reg serenades Brenda in their London flat, 1968. Happily, this turned out to be one of showbusiness's longest-lasting marriages and still goes strong today.

Above: Riding the range in the United States.

Below: Sweden, 1969.

Above: The inimitable Ronnie Bond behind the kit.

Left: Striped jackets became a Troggs trademark for a while.

Above: The Troggs meet one of Dr Who's Daleks.

Above: Pete Lucas (left) with Tich Amey, who became a Trogg in 1977.

Below: Take that Rod Stewart! Reg pumps iron.

Right: In the studio with the REM boys for 'Athens Andover'.

Below: The anvil chorus – today's Troggs play up to the 'country boy' image.

Left: Gotta light, Mac? A predatory Presley gives it his all.

Below: On stage in the 1980s.

Reg poses with chart-toppers Wet Wet Wet (**above**), and picks up the Ivor Novello awards for writing their record-setting hit 'Love Is All Around' (**right**).

Opposite: Acting with Suzi Quatro (**top**) and composing in 1991 (**bottom**).

Above: The Troggs of today. Joining Chris (front left) and the ever-present Reg (top right) are Dave Maggs (top left) and Pete Lucas (front right).

have displayed in the studio was lost on the boards where high decibels and heads-down-no-nonsense rock was the order of the day.

If as gut-wrenching too in their way, The Troggs often found the going difficult in front of crowds who expected Sabbath-like heavy metal for the price of admission, and said as much between songs. Yet had they adapted enough of the trend – as maybe a UK 'answer' to Canned Heat – The Troggs might have had, if not a walkover, then a smoother gaining of their toehold in the colleges as loveable curios from the recent past as Gary Glitter would be on the same circuit in the 1980s.

Before they figured out too, that a lot of the youngsters who'd grown up to their hits were now young adults in higher education, 'we didn't fit in anywhere that was going on,' shrugged Reg Presley, 'all those long instrumental solos in which you could marry, have kids and divorce before they were over...we stretched out "Gonna Make You" like that to be trendy, but it really wasn't our scene. You bled in and out of those fads as much as you dare go without either feeling a prize prat or alienating old fans. To me, it was musos getting their rocks off. It was for the benefit of the group rather than the audience. We didn't fit into nostalgia cabaret either. I wasn't happy on stage. Nothing seemed right in any shape or form.'

Another year with no hits, and The Troggs might be in danger of being forgotten in Britain and the USA, but 1973's 'Strange Movies' would claw into the Top 10 in Germany and the Netherlands, going to the very top in Spain. Three years earlier, unsolicited snippet coverage in a South African TV commercial of 'Feels Like A Woman' – which began life as B-side of 'Everything's Funny', a unique Britton-Presley collaboration – catapulted it to Number One in that territory too. If caught off-guard by this windfall, the group raised liberal eyebrows with a tour of the Transvaal, where the subject of race was as sensitive as that of religion in Northern Ireland. They refused to appear before segregated audiences, though authorities circumvented this as best they could by herding blacks on one side of the hall, whites on the other.

The protraction of this winning streak in South Africa may be attributed to the right-wing militancy that had precipitated the removal of Beatles records from radio playlists since 1966 when the republic's newspapers had picked up on the story of John Lennon 'boasting' that he and his outfit were more popular than Christ (though the arch-Beatle was actually bemoaning the increasing godlessness of the times). With this major competitor out of the race –

and 'I Can't Control Myself' a hazy memory, and the existence of the Troggs Tape not yet common knowledge – adult Boers reasoned that, if their children had to like British beat groups, let it be ones who didn't blot their copybooks with blasphemy and churned out resolute three-chord pop rather than this marijuana-smoking nonsense that those amoral Beatles and all the bands that took their cues from them were playing.

While euphoric with the success of 'Feels Like A Woman' in this equatorial clime, Reg was to be confounded in his opinion that 'If any number can put us back in the British charts, that one can. It is aggressive rather than progressive, which is a type of music we share with people like Slade and the Stones.' With Jagger *et al*'s latest 45, 'Brown Sugar' ruling the US *Hot 100*, and Slade, a four-piece from the Black Country, slugging it out with Gary Glitter, T Rex and David Bowie for glam-rock domination, there was sufficient grounds for The Troggs as a whole to hold on hoping that fortunes would revive.

This, however, wasn't hopeful enough for Chris Britton, a being apart geographically as well as philosophically. Living in Walton-on-Thames again, he was thinking aloud to his second wife about a more sedate pace of life now that an opportunity had presented itself to invest in and run a disco-*cum*-nightclub in Portugal. Besides, after growing to manhood in the hothouse of The Troggs, he was sick of being treated like a food pigeonhole in a self-service cafeteria. No more was it to be taken for granted that Chris Britton existed only to vend entertainment to people who thought a thousand miles was just a few inches on a map.

It was a typical journeyman musician's lot, but Chris was recalling too many drained moments when he'd put down the challenging book he'd scarcely peeked at since a given string of bookings began, and glowered from his room in this Holiday Inn or that Trust House, his sun-blanked spectacle lenses flashing like a heliograph over the concrete desolation of the car park. Was this all there was? A Ramada in Belgium was just like a Crest in Scotland. The Coca-Cola tasted exactly the same. If it's Tuesday, it must be Stockholm.

Let's tarry for a while on the latter-day Troggs' tour coach with a tired driver. You're suffering from a headache, an eye-crossing cough and a certain queasiness after that last plateful of overpriced lard-and-chips, hours of torpid warmth ago in a nameless service station on the autobahn. Now you are on a flight to a soundcheck somewhere in Scandinavia. Eyes glazed, brain numb, you could soundcheck forever. After the show – and contrary to what was sensationalised in the tabloids – you're more likely to drink in a what's-the-best-pint-you've-ever-had? ennui that anything resembling either *Satyricon* or a BBC mock-up of an imagined pop group drugs-and-sex debauch with pushers, groupies and loud-mouthed showbiz periphery almost smothering the blues jam on an improvised stage.

In tomorrow's dressing room, you'll wait in bored despair as shiftless equipment changeovers keep the second house in Innsbruck waiting. The stagehands loaf about, eating pork pies and smoking. Isolated in the midst of it, what was there left to enjoy about such a debasing job in which, like them, you couldn't wait until knocking-off time?

Nevertheless, enough pride and concern about the group lingered to deject Chris Britton. It wasn't merely fear of seizing up as a stage performer either as, when he finally got to bed, stress-related tension in his bones and muscles might have him lying as rigid as a crusader on a tomb. There was also the disturbing psychological undertow that, according to the laws of averages and superstition, there was bound to be a serious accident sooner or later – as there'd been for Johnny Kidd, killed in a road accident near Preston, and crash-landing soulman Otis Redding, whose career had taken a turn for the better with a posthumous US chart-topper, albeit not entirely on 'sympathy sales'. More recently, he'd read in *Melody Maker* of a guitarist in Stone The Crows absorbing more than enough high voltage to kill him after touching a microphone because persons unknown had been tampering with the wiring of the PA system.

After Chris chose the scent of Iberian suntan lotion over dressing-room fug, The Troggs suffered a dreadful week in Poland with a stop-gap guitarist from Andover whose principal virtue was availability. Vacillating between despondent chagrin and guarded enthusiasm in his capacity as *de jure* leader of a once world-famous group with its heart ripped out, it was Reg Presley's judgement that 'the guitarists that came after were better, but didn't understand what The Troggs were all about.'

The cream of the crop was Richard Moore, a Canadian whose earnest dedication to his craft had its downside when, if he considered that the item that Reg was announcing wasn't suitable for that particular point in the set, he would launch impetuously into one that he reckoned was, an unhelpful practice that had Ronnie and Tony exchanging nervous glances, and, on one occasion, would goad a piqued singer to quit the stage, the building and the town immediately, leaving the other three to face the music.

A more absolute departure had been that of Stan Phillips who, well into his fifties, had the removed look of a dying man – which he was. Since then, the destiny of the Troggs had been bound up for not quite two years with that of Peter Walsh, recommended by fellow Mancunian Danny Betesh. One main point in Walsh's favour was his reputation for keeping fading 1960s groups in work, even if it was only staving off a drift back to whatever local venues were still standing by flinging them into an outer darkness of the supper clubs and out-of-the-way dance halls from Eire to Yugoslavia. Nevertheless, holding on to their flashback grandeur by running through their best-loved songs for those who still loved them wasn't such a bad place for The Troggs to be in the mid-1970s.

By the time they parted – fairly amicably – from Peter, the group had moved a little closer to a qualified renaissance via the patronage of fashionable journalists who'd decided that, like the restoration of 'Merry Monarch' Charles II after Cromwell's joyless Protectorate, there had to be a swing back to the cheap thrills of the *in-yer-face* shouting and banging of disaffected youth as a reaction against the ghastly present with its stadium 'superstars'. With glam-rock and pub-rock as milestones, and punk the final destination, this judgement was to prove correct, though those who'd made it were mostly from a school of over-analysing pundits that intellectualised the unintellectual; turned perfume back into a rotten egg, and told you what Greil Marcus had written about 'innovation and continuity in Little Richard's vocal style', and what Simon Frith thought he meant.

This accelerated infiltration of academia into pop becomes relevant to this discussion through the late Lester Bangs, a 'respected' US rock writer, who dismantled The Troggs and stuck them back together again in a 28-page eulogy in *Who Put The Bomp?*, a Californian magazine catering for the kind of person who was breaking into an anticipatory sweat on spotting a pile of scratched 45s on a bric-a-brac stall – a foot-soldier in a growing and increasingly less silent global army of disenchanted musical renegades who turned their noses up at both James Taylor and Black Sabbath to scour second-hand bazaars and the few vintage record shops around, for artefacts from earlier and more exciting musical eras.

Had Reg Presley read Lester's effort – which he hasn't to this day – it might have affirmed his conjecture then that 'we're a cult thing in the States. It has always been the case. We are far more respected over there for having started the heavy sound, while Britain treats us as a joke. I don't mean the fans, but the business people down us.

Producers, DJs, other groups – they've all had a go.'

It wasn't quite 'all'. One most conspicuous champion was Radio 1's 'underground' disc-jockey, John Peel, while systemising fine feelings about The Troggs more coherently than Bangs was a 1972 article in the now radical *NME* that paraded the party line of grassroots backsliding. Next, *Time Out*, the metropolitan events guide, front-paged Reg, a most game interviewee, from the open-air café in the middle of Regent's Park.

Partly because of the enthusiast reports in *Who Put The Bomp*, the *NME* and suchlike, the Troggs were cool – sort of – and certain evenings were not unlike those that Reg and Ronnie had known back in Andover with the old line-up. Involved onlookers might cheer after an especially *bravura* 'I Can't Control Myself' with Reg taking it down easy for the bridge before piling up the tension to explosive panic for the re-entry of the *'ba-ba-ba'*s that brought the house down. As memorable in its way as that Boxing Day night at the Moore Hall in 1965 was an engagement in a holiday-camp ballroom 'and there were about a thousand people there,' estimated Reg. 'Everything was spot-on – the audience was perfect, you could not fault anything. It was absolute perfection.'

Word got around, and brought out odd and conflicting accounts of what people claimed to have seen or heard about the mere mortals behind the Troggs Tape, but many could not cite an explicit source of such intelligence. Hoarders of pop trivia would relate what were derided then as tall tales about Chris Britton's prowess as a flamenco guitarist, and Reg inventing the motorway fog warning light. Such apparent myths – though both were absolutely true – improved with age in the teeth of dull truth like Ronnie's excursions up the road for a darts match; Brenda and Reg redecorating their front room, and Pete Staples ploughing back his royalties from bygone recordings into a joinery and antiques business before streamlining it into general joinery.

Pete's recoupings of more than golden memories from the hits were modest compared to those of Reg, who had appointed the same supposedly efficient financial consultant that Peter Walsh used to superintend the mazy balance sheets, computer run-offs and ledgers accumulated since 'Wild Thing', and minimise the ravages of Inland Revenue supertax.

Blissfully unaware that the net was already closing with a vengeance – and that the economic slump caused by the 1973 oil crisis was looming – Reg and Brenda's search for a house commensurate with the means they'd been assured were at their disposal concluded with the purchase of land just off the A303 for the fulfilling of Reg's long-held dream to build his own house. The mock-Swiss chalet – 'Harewood Lodge' – was, therefore, an outlet for all manner of structural intricacies as he astounded the architect with erudite critiques of the survey report: his spinning of learned technicalities about the advantages of an iron girder over a concrete lintel on a supporting wall, and his unsettling awareness of the difference between top-of-the-range and shoddy building materials.

As to what had paid for the bath with gold fittings, the sunken bed area, and the brick-and-flint bar, you only had to look at the unbelievable outcome of a showbusiness career that seemed to promise Reg and his wife a dotage rich in material comforts beneath untroubled skies as the Number Ones, the money down the drain, the Troggs Tapes and so forth were transformed to matters of minor importance.

Situated where he was, however, the past was never far away. Down in the town, however, many of the old haunts were no more. The Fiesta was now a car park; the Moore Hall bore another name, while the TA Centre had been torn down after a fire had set the wheels of demolition paperwork in motion as the staircases fell in and, bit by bit, the walls crumbled. If it had been a scene in a horror film, you'd have heard 'Walkin' The Dog' as if from a seaside conch, and seen a spectral Pete Mystery wailing and rattling chains to the beat. Nevertheless, with a modernised interior, the Savoy Cinema still stood, and there existed *a* Copper Kettle (though the original site now accommodated the Woolwich Building Society), and the likes of Dave Wright were barring the chord changes of numbers they'd played since the 1950s in venues like Lance Barrett's Country Bumpkin club.

It was imagined that The Troggs were still too expensive for Lance or any other parochial impresario. Yet it was feasible to experience the group for less than half the discomfort and inconvenience of the scream-rent Salisbury City Hall engagement in dear, dead 1966.

The parameters of The Troggs' work spectrum had narrowed sufficiently to bring them as near as Farnborough Technical College in 1974. The PA desk and the rest of the hardware had been assembled but was still being tested, *one-two one-two*, when the musicians strode through the swing doors into the dusty, curtained half-light for what would not be a routine dance in another nondescript Students' Union hall, but the most harrowing ordeal of their public journey – and its only instance of direct violence.

For a swaggering phalanx of eight youths from Calcot, one of Reading's pokier suburbs, whatever was happening on stage would be secondary to getting fighting drunk on cheap spirits, and seeking more brutal sensual recreation than merely cavorting in the gloom past the footlights. If you so much as glanced at them, the action could be *you* – and if there wasn't even that much justification to start a punch-up, they'd make some. Ugly people who wanted to make everything else ugly too, they procured ice-cubes from the common room bar to push down the cleavages and hot-pants of girls so that incensed boyfriends would end up writhing around in a forest of kicking 'bovver boots' to amused jeers from bestial faces out for an eyeful of unofficial spectator sport.

Still itching to start something, the gang's butterfly attention fixed on the main attraction. However, their heckling failed to spoil an uproariously joyous evening as The Troggs rode 'em on down. Though they'd never say so, no such yob could fault the playing or the group launching into unashamed classic rock if they felt like it. Neither could he complain that they hadn't done his favourite from the backlog of hits. The air of menace was defused – or so it seemed – and the four principals ambled back on for an encore that was marred by a travesty of legitimate admiration when a couple of the mob from Calcot, Chad-like in front of Richard Moore's feet, yanked a carpet from under him, causing the guitarist to topple backwards into his speaker stack.

Thus far, Reg Presley, a past master at verbal fencing, had restricted himself to the odd mild reproof from the footlights, but this last straw had him down in the throng, seizing the principal culprit by the lapels and administering face-slapping retribution. This was the thrill divine, what the Calcot contingent been waiting for since entering without paying through a toilet window – and there wasn't a moment to lose. A metal-framed chair came down on Reg, but, as blood cascaded from him, bouncers waded in and he was able to beat a quick retreat to the stage where, underestimating their number, he dared the trouble-maker to come and get what he deserved in the bunker-like dressing room. Surely he'd never take Reg up on it in a million years?

He did – and so did his seven mates – and the subsequent scuffle left Richard Moore with a punctured lung and another knife wound in his shoulder. The assailant was a gentleman – so it would be divulged in Winchester Crown Court – under investigation already for rape. He tried to run from this latest felony, but was restrained by college security officers until a police squad car bore him off into custody to await an eventual four-year prison sentence for grievous bodily harm.

The incident filled many column inches in the *Aldershot News*, but only stray paragraphs in most of the nationals. Despite fullish houses whenever they appeared, The Troggs weren't big news anymore. As poor sales of new recordings against healthy returns for reissues demonstrated too plainly, all that fans, old and new, wanted were the sounds of yesteryear.

Not forestalling deletion either was an *in extremis* reggae remake of 'Wild Thing' after The Troggs changed labels for the third time in four years. From DJM via Pye – and a one-shot Reg Presley solo 45 on CBS in 1973 – they would end up on Penny Farthing, perhaps the last bolt-hole anyone might have expected to find them. 'We went back with Larry to see if there was any sparkle there,' explained Reg – but, with half-a-dozen pot-shots at the singles chart and an equally unviable eponymous LP spread over three years, The Troggs would know more indubitably than ever that the mid-1970s was not the time for a comeback.

A sure sign of creative as well as commercial insolvency was an increased reliance on revivals, either of numbers in the set from the year dot like 'No Particular Place To Go' and 'Got Love If You Want It' – or items from the hit repertoires of contemporaries, notably an extraordinary 'Good Vibrations'. The arrival of an amused telegram from Beach Boy Bruce Johnston climaxed the nine-days-wonder that was The Troggs' treatment, seen today as a none-too-subtle novelty during an era when British television sitcoms were fraught with innuendo about tits and dildos. If impregnated with a little 'I Can't Control Myself' suggestiveness via minor fracturing of the lyrics in Presley's half-spoken Andover twang, it approximated closely to the blueprint's layers of treated sound, and certainly it was more entertaining than the version The Beach Boys' themselves were doing in concert, complete with chief buffoon Mike Love's asinine remarks during the quiet section.

Like both The Beach Boys and The Troggs, other artists better known for their own work were releasing non-originals in the mid-1970s, either to display their skills as 'interpreters' or simply because they too were running out of ideas. Bryan Ferry, Jonathan King, John Lennon and The Hollies were to issue entire albums of oldies after David Bowie set the ball rolling with 1973's *Pin-Ups*, an affectionate trawl through British beat group classics.

While no Troggs opus was selected for *Pin-Ups*, Bowie made

amends by requesting the group's presence before an invited audience on 1974's *Midnight Special*, a TV extravaganza to be networked in the USA – timely as another overhaul of 'Wild Thing' (by Fancy, an entity connected to the Plastic Plastic-Loot-Hookfoot clique) was a 'sleeper' hit in the current US Top 20.

Midnight Special's star had *carte blanche* to turn his every whim into audio-visual reality – and Bowie, the most outrageous glam-rocker of them all, had some exquisite whims. During the three days set aside to film the show on location at the Marquee, among many transfixing sights were a cameo by the transsexual Wayne County dressed as a lady; Marianne Faithfull in a cross between a nun's habit and buttock-revealing mini-skirt, and, for the finale, Bowie himself, a sartorial vision in stiletto heels and a black fishnet number that, from certain angles, displayed his genitalia to the front rows.

Keeping North America's viewing public in tasteful focus, the latter sightings fluttered on to the cutting room floor, and a watchdog of decency asked Reg Presley to tone down the 'everyone was in bed' line of 'Strange Movies'. Obligingly, Reg had made it 'everyone lost their head' while The Troggs steeled himself to face facts in front of a teenage audience, some of them aware of 'Wild Thing' as just a playpen memory. The four needn't have worried. Coming belligerently alive when the lights hit them, The Troggs' five-song turn was a triumph because everyone there wanted it to be. Quite a few had a glimmer of how much the long-gone 1960s hitmakers had on their plate, and so adored them for wanting to please.

Three items – 'I Can't Control Myself', 'Wild Thing' and 'Strange Movies' – featured on the finished product, and to a lot of *Midnight Special* consumers, The Troggs stole the show from all those weirdos. Yet the impact abated quickly, and those who'd been thrilled that the old boys still had it in them, weren't thrilled enough to buy their records.

In a similar situation, a reconstituted Dave Dee, Dozy, Beaky, Mick and Tich had resumed their recording career that year with a single, 'She's My Lady', before fragmenting once more; Dozy, Tich and Beaky as part of an amalgam called Tracker with 24-year-old Peter Lucas, who, since Bethany, had drifted with his guitar from pillar to post, from band to unsatisfactory band such as Charlie Harwood and the Pub Beats, around too soon for the pub-rock craze that paved the way for punk. Prospects weren't much brighter for Peter in Tracker for all the long rehearsals, four days a week, that resulted in a show-stopping Beatles medley, sterling covers of Steely Dan, Cat Stevens and other toasts-of-the-campus plus fiery originals that mined the same seam.

With the exits of Beaky and Dozy in 1975, Tich and Peter kept the faith with Reginald Maggs – once Bethany's drummer – and Steve Collingson, a bass player from Amesbury (and the elder brother of one of Chris Britton's skifflers in The Hiccups) before bowing to an eventual and inevitable reformation of DBMT in 1977 with three of the old personnel plus Lucas as 'Mick'.

Along the way, Pete and Tich had been moonlighting in a Troggs now bereft of Tony Murray and Richard Moore, for dates in Germany in summer 1977, and – indicative of careless research by the record label concerned – would even be pictured on the sleeve of a re-issued album in the wake of the group's not unfruitful foray into pub-rock. The Troggs had seen for themselves the street level acclaim – and chart action – granted to Dr Feelgood and Ace. What with The Searchers, Johnny Kidd's surviving Pirates and The Downliners Sect cashing in on it, surely there was a place in the nicotine-clouded pub-rock sun for The Troggs too?

Indeed, there was, judging by the clusters chattering excitedly as they spilled out onto the pavement after a sweatbath with The Troggs upstairs at High Wycombe's Nag's Head or when the group headlined at West London's Nashville Rooms in the same May week in 1976 as Rocky Sharpe and the Razors, The Stranglers and France's roly-poly Little Bob Story, all agreeably retrogressive and playing with more thought for the paying customer than any millionaire superstar forever in America and throwing a wobbler at Madison Square Gardens because of the promoter's misconstruing of a backstage amenities rider about *still* rather than *fizzy* mineral water.

By definition, pub-rock precluded primadonna tantrums – and so did punk after the decade came to be divided in two – pre- and post-Sex Pistols. As their banned 'God Save The Queen' 45 raced towards Number One, 1977 would prove a bad year for most of UK pop's elder statesmen as guitars were thrashed at speed to machine-gun drumming behind some ranting johnny-one-note who acted as if he couldn't care less whether or not you liked it.

Just as it helped if you could talk Scouse in 1963, and convey an intimation of bisexuality as a glam-rocker, so it was hip to assume the take-it-or-leave-it attitude that had been borrowed – perhaps unconsciously – from The Troggs as was the guitar-bass-drums-lead vocals set-up of the trendsetting Sex Pistols, and the exhilarating margin of error that had put teeth into the older outfit's still-potent smashes. 'Punk rock?' said Reg. 'We invented it!'

The Pistols' exploratory stumblings had included a go at 'Wild Thing', and both The Buzzcocks and – though not strictly punk – Clayson and the Argonauts were piling into 'I Can't Control Myself' while another outfit from that fierce time, True Life Confessions, resurrected a 'Give It To Me', panting not so much with 'Je T'Aime...Moi Non Plus' *carezza* as a hammer-and-tongs knee-trembler.

Whereas other old groups were being lampooned in the *NME* as 'dinosaur' – over-the-hill like The Grateful Dead or wholesomely Americanised like Fleetwood Mac – The Troggs were rated in the punk explosion. In reciprocation – and with reservations – Reg Presley as spokesman for the group 'loved it. I saw it as energy, but I didn't see any melody. Just afterwards you got the melody back with the energy. That was a good time was that.' It was such a good time that The Troggs were quite amenable to such suggestions as being special guests of The Damned at the Strand Lyceum where they brushed aside the millennia that had passed since 1966 like so many matchsticks with an act that was as new and disquieting to most punks as it had been for their Swinging Sixties forerunners.

This was gratifying, but much was rotten in the state of The Troggs at this juncture. As well as a rapid and disheartening turnover of transient guitarists and bass players, a metaphorical pistol had been pointed at the very head of the group through the burdensome Inland Revenue demands on high earners in a high-risk business that had already driven The Rolling Stones to temporary exile in France; Dave Clark to a fiscal year in California, and Maurice Gibb of The Bee Gees to the Isle of Man. Reg Presley wasn't in the same bracket, but was still considered wealthy enough to be stung for a £23,583 tax bill – a sky-high amount a quarter of an inflationary century ago – that had snowballed over 11 years of stardom. Just as stomach-knotting was the discovery that Peter Walsh's financial paragon was no longer as trustworthy or as confident in his ability to soften such a blow – but perhaps he never had been in the first place.

Far too little had been set aside for such an unthinkable catastrophe. Reg was not amused by his incompetent adviser's pathetic quip about claiming for the paper on which 'With A Girl Like You' *et al* had been written while he searched in vain for more plausible avenues for rebate or playing for time as the date of his client's bankruptcy hearing neared.

With terrifying sureness, it would leave a humiliated Presley trying to put a brave face on the realisation that Harewood Lodge wouldn't be his for much longer, and he was to be allowed 'just enough to live on. It's awful not being able to buy things for your wife and family.'

During this lowest ebb, it seemed fanciful to look to future victories – and, in some respects, the worst was yet to come. So it was that the usually level-headed and pragmatic Presley began staying the phantoms of his mounting desolations with alcohol, consumption of which became so immoderate that 'I woke up one morning and I fancied my favourite drink. A bell went off in my head which said, "You fancy a Scotch-and-Coke at quarter past eight!?" From that day, I knocked it completely on the head, apart from the occasional glass or two of wine later.'

Reg might have mastered his inner chaos and pulled back from the abyss – but Ronnie was as doomed as his distant friend Keith Moon, whose body rebelled with fatal results after a lifetime of abuse in 1978. The Troggs' sticksman had long been as prone to the short-lived magic of booze, but whatever the tipple of choice, it was but a temporary analgesic, an alleviation of the pangs of an unexplainable depression that had been gathering in intensity of late.

The majority of the sick are not in bed – and, in the early 1980s, Ronnie was fit enough still to turn on the old breezy vitality on the boards, even when he'd knocked back more than he should. When the show was over, the tension would flow out of him as the liquor flowed in, and he'd burble away convivially, bonding with others who weren't in the mood for sensible conversation either. His head thrown back with laughter at some vulgar joke shared in the beer-sodden jollity of a lock-out after a performance at the Nag's Head, how could Ronnie Bond have known that he had only ten years to go?

Chapter 9
When Will The
Rain Come?

'We're making more money now than we did in the 1960s
when our discs sold in millions.'
Reg Presley

When had twilight descended upon The Troggs? Could you date it from 'Give It To Me' missing the Top 10? The bust-up with Larry Page? 'Surprise Surprise'? The exit of Pete Staples? You can be as divergent in picking the moment when the first rays of the rising sun heralded the end of their long and seemingly impenetrable night.

Punk had been a false dawn, and after the record industry stole and sanitised its most viable ideas, The Troggs had been out in the cold again. A more direct and personal upset had been the death of Stan Phillips in August 1977. His relationship with the group had been based as much on friendship as profit – and, had he recovered his health, his return as their full-time manager would not have been improbable. At the funeral at Weyhill Parish Church – where a wreath from Rod Stewart was among those displayed – the older Troggs felt their anguish all the more sharply on realising how many functions Stan had fulfilled for them; careers advisor, father confessor, ego massager, shoulder to cry on, trouble-shooter – most spectacularly when he'd extricated them from the clutches of the New York vultures in 1967 – and someone who'd give honest, constructive answers when ideas were bounced off him.

On 24 September 1977, a month after the interment, The Troggs performed what some may have regarded as an unofficial memorial concert for Stan. It took place in front of about 400 rain-drenched locals in the open air of the Walled Meadow, a stone's throw from the car park where once the Fiesta was. The disappointing turn-out could be ascribed to the weather – windy drizzle that was almost but not quite a gale – and the short notice that precluded more than the most cursory advertising by the organisers, Andover Football Club. It was Reg's belief too that the individuals in the group were such over-familiar figures around the town, shopping or knocking back a quiet lunchtime beer in a high-street tavern, that it was like 'playing in front of your mother'.

Supporters of the younger outfits on the bill – Papillon and Breaker – may have been ignorant of the headliners' international stature in the 1960s, but for those who remembered, the Local-Boys-Made-Good's first 'home game' for 11 years, was, if not on the scale of Moses re-appearing before the Israelites from the clouded summit of Mount Sinai, at least on a par with the original Animals reunion bash at Newcastle City Hall or Paul McCartney's post-Beatles debut with Wings at the Liverpool Empire.

Adoration had been years a-dwindling, if at all, for some who'd stayed in the picture about The Troggs' activities since 'Lost Girl' and before. For them, those 50 minutes on the squally stage were the proverbial 'something to tell your grandchildren about'. Others were more level-headed. Sagging on the ropes as The Troggs were then, only a miracle could have rescued the show from anti-climax when the buzzing tribe filed out of the muddy field, blood pressure dropping in the unseasonable cold – and, by most accounts, the group had put on a show that was no better or worse than any other dished out during that erratic round of British engagements. All the same, a spirited 'Wild Thing' finale had sparked off an ear-stinging bedlam of applause, just as all the renderings of the other hits had likewise lent credence to the homily, 'I care not who makes a nation's laws as long as I can write its songs'.

Songwriting royalties, if diminishing, and his cut of net income from bookings were giving Reg Presley's financial graph an upward swing, and the Inland Revenue were so convinced that he would be able to earn enough to pay off his debt completely that he would be discharged as a bankrupt in October 1982.

A place as grand as Harewood Lodge might have been out of Reg's reach then, but he wasn't short of a penny or two anymore even if the unostentatious family home at 12 Weyhill Road, along one of the town's main suburban thoroughfares, emitted no immediate impression that the tide was turning with more than its expected majestic slowness.

Ronnie's domestic situation had improved too after the establishment of a pattern whereby he, his wife Pat and their now three sons – David, Darren and Gary – had gone onwards and upwards from the council house to ownership of homes that were nearly always improvements on the ones before. Three-piece suites and wall-to-wall carpeting were in the scheme of things too for Pete Staples, who, with moonlit miles as a professional musician firmly behind him, had uprooted to the outskirts of Basingstoke where he carved out a niche as a self-employed electrician. This had followed a brief period as a pub landlord where he'd foreseen how weary he would become of pulling pints while recounting for inquisitive drinkers how crazed females had stormed the stage at Salisbury City Hall when he was a Trogg.

Meanwhile, Chris Britton had left his Portuguese club to fend for itself on moving back to the old country in 1978 – to Guildford before a prodigal's return to Andover, and an ivy-clung cottage with exposed rafters and stone-flagged floor – though alien to a post-Restoration man-of-the-soil was the extension Chris himself would build long after a summons to rejoin The Troggs that took rather too long to arrive for his liking. 'When Chris came back to England,' chuckled Reg, 'I was so pissed off with him going the way he had that, even though we used guitarists that weren't that good, I went all that time before I even mentioned to him about coming back into the group.'

Still in and out of the Troggs, Tony Murray tagged along when the band basked in a heroes' welcome back to New York in 1980. This Stateside sojourn came about because one of Ronnie's relations in Brooklyn had the ear of the booking manager of Max's Kansas City, one of the downtown clubs where the Big Apple wing of the punk movement had fermented, and where genre luminaries The Velvet Underground – the 1960s edition – and ex-Sex Pistol Sid Vicious had each immortalised tired farewell recitals on disc.

The Troggs were to stoke up more excitement via their in-person album from Max's (with a cover illustration of a nude woman standing on the palm of a hand), taped over three nights during which the audience blossomed from a handful to a word-of-mouth queue round the block. While this residency paid for the musicians' air fares and accommodation, the enterprise would be in a profit position after a short tour, arranged by the club, that spawned a bootleg LP with a title that repeated a much-asked question: *Was This The First Punk Rock Band?*

The same enquiry had been made with respect to The Pretty Things who, having resisted enticements to work a passage round Europe on the nostalgia ticket, would be knocking 'em dead back in London every Tuesday throughout 1984 in a room above the Bridge House, a fashionable Little Venice pub. For 50p admission, a comparatively youthful clientele would witness not only the band but guest players of such diversity as Pink Floyd's Dave Gilmour, Mick Avory of The Kinks, Glen Matlock – another former Sex Pistol – and drummer Bruce Brand from Thee Headcoats (*sic*).

Even more of a bargain was Wednesday nights in the Station Tavern along Latimer Road with The Jim McCarty Blues Band – as near as you'd get to The Yardbirds, leaning as heavily as it did on that august group's repertoire as The Blues Band – formed by Paul Jones and Tom McGuinness in 1979 – did on that of Manfred Mann.

Rather than the scattershot approach of a residency, The Troggs pursued precision bookings in the capital that, because of their very infrequency, had more of a sense of occasion as, like a halo of flies, fans and critics alike droned round, say, the Rock Garden in Covent Garden, the place for all London's bright young things to be on the humid summer's evening when The Troggs mounted its box-like stage.

Perhaps the story could have ended with this regaining of native popularity, a settling down to a prosperous lassitude as British showbusiness treasures, guaranteed work for as long as they can stand – with another record in the charts a mere sideshow. Like the 'happy ending' in a Victorian novel, all the villains had been bested and the inheritance claimed.

In truth, it was a period that at least Ronnie, now a grandfather, might have recognised as the nearest he ever came to contentment. For balance, there were hiccups like the theft of every item of uninsured equipment – even the ocarina – just after an engagement in Marseilles, and, grimaced Chris Britton, 'the following three months of agony using hired junk for the rest of our European tour.' Adding insult to injury, a British customs official was quizzical about the Marseilles incident, wondering aloud if they'd sold the stuff to some French outfit. 'Never again', muttered The Troggs when they were finally waved on. For future trips abroad, all they'd take would be instruments and a pair of drumsticks. Let the promoters provide the 'backline' of amplifiers and drum kit. Hang the expense.

Money was very much on Tony Murray's mind – and after the cancellation of a subsequent three-month tour of the States, he did heartsick sums and gave notice to The Troggs. Within a fortnight, he was installed as a full-time representative for a local brewery.

The gifted Tony's withdrawal was regrettable but not disastrous. Without a pause, The Troggs got by with transitory substitutes until Peter Lucas was persuaded to transfer permanently from DBMT. The opportunity was taken too to beef up the sound with a keyboard player for a while – in particular, synthesised strings on 'Any Way You Want Me', 'Love Is All Around' and, back in the set after a long absence, 'Little Girl'. Another keyboard player, Steve Benham, was to be the motivator of a 1986 revamping of 'Wild Thing' for the disco floor as a duet by Reg Presley and Suzi Quatro, a Detroit lass who'd cut a dash in European charts during the 1970s.

More importantly, there'd been an administrative adjustment. The management of the operation was now by Stan Green, a Salisbury concert promoter who'd breathed the air round 1960s acts over two decades as the Greater London Council's director of outdoor pop festivals. He was, therefore, *au fait* with developments since The Troggs' fall from the charts to warranting not a single mention in *The Rolling Stone History Of Rock & Roll* (Picador, 1981), and being slotted between The Toys and Ike and Tina Turner in *Whatever Happened To...: The Great Rock And Pop Nostalgia Book* (Proteus, 1981).

Yet the nostalgia circuit was no longer such a netherworld by the mid-1980s. All it took, it seemed, was for a swarthy youth to remove his jeans in a launderette in an ITV commercial to the sound of an old record, and Britain was awash with yearning for the Swinging Sixties. Snippet coverage in a lager advertisement sent a 19-year-old Hollies single to Number One in 1988 – while even older mementoes by The Kinks, Dave Clark Five, Rolling Stones, Swinging Blue Jeans – and The Troggs likewise broke up evenings that were sabotaged then by championship snooker.

On the silver screen, 'Wild Thing' popped up in *No Way Out*, a movie starring Kevin Costner and Gene Hackman, and a new Troggs single, 'Every Little Thing', was issued by Virgin in 1984 – though the company's gamble in signing them did not pay off especially handsome dividends. Furthermore, *Black Bottom*, the first studio album since 1975, was not deemed worthy of release in either Britain or the USA, even after it sold steadily if unremarkably in Australia where memories lingered of a nationwide television appearance during a trek Down Under in spring 1983.

Black Bottom, nevertheless, shifted 30,000 copies in France. A more general interest in the Troggs was higher in Germany as attested by the increasing demand for them for 'Oldies *Nachts*' – most of them co-ordinated by Rainer Haas, Suzi Quatro's husband – where Cecil B de Mille-sized crowds of all ages would be enthralled by up to 12 hours of performances by pop methuselahs, one after the other, on stages framed by sky-clawing scaffolding, giant video screens and lighting gantries like oil derricks. When had the Troggs – and, indeed, any other beat group – ever been as loud and clear or seen so well?

Such occasions dwarfed any given 'Sounds Of The Sixties' evening in Britain, but Dave Dee tried hard on behalf of the Nordoff Robbins Music Therapy with his organisation of a fund-raising extravaganza entitled *Heroes And Villains* at London's Dominion Theatre in October 1985, perhaps the most pivotal event to nudge the 1960s revival out of neutral. As well as the acts – and there were so many of them – that shared the stage, the audience contained the future editors of *The Beat Goes On* – now the UK's mouthpiece of 1960s pop in the 1990s – and fanzines like *Zabadak!* – 'the magazine about Dave Dee, Dozy, Beaky, Mick and Tich' – *Hostage To The Beat*, *Yardbirds World* and *Carousel* (concerning The Hollies).

The show had long been underway when Alan Clayson reeled into Dave Berry's dressing room in a disenchanted state after sunset had found me on the M4's hard shoulder, howling at the moon because of an overcharging alternator of a now extinct Mini. A sympathetic Dave steered me into licensed premises where Ronnie Bond was holding court.

As a result, my recollections of the next few hours are now necessarily vague, but during his roaming of the backstage wastes of the Dominion, I passed a dozen famous faces along a single staircase; stood in the wings beside a portly gentleman who strode onstage to metamorphose into Chris Farlowe – and breathed lagered platitudes at a preoccupied Reg Presley.

Though it didn't seemed like it at the time, this turned out to be one of those Momentous Encounters. I next saw Reg with his group firing on all cylinders at a smaller bash at the Hammersmith Odeon, against stiff competition from The Equals. Then again, the Troggs popped up on *Unforgettable*, a Channel Four nostalgia series, at the lonely mid-week hour of 3.45 pm, and with Dave Dee, The Dowlands and Terry Dene on a light-hearted Southern TV documentary, hosted by Zoot Money, about the old days of Dave Dee and the Bostons, 'Wild Thing' and Zoot ritually hurling hundreds of pounds worth of equipment off the end of Bournemouth pier after one gremlin-infested show at the Pavilion in 1963.

122

Yet an era that had once seemed almost as bygone as that bracketed by Hitler's suicide and 'Rock Around The Clock' was faraway no more – as exemplified by my employment as boffin-at-the-high-school-hop shortly after the publication of my first book, 1985's *Call Up The Groups!: The Golden Age Of British Beat, 1962-1967* (Blandford, 1985). An unsolicited letter arrived inquiring whether I'd be interested in running a course called *The Sound Of The Sixties* at a Watford adult education centre. This spurred me to seek similar work, and I amassed an itinerary stretching months and then years ahead. Those enrolling included both pensioners and those for whom even 'Strange Movies' predated consciousness.

Among *bona fide* icons of the era invited as guest speakers was Reg Presley whose thought-provoking (and unadvertised) seminar in an austere cream-painted classroom at Swindon College on 24 April 1987 had a bizarre repercussion when Nora, a very intense student in her mid-forties, rang me from her Cirencester home the day before to ask if I could retrieve the butts of any cigarettes he might smoke during the lecture. She wanted to keep them, she explained, as a joy forever, having tracked The Troggs since 1965 when she saw them second-billed to The Big T Show in Basingstoke. She became completely hooked, she said, at a party a year later when 'Wild Thing' soundtracked her first bout of snogging.

I more than responded to her request by mailing her the Silk Cut fag-ends with which Reg had filled my car's ashtray when I drove him to Swindon that evening as well as those he'd got through during his talk. A freelance reporter scooped the story for a local journal, and the following week, the newspaper *Today* picked up on it.

Though it was all grist to The Troggs' publicity mill, Nora's desires were infinitely less interesting to me than Reg's most diverting account of The Troggs' professional career, his songwriting methodology and co-related topics. Accompanied by recorded examples – including the only 20 or so consecutive seconds of the Troggs Tapes that didn't contain swearing – Mr Presley walked a tightrope between historical and cultural narrative, and anecdotal entertainment for a cramped audience of around 40. Enthusiasm was such that the question-and-answer session overran by just over an hour.

During the journey back to Andover, Reg and I spoke of many things including the fog warning system he'd invented which became operational on Heathrow Airport runways the day after his patent ran out. He told me about this with some bitterness. Though I have forgotten precise details, Reg also mentioned an intriguing idea for reclaiming desert regions.

When I dropped him off at Weyhill Road, he presented me with a Suzi Quatro 'Wild Thing', a gift that seemed of more intrinsic worth than his cigarette stubs – but the last thing I remember thinking before I fell asleep that night was that I'd never walked in Nora's shoes, so what the hell did I know?

However, the packaging of the new 'Wild Thing' cried 'buy me!' more shrilly than the jiffy-bag I sent to Nora – but was it a hit? These days, see, merely making the record was the least of it. What about the plugger paid to get in on Radio 1's playlist? How about the video? Any news on the TV advertisement to be scheduled before the last part of the Chart Show on Friday between 'Britain's noisiest crisps' and the government health warning about AIDS? If all you did was post review copies to the music papers, you might as well throw the record out of the window.

In any case, Steve Benham's too premeditated reconstruction of 'Wild Thing', in which 'Art' intruded upon guts, left a peculiar afterglow for those like Nora for whom The Troggs' original on a dusty old Fontana 45 held emotional significance. Nothing was ever as great as it'd been in the 1960s. 'I had a long conversation with Van Morrison the other day,' Steve Winwood had grumbled in 1981 to *The Times*, 'and we found that we have that in common. He's always been told that *Astral Weeks* is his best record. How's he going to beat that? I have the same problem with what The Spencer Davis Group achieved.'

Yet there would be fiscal advantages. As commodity began to assume more absolute sway over creativity, the history of pop would be seized upon as an avenue for shifting records beyond simply getting information about compilations inserted in retailer catalogues. Saturation television commercials could hoick up sales from tens of thousands to a quarter of a million a year in the UK alone. Come 1987, and Winwood's *Chronicles* would see as much action in the charts as other 'greatest hits' offerings by Paul McCartney, George Harrison, The Kinks and The Dave Clark Five – and The Troggs' time would come too.

No matter how it was tarted up – on 12-inch 45 like the Presley-Quatro 'Wild Thing', or pressed on polkadot vinyl, the pop single had become a loss leader, a mere incentive for adults to buy an album on one of these new-fangled compact discs – on which you could nearly make out the dandruff falling onto an engineer's shoulders on 'With A Girl Like You'. Teenagers, you see, were no longer pop's most courted consumers, having been outmanoeuvred by Swinging Sixties parents who had sated their appetites for novelty.

Nevertheless, as well as triumphs of repackaging in the album lists, there'd be *Top Of The Pops* visitations – either on video or in the chicken-necked flesh – with their latest releases by such as The Rolling Stones, The Steve Miller Band, The Kinks, The Beatles, Roy Orbison and Cliff Richard. All this justified the words of John McNally of The Searchers: 'You don't have to be young to make good records.'

Even on 1960s nights in the most dismal working men's club, The Searchers, Dave Berry, The Troggs and those of corresponding vintage would lure a strikingly young crowd by counterpoising contemporary offerings with the ancient chestnuts. The daringly hard-focus cover photo of 'Wild Thing' had had Reg looking hale, hearty and almost slim, but 'good' foreheads, crow's feet and belts loosened to the last hole were no bar to the worship of old campaigners by those envious of their more vibrant past.

Partly, it was a symptom of artistic bankruptcy among young artists, content to imitate or exalt middle-aged legends whose lasting influence was illustrated by entire albums of various artists elaborating on – or just plain copying – chosen examples from the portfolios of Syd Barrett, Captain Beefheart, Peter Green and like greybeards. Several new hitmakers even depped for the Lonely Hearts Club Band on *Sgt Pepper Knew My Father*, a charity rehash of the Beatles' most famous record; Wet Wet Wet scoring a Number One with the 'With A Little Help From My Friends' off-cut single.

Names of lesser commercial magnitude were to be among credits for *Groin Thunder*, a salute to The Troggs consisting of items accumulated over the previous 15 years from locations as diverse as Sydney and Barrow-in-Furness. The most outstanding of these were a 'When Will The Rain Come' and an 'I Want You To Come Into My Life' from respective paladins of post-punk resurgences of psychedelia and garage-band rock, The Bevis Frond and Thee Headcoats – whose rendition on the boards of 'Meet Jacqueline' – from *Trogglodynamite* – was sometimes 'dedicated to Uncle Reg'. The Troggs were also the inspirational source of a US hit by Tone Loc. Their 'Wild Thing' was an essay in the brutish *braggadacio* of rap, but closer to the old definition would be a 1992 duet by Oliver Reed and snooker champion Alex Higgins – with assistance from The Troggs – and one that would herald the Grand Entrance of 'Wolf', mainstay of ITV's *Gladiators* series.

To Reg's bank manager, it was a shame it hadn't been 'With A Girl

Like You' that had merited such continuous royalty-reaping attention. The covers of his songs by The Truth, The Nerve, True Life Confessions, the *Groin Thunder* bands *et al* had been pin-money. Even cumulatively, they couldn't hold a candle to the car-buying, Presley mortgage-paying, foreign holiday-making lump-sums for any given classic by the Troggs themselves.

However, the group would be far less likely to be lynched for quitting the stage without giving 'em 'Give It To Me', 'Night Of The Long Grass' or 'Love Is All Around' than they'd be for missing out Chip Taylor's 'Wild Thing'. A milestone and a millstone, it had so swiftly become to The Troggs as 'Be Bop A Lula' to Gene Vincent, 'You Really Got Me' to the Kinks, 'A Whiter Shade Of Pale' to Procol Harum, and 'Mama Weer All Crazee Now' to Slade.

Reg, Chris and Ronnie couldn't afford to be tired of 'Wild Thing' – or of finding themselves, time and time again, at the same venues – Caerphilly's Double-Diamond, Blazers in Windsor, Hamburg's Easy Rider, Luton's Caesar's Palace, the Sixties Club in Marbella, you name 'em – where incorrigible old Mods, Rockers and hippies (and their offspring) didn't mind squeezing into the 'smart casuals' that were the norm. Still, at least there was the opportunity for the entertainers to form genuine friendships with management, staff and patrons, rather than play backstage host to starstruck fans. The same applied to professional cronies on the same bill or showing up simply to watch.

While The Troggs could be proud, even boastful, about how well they still went down after all this time, there were no rockstar-ish dark nights of the ego about obesity, middle age and galloping alopecia – or rockstar anything else. Mingling with the customers in the foyer after the show, Ronnie, with a stiff drink close at hand, might be chatting freely and offending none by refusing to autograph a *Black Bottom* straight from the merchandising stall or a dog-eared *Troggs Tops* sleeve, depicting Chris with most of his hair still on his head.

There was more hail-fellow-well-met familiarity than usual when Tich and the first Mick – now proprietor of a driving school – turned up at a Troggs recital at Concorde's Night Club in Salisbury in 1989. For all the outlines that had dissolved between the twinned outfits over the years, this was the first time Mick had seen The Troggs since the 1966 tour with The Walker Brothers.

Having re-formed in the mid-1980s, Dave Dee and Dozy-Beaky-Mick-and-Tich were now recording and performing separately once more; Dave, more often than not, as 'featured singer' with

Marmalade. At this point, The Troggs weren't much of a group either as constituent parts had started dipping their toes into other pools.

Reg was perhaps the best-placed to do so. After doing his duty by Suzi Quatro, he next allied with Brian Poole, Tony Crane of The Merseybeats, Mike Pender from The Searchers and The Foundations' Clem Curtis in what was known collectively as 'The Corporation' with lead vocals doled out equally on a sprightly reworking of 'Ain't Nothing But A House Party', a much-reissued 1968 hit by The Showstoppers. With its accompanying video, it was launched at London's plush Hippodrome ballroom to tiptoe into the lowest reaches of the chart, the first such entry for any of its participants in many a long year.

Like Noddy Holder, soon to be estranged from Slade, Presley had been thrown down a line in a different medium altogether as the echoes of the 1960s grew fainter once more. Passing a screen test, he landed a bit-part as a guitarist in *Hearts Of Fire*, a vehicle for Bob Dylan – who some reckoned had been typecast as an ageing pop star. Dylan had been introduced to the Troggs Tapes by Ron Wood, and it was the latter-day Rolling Stone who effected an off-set introduction between the messianic symbol of 1960s cool and the leader of the Unthinking Man's Pop Group – who cracked the old quip when Bob asked how long he'd been playing guitar.

Reg's next acting job was even less substantial – a blink-and-you'll-miss-him role as a supermarket manager in a *Ruth Rendell Mystery* on ITV. Nonetheless, he'd proved able 'to other be' more effectively than many other pop musicians who'd fancied themselves as screen attractions – and, if Reg Presley isn't quite the next Sir Laurence Olivier, there may be surprises to come.

While Reg made this small beginning, Ronnie was closing the door – however involuntarily – on The Troggs completely. His health had continued to deteriorate and on more than one night he'd looked as if he'd never totter on stage. He always did, but it might have been better sometimes if he hadn't.

Finally, Reg could grope for no more excuses for poor Ronnie's conduct than Chris had done for that of Pete Staples and in Andover on a March evening in 1987, Presley's frank nature could not allow him to stay silent any more.

He had, he said, something serious to say to Ronnie. Then he disguised an ultimatum as a gentle suggestion that his old friend ought to take a six month sabbatical from the group, to sweat out the blue devils. In his heart-of-hearts, however, Ronnie understood that this was the end, and cried silently into the night.

The following day, a telephone rang in the Amesbury home of 36-year-old Reginald Maggs, Peter Lucas's Tracker *confrère*. If a beer-and-skittles type, and married with teenage children, Maggs was no biological duplicate of Ronnie Bond, but he was as reliable as he was experienced.

His father and grandfather before him had drummed in silver and brass ensembles, and Reginald had followed the same star as a member of over 30 professional outfits of every variety and size from dance orchestras to jazz trios – and had served DBMT for 18 months just prior to Reg Presley mincing no words in asking him to join The Troggs.

To avoid confusion, Reginald let his new paymaster introduce him on the boards by his middle name. As 'Dave Maggs' too, he was pictured on the cover of 1989's *Au*, an album that encapsulated the paradox of The Troggs in the late 1980s in its uneasy reconciliation of reprises of four of their own hits – including another 'Wild Thing' – an exhumation of Sandie Shaw's chart-topping 'Always Something There To Remind Me' from 1964; a second 'Strange Movies'; 'Walkin' The Dog' after all this time, and, for good measure, a couple of previously unheard Presley originals.

The Troggs were apparent has-beens, but were more often in the public eye these days than they'd been since the 1960s. There they were, wowing 15,000 ticket-holders at a jubilee in Belgium that brought together pioneers from every trackway of pop's turbulent history – and again on *The Trouble With The Sixties*, a British televisual romp transmitted in January 1993, with all manner of diverse living relics of the decade such as George Best, Dave Berry, Jane Birkin, Henry Cooper, Oliver Tobias, Alan Freeman, Henry Cooper, Sandie Shaw, Screaming Lord Sutch and Mary Whitehouse. Musical illustrations were provided in 'Hippy Hippy Shake' from The Swinging Blue Jeans, Donovan's querulous 'Catch The Wind' – and, finally, The Troggs, once more with feeling.

Wasn't that them doing 'Wild Thing' again on *Bygones* on BBC 1 – and over on the other side in Cilla Black's *Surprise Surprise*? A more private surprise treat saw the Troggs as the star turn at the gala reception that followed rock megastar Sting's wedding to Trudy Styler on 22 August 1992, where you'd unzip yourself in an adjacent urinal in the gents to Peter Gabriel or one of The Eagles.

No-one knew for certain whether the newly-weds appreciated The Troggs in absolute terms or for reasons connected with a feigned unawareness of the camp humour in booking such an act from the very morning of Sting, Gabriel *et al*'s pop careers. Whatever the motives too, those of The Troggs' own vintage were also both loud and pragmatic about their partiality for the group; Roger Daltrey of The Who inviting them to use his recording facilities, and Paul McCartney voicing a preference for them on a BBC1 chat-show.

A more current seal of approval came The Troggs' way from REM, a guitar-bass-drums-lead vocals quartet from Athens, Georgia, who had cemented an elevation from cult luminaries to mainstream stardom with 1991's *Out Of Time*, a multi-million-selling album that created among their fans an almost unendurable anticipation for the next one.

Beyond garrulous eulogy and buttressing their own standing with credible influences, REM's known fondness for 'British Invasion' pop was lent practical expression in an in-concert revival of 'Love Is All Around' as B-side to an *Out Of Time* single, but its composer was not flattered for the excellent reason that he'd never heard of REM until 'We were working at a hotel up north. I'd just come off-stage, and people were gathering round while I was waiting for the lift. A bloke at the back shouted, "Do you know REM have done one of your numbers?" I thought he said "EMI". REM meant nothing to me then. Next thing I knew, Larry had fixed it for us and REM to do something together.'

While Larry Page was not to have the all-powerful authority he'd enjoyed in the mid-1960s, Reg and Chris couldn't help liking him for all the joys and sorrows they'd shared. After media interest both at home and in North America had brought home what a coup he'd made by conjoining them with REM, Page would be put in charge of production when Presley and Britton, armed with *Out Of Time* and other relevant records, underwent a crash-course in the music of REM in preparation for flying to Georgia in autumn 1991 to commence work on *Athens Andover*, the LP that, depending on your taste, would be either ersatz REM (as all the band – apart from singer Michael Stipe – donated both instrumental skills and a songwriting collaboration, 'Nowhere Road') or how those who hadn't heard much of The Troggs since *From Nowhere* may have imagined them sounding a quarter of a century on, right down to a hand in the matter by Chip Taylor, who, since 'Any Way That You Want Me' had not been idle either, whether penning 'Angel Of The Morning', a US smash for Merrilee Rush, and a Top 30 finale for PP Arnold in Britain – or superintending the twiddling of console knobs for singer-songwriter

Neil Diamond in the 1970s.

Larry Page would again be involved when work-in-progress on *Athens Andover* was brought to a studio near Farnham, Surrey by Chris and Reg who, after spending their days in REM's studio, had mixed work with pleasure; being shown a good time in the Forty Watt – to REM what the TA Centre had been to their guests – the Shoebox, the Half-Moon and other local clubs, and answering questions for an interviewer from *The Flagpole*, the Athens equivalent of *Time Out*.

Though a winner with both Troggs and REM devotees, *Athens Andover* wasn't to put The Troggs back on *Top Of The Pops* as a yoking-up with The Art of Noise had for Duane Eddy and then Tom Jones in the late 1980s, but it slid into the German charts; its placid spin-off A-side, 'Don't You Know', was a 'turntable hit' on BBC radio, and there was no doubt about overall favourable reaction from the critics that prompted the insertion of a couple of *Athens Andover* tracks when The Troggs raised the roof with the hits at this Harvest Home dance or that stop on a British tour with Animals II (formed by the guitarist and drummer from the Eric Burdon days) in 1994.

Passing too many hours in front of the television, Ronnie Bond was torn between drinking his old group's health in silence and glooming about not being in on their present good fortune. So much was still unresolved, but brimming with medications for a debilitating condition that was losing him his race against death was not the firmest foundation for Ronnie to give The Troggs another whirl.

Death took Ronnie Bond without effort on Friday, 13 November 1992. There were more obituaries in 'quality' broadsheets like *The Guardian* and *The Times* than the tabloids in the interim week before the send-off at the necropolis in Salisbury. Behind the Bullis family and the officiating priest walked Reg, Chris and the other two; Dave Dee, Dozy, Beaky, Mick and Tich; members of Marmalade and The Tremeloes, Stan Green – and Larry Page who was to pace to the lectern, adjust his spectacles and deliver a eulogy so poignant that, accosting Larry after the service, Reg commented, 'If you'd been selling anything then, I'd have bought it.'

Epilogue

Andover To Alpha Centauri

'"Wild Thing" is the Andover anthem.
Even kids of today know "Wild Thing".'
Dave Wright

The Troggs and Dave Dee, Dozy, Beaky, Mich and Tich – reunited for the first time since 1989 – were on the bill of *Sixties Gold II* which covered British theatres during the weeks building up to the end of the century. If I had had possession over judgement day or whatever the expression is, not only would Dave Berry's set list at Oxford's Apollo on 14 October have been rewritten, but also the running order would have been reshuffled, partly because there was little constructive comment that could be made about the headlining Tremeloes, except that they did their hits.

The other three acts did too, but the form and content of each had an in-built individuality that was lacking in the Essex boys – as was a focal point of the calibre of a Reg Presley, a Dave Dee or even a Brian Poole. Never mind, The Trems were adored by their fans, even if certain ticket-holders who weren't that keen, left after The Troggs opened the second half.

If ravaged by age, Andover's finest delivered the goods with the enthusiasm of their younger selves. Any grumbles I had were minor – like the too-staccato *b-b-ba-ba-ba*'s in 'With A Girl Like You' – but a lady in the same row looked po-faced when Reg fondled his mic stand in keeping with 'Strange Movies'. Yet I must add the raw information that, during 'I Can't Control Myself', someone else couldn't – to wit, a man who cavorted crazily up and down the aisles, probably belying a daytime sobriety as a computer programmer or school janitor.

131

While Presley is a learning experience for every aspiring pop performer, a more unsung hero of the group's spell on the boards was Chris Britton. You might think I'm being silly, but he is as much a virtuoso in his way as, say, Jimmy Page, Ritchie Blackmore or Eric Clapton.

Grandparents now and travellers of a mighty rough road since 'Little Girl' tumbled from the UK charts, Chris and Reg look no worse outwardly than anyone else of around 55.

Reg is a bit thicker round the waist, and there are silver threads in his dark hair. He still smokes like a chimney in spite of a public warning issued in June 1997 by a doctor on BBC1's *Watchdog* when he, international playboy Peter Stringfellow and a guitarist from Status Quo submitted to exhaustive medical tests to determine their fitness – or lack of it.

Chris, however, has all but given up tobacco in the aftershock of a coronary the previous January. To the agitated clang of an ambulance bell, he was rushed, breathing like a bellows, to the same Winchester hospital where Ronnie Bond had shuffled from this mortal coil. Off the danger list by the following afternoon, Britton's sticky eyes parted as if slit with a knife. There was a whisper of a smile as his hand tightened in his wife, Elaine's. Neither a hypochondriac nor malinger by nature, a rise from his half-death became more perceptible in his own gruesomely hilarious remarks – and, after a week of well-wishers bearing grapes and flowers, he was discharged. 'It was not a major artery in the heart,' Reg assured the *Andover Advertiser*, 'so it is not as serious as it could have been, but he will have to try to take it easy.'

In the context of the oak-beamed rural gentility of his home in the Clatfords, Chris resembles less the flaxen-haired Norse warrior of old than a professor who'd lived all his adult life in an atmosphere of books, armchaired symposiums and dialectic gymnastics. Though within an hour's drive from London, only the whoosh of the odd Concorde from Heathrow need remind the Brittons of the 20th century.

On the outer rim of Andover too, the office-cum-studio of Reg's Four Corners Vision film company, several technological steps ahead of the average London complex, stands in his garden. In the main building, however, a fireplace with space for half a tree to blaze in it, and a suit of armour are among first impressions of the Balls' mock-Tudor pile in Andover Down, a village sprung from land sold in 1825 by the council to help pay for the third Guild Hall.

Reg has become something of a town patrician, intervening in parochial affairs with yet-unrealised visions for a pedestrianised high street and a dry skiing slope, but his most publicised extra-mural activity has been the ploughing back of some of the vast Wet Wet Wet earnings into scientific and mystical research. In particular, his findings and theories concerning crop circles are worthy of a separate book – and a very thick volume too – that Reg is better qualified to write than either author of this present tome.

Whereas Spike Milligan threw himself into animal rights, George Harrison waxed evangelical about Krishna Consciousness, and Cliff Richard spoke up at rallies of muscular Christianity, Reg Presley's name has become as synonymous with crop circles since a 1990 outing to Alton Barnes, a settlement between Marlborough and the confluence of prehistoric monuments further along the A4, *viz* man-made Silbury Hill, the West Kennet long barrow and Avebury's stone amphitheatre.

Patterned formations of flattened crops had been appearing overnight all around Alton Barnes – and no-one had come up with a satisfactory explanation why. The discovery of one shaped like a question mark fuelled the common notion that they had resulted from the antics of all-too-human mischief-makers.

Others weren't so sure. A fellow was testing the ground with a dousing rod when Reg and Brenda's car pulled up. Using such a device was second nature to a former bricklayer, and, having a go himself, Presley's registering of magnetic disturbances marked the beginning of a passionate investigation. 'Up until then, I'd lived in this area without ever sensing anything strange, but I was drawn towards it. I met people at the site, and started talking, and I got more and more into the whole thing.'

After digesting a definitive work, *Circular Evidence* by Pat Delgado and Colin Andrews (Bloomsbury, 1989), and noticing for himself phenomena like the characteristic V-formation of flying geese scattering randomly over a crop formation – as if against an invisible three-dimensional force – Reg went out of his way to contact Colin Andrews, sometime resident in Andover before continuing his studies in the United States and Mexico – where Presley was to spend a holiday-*cum*-cosmic safari.

The two became friends – and what times they had photographing England's own Bermuda Triangle from helicopters hired from Thruxton; organising a thoroughly diverting evening at Salisbury City Hall, divided between The Troggs and a lecture on UFOs, and hosting a UFO Roadshow at Andover's Cricklade Theatre, embracing Reg's film short about alien craft sighted over Alton Barnes, and a tutorial by noted UFO-ologist, Timothy Good.

'It's really exciting to be able to present this evidence from not an amateur but a highly respected scientist,' enthused Reg to the *Advertiser*. 'I know from the evidence I've seen that there is something going on out there and I'm just trying to make sense of it all and find out what it's all about. There are still new patterns being created all over the world and some are hoaxes, but at least 25 percent aren't. To say the whole thing is caused by blokes having a laugh is ridiculous.

'The royalties from "Love Is All Around" mean that I don't have to worry too much about doing this kind of thing now. At the end of the day, this is a hobby for me, but one with a serious aim. I believe it's crucial that we decipher these messages that are being left for us.'

He'd united with others searching the beyond by climbing a tor ten nights running to look for extra-terrestrials. Many hours passed with no signs from outer space until the watchers saw a light 'with the brightness of a star, but throbbing like someone was operating a dimmer switch. It crossed the valley very slowly then it went "woof-woof". It became four or five times brighter than a star, and its colour changed to orange. It stayed in the same spot for about three minutes. The very next day, there was a formation of a triangle with circles in a field exactly where that thing had stayed for that amount of time. I'm a pretty level-headed bloke, but when you see things like that you start thinking. I often wonder what I would do if I saw one of them close to – one of the little fellows – the ones with the big cow eyes which, in UFO circles, we call "the greys".'

Reg's observations and well-argued points could have come as easily from a street-corner orator warming to a pet theme amid jeers from the few who stop to listen. Yet because of who he was, Reg was invited to air his views to a broadsheet scribe's tape recorder, and to Jonathan Ross on *The Aliens Are Coming* on ITV as well as present a weekly show, *Is Anyone Out There?*, on Town TV.

Among leading lights of this cable television station local to Andover were Tony Murray and former Redwood Alan Grindley. Both had blown the dust from their instruments to inaugurate Still Crazy, a weekend quintet with Dave Wright, drummer David Bullis and an Eddie Vincent. In February 1996, this weekend combo opened for The Troggs at Bob Potter's plush Lakeside Country Club near Camberley's Agincourt where he'd first booked four callow youths from deepest Hampshire.

Pete Staples remains in touch with both certain of his former musical acquaintances from Andover, and the record business as he balances agency work for British Telecom and submitting the songs he still composes for consideration by suitable artists. To many, he will always be a Trogg as Pete Best will always be a Beatle. Like Best, Pete takes on board numbers by his old group on the rare occasions he performs these days – as he did at a friend's 50th birthday party. On a holiday cruise with Hilary in 1992, he was recognised and coaxed into taking the stage with the liner's band to clamorous applause from onlookers that included a booking agent from Moscow.

'He explained that the Russian authorities were anxious to broaden their knowledge of western art, culture and music,' Pete would inform the *Basingstoke Gazette* on his return. 'He asked me if I'd be prepared to go there to perform, talk to groups about how the English pop scene had evolved and discuss ideas for developing pop music in Russia. I told him that it sounded a fascinating project, and he said he'd be contacting me later this year.' However, Pete's diplomatic mission to Russia had yet to take place when he was a prominent interviewee during a half-hour devoted to The Troggs in an edition of Channel Four's interrogatory *Without Walls* series in 1995.

When Reg's face filled the screen on the same programme, Mother Nature seemed to have been a little less kind to him than to Pete, but it didn't work against him because we British like our entertainers to be survivors – and Reg was nothing if not that. As such, he has emerged as a participant in televised celebrity panel tournaments like Michael Aspel's *The Music Game* – and joining in the biting of the biters on *Sixties Sing Nineties*, a 1999 album instigated by ex-Tremelo Chip Hawkes, on which the masters' touch was given to hits by contemporary 'Britpop' acts who had borrowed ideas from the golden age of British beat. Invested with more guts than the originals were Dave Dee's 'Don't Look Back In Anger' – from Oasis – and Billy J Kramer's 'Losing My Religion' (REM) and the circle remaining unbroken with Wet Wet Wet's arrangement of 'Love Is All Around' by Reg Presley: jovial voice-of-experience taking on cheeky young shavers.

Wet Wet Wet, Oasis, Pulp, The Bluetones and all the rest were regarded by tidy-minded (or lazy) journalists as modern-day equivalents of whatever 1960s outfits they could be heard echoing on any given record. There was no escaping it. As well as the omnipresence of the original perpetrators at a venue near you, there were Channel Four's *Ready Steady Go!* and *Beat Club* re-runs; Radio Two's *Sounds Of The Sixties* with veteran *Thank Your Lucky Stars*

MC Brian Matthew; the Beatlefests that were annual fixtures in cities across the continents; not a week going by without the formation of another 'tribute band', and the back-to-back oldies on juke-box, disco turntable and television commercial.

All over the world, it seems that you can't turn on the box without catching an excerpt from an old Troggs song, whether 'Anyway You Want Me' rewritten as a jingle for a brand of yoghurt, or 'With A Girl Like You' beneath a voice-over for some other dairy product. Above all, there was the incorporation of 'Wild Thing' into the sloganeering, the hype and the cramming into less than a minute of everything particular merchandisers wanted saying about cars, coffee, confectionery, relish and insurance as it encroached on public consciousness to the degree that the most unlikely people would find themselves humming it.

Back in Andover, even the grandchildren of those who'd spent evenings with The Troggs in the Copper Kettle knew an anthem as peculiar to the town as 'You'll Never Walk Alone' to Liverpool, Joy Division's 'Love Will Tear Us Apart' to young Manchester or 'She's Not There' to The Zombies' St Albans.

Prompted by Harp Lager – the firm behind the publication of Pete Frame's *Rock Gazetteer Of Great Britain* (Banyan 1989) – Andover had displayed its pride in its cradling of The Troggs by attaching an honorific plaque on the wall of what had been the old Copper Kettle. Present with Chris at the unveiling on Thursday, 21 January 1993, Reg commented: 'This was where everything began. All our dreams were made here.' Unaware then of what fate – and the director of *Four Weddings And A Funeral* – had in store for him, he added, 'I'd like to buy it back and turn it back to how it was.'

As overseas representatives of Britain's performing arts, The Troggs had played 'fly in-fly out' dates in the USA that summer. These ranged from a night in the Florida air base that was the operational hub of the Gulf War to a 'British Invasion' festival among a delegation that included The Searchers, Billy J Kramer, Eric Burdon with rather too youthful Animals, Peter 'Herman' Noone (minus The Hermits), and an act that was quite open about not being the full shilling, namely 'Eric Haydock's Hollies'. Either not noticing or not minding, the customers also patronised the site's 'British Village' with its fish-and-chip shop, 'Henry VIII' pub, hello-hello-hello policeman and further gleanings from Hollywood movie notions about this sceptr'd isle.

From this clotting of kitsch, The Troggs globe-trotted to a German television spectacular on behalf of UNICEF. An earlier sea-mark on rock's voyage to respectability had been the opening of the eastern bloc in 1989 that had since seen The Troggs in territories once *verboten* to all decadent beat groups from the west.

On 7 August 1993, The Troggs had gone ahead with an engagement in a German hotel on the nearer side of the demolished Berlin Wall, having uniquely resolved the quandary of Dave Maggs being double-booked to give away his daughter at her nuptials in Amesbury. Introduced as 'somebody special' by Reg, the substitute was none other than Darren Bullis who, like brother David in Still Crazy, was very much a chip off the old block as a drummer, just as the similarly-placed Jason Bonham had proved to be when enlisted to join a briefly-reunited Led Zeppelin.

Once Darren's moment of glory was over, The Troggs slipped into a more accustomed domestic routine of one-nighters – and raking in more loot with less effort as part of mass celebrations of the Swinging Sixties, whether in holiday camps in Sussex, Wales and East Anglia – where, jabbing at his watch, the stage manager of Caistor's Memories Music Club had them on stage within ten minutes of their late arrival – at Aldershot's Rushmoor Arena on a wet, wet, wet August day in 1996 or as the only non-Mancunian attraction on a money-spinning 'Solid Silver Sixties' summer tour in 1996 on which Freddie and the Dreamers were compelled to lengthen their set one evening at High Wycombe's Swan Theatre after both Reg Presley and Peter Lucas were poleaxed with food poisoning. When the news was announced in the foyer, an audible groan signified the profound collective disappointment.

After this second instance in 30 years that ill-health had forced the cancellation of a Troggs performance, the group returned to this round-Britain wallow in nostalgia. Coming to terms with both their past and present situation, The Troggs and the rest of the bill – Freddie, Wayne Fontana and Herman – had long understood that, whether a newly-reconstituted Ten Feet Five (which includes Chris Penfound, Dave Smith and occasional 'special guest' Chris Britton plus Johnny Walker on drums) in the Clatford Arms; Johnny Walker at Lakeside with Terry Ward and The Bumblies, once production clients of Jonathan King; or The Troggs, cynosure of tens of thousands of eyes at the 'British Invasion' festival, all an act still intact from the 1960s had to do was be an archetypal unit of its own, spanning every familiar avenue of its professional life – all the timeless hits (or ones by association in Ten Feet Five's case), every change of image, every bandwagon jumped.

Even those still established on a contemporary footing are often supported only out of habit by the kind of consumer for whom information that a preferred performer's latest disc is just like the one before is praise indeed. Moreover, with repackaging factories in full production now, it makes as much sense to plug recordings 30 years old as hard as the most recent efforts.

Thus the future is the past all over again. Yet, for the faithful – whether there from the beginning or *Athens Andover* latecomers – every new Troggs release still remains a special event – if only because the group keep you guessing as to what they'll be up to next, unlike certain more feted contemporaries who churn out increasingly more ordinary albums that devotees have to own to complete the set like *Beano* annuals. Polished and ostensibly unobjectionable, such records are never expected to be astounding but suffice because skilful arrangements and technological advances can help conceal nondescript songs in need of editing.

It's a sweeping generalisation, but as console facilities improve, standards of composition fall in favour of the blinded-by-science sound at any given interval. If this is to be the rule, then The Troggs might be among the exceptions to it. 'The more I get out and about, the more I know I can produce,' acknowledges Reg Presley. 'I like to create while I'm doing something. It releases the music. They're all good ideas and it's a race to get them down on paper.'

The Troggs' re-emergence as a chart concern has never been out of the question – especially now that, thanks to Reg's Wet Wet Wet windfall, they are in a position to call shots about marketing procedure through the founding of their own Trogg Records with Christmas 1999's 'Let's Drink A Toast', its first release. 'If we'd have had the right managers and producers and been paid what we earned, we'd have been able to invest in our own recordings much sooner, and have had more say in what we did,' mused Reg. 'We'd have had more hits, remained on the scene longer – and Chris would have stayed in the group. Most artists are in the lap of whoever comes along and pays for the studio, and don't have much say in what they really want to do. If they do say too much, they haven't got a deal, they don't have a record out and nobody hears them. The whole world works that way.'

The Troggs Tapes

Location:	**Dick James Music Recording Studios, London**
Date:	**May 1971**
Purpose:	**To record new song "Tranquillity."**
Cast:	**In the recording room – Ronnie Bond (Drums); Chris Britton (Guitar); Tony Murray (Bass). In the control booth – producer Dennis Berger; Reg Presley.**

After a number of attempts at the instrumental backing track, the musicians stop playing, and the following conversation takes place. All the while, the engineer keeps the tape rolling:

Ronnie Bond: "...get into it. It's a fuckin' Number One. It is...whether you think so or not, that is a Number fuckin' One. If that bastard don't go, then Oi fuckin' retire. Oi fuckin' do. Bollocks!"
Dennis Berger: "I think it is a good song. I agree, it is a good song..."
Ronnie: "But it fuckin' well won't be unless we spend a little bit of fuckin' thought and imagination to fuckin' make it a fuckin' Number One. You've got to put a little bit of fuckin' fairy dust over the bastard! You know!"
Dennis: "Well, we'll get some fairy dust over it... I'll piss over the tape."
Tony Murray: [quietly] "I'm not doing this..."
Ronnie: "Do you know what I mean?... Oi don't know what it needs, Den..."

Dennis: "Ahh! I know that it needs strings – that I do know. Right? And it needs something at the beginning of that number to make someone remember it...?"

Tony: "While we're arguing here, we could be trying to get some sounds out there, trying to get something right... So what do you suggest we do Den? Give up on it?"

Dennis: "No! Not at all. I don't say give it up. I'll stay here till tomorrow night... [background groaning]... just provided we get something going."

Ronnie: "We will... it's just, that what he was playing...agreed...the sound was..."

Tony: "We've got, one, two, three, four, five, about six producers in here tonight."

Dennis: "[sighs] We haven't got six producers..."

Tony: "Yes we have... If we had one producer here, we might get it right – or he would get it the way he thinks it should be. But because we haven't got one producer, we're all fuckin' pitching in ideas..."

Dennis: "Well we always do that..."

Tony: "But most of them are rotten. You know."

Dennis: "Not necessarily wrong ..."

Tony: "Most of them are wrong... It makes his life fucking hell... But we haven't got a producer... we were supposed to have a fuckin' producer, but we haven't got one."

Reg: "This is what's been going fuckin' wrong. You've got to have a fuckin' bloke that says, Oi've got a fuckin' sound in here that's fuckin' great. Come in here and have a fuckin' listen to it... and you can come in 'ere and it's probably a different fuckin' tune nearly, but if it's fuckin' good, Yep that's it. But when we go through that door ..."

Dennis: [interrupting] "But what would you have said if the producer had been here and he would have left it exactly as it is – exactly as you've got it now."

Tony: "What sort of producer would do that?"

Dennis: "I dunno...might be, I dunno. He might say, keep it like that and put what ever else, strings or whatever."

Tony: "Well, we wouldn't have signed a contract with him in the first place."

Dennis: "Who?"

Tony: "Any producer."

Dennis: "You don't have to sign a contract with him. You don't have to sign a contract with a producer to have a record produced."

Tony: "It'd be thank you and good night, if he left it like that..."

Dennis: "Ah, you see, then you'd argue with him..."

Tony: "Yeah!"

Dennis: "There you are!"

Tony: "But no-one would leave it like that. No producer would..."

Dennis: [interrupting] "You don't know. He might say, put other things on it, or strings or brass or whatever his ideas are, or a fuckin' wobbleboard, I dunno. But would you agree to that?"

Tony: "Well for a fuckin' start, I don't suppose he'd even..."

Dennis: [interrupting] "Ohhh! Yeah! Sure! Would you agree? Would you have a producer sit here and say 'That's it!'".

Reg: "After the first half an hour, I'd either have faith in the cunt, or I wouldn't."

Tony: "Of course. That's what we need. We need a producer who says, No. You're not doing this; you're fuckin' doing this. That's what we need."

Chorus: "Yeah."

Dennis: "Well I don't think you'd wear it."

Chorus: "We would."

Reg: "We would, if we had faith in him. And we'd know if we had faith in him within the first fuckin' half an hour."

Dennis: "Did you do exactly what Larry Page said?"

Chorus: "Yep!"

Tony: "That's how they had hit records."

Reg: "Because there was just one fuckin' mind on it – not fuckin' seven or eight."

Ronnie: "We didn't even fuckin' get a say in it – it was fuckin' wham, it was in the can regardless. You reckon that was bad. Fuck me! One take, that's it. Finished! You never 'ad a fuckin' say – it was out. As weak and fuckin' insipid we used to think, well fuckin' 'ell.

Reg: [over background shouts from Ronnie] "We thought 'With A Girl Like You' was fuckin' terrible and let's go and do it again. And that was the only fuckin' time 'e let us have ...

Ronnie: "...our way..."

Reg: "...Our fuckin' way. And could we get anything fuckin' better?"

Ronnie: "No."

Reg: "Fuckin'...the first thing he fuckin' did was it."

Ronnie: "All fuckin' day. All fuckin' day. We went in there at nine o'clock and we didn't come out till, fuck, about three o'clock the next fuckin' morning, and they had Mick Jagger, you name it, they were fuckin' in there to try and make it better. And they couldn't."

Tony: "…What are we gonna do?" (There is a pause.)

Reg: "What about a fuckin' 12 string on it? Doing what he was doing?"

Dennis: "Play the beginning again, Barry. Play the beginning again."

Reg: "That sounds empty, and unless you can really get something exceptional…"

[Barry, identity unknown, vigorously strums some guitar chords, punctured by Reg shrieking, "Yeah!" and then "No!".]

Reg: "You 'ad it there at the beginning, Ron. It was sounding good. Ron? Ronnie? Just listen for a sec…"

Ronnie: "You can say that all fuckin' night, but Oi just cannot feel it any other way than what Oi've been fuckin' doing it."

Reg: "You have played it tonight."

Ronnie: "…I'll tell you this now, I cannot fuckin' do it. [barely audible mumbling] I don't know, because if that is the case, we should find out before we even get to the fuckin' studio. If we wanna do that, that and fuckin' that. [a door slams] I mean, we've been doing it all night…"

Reg: "It's easy."

Ronnie: "Don't expect fuckin' miracles just like that, Reg. It's fuckin' there – embedded in there. Oi can't fuckin' hear it any way but that."

Reg: "You have done it. You did it."

Tony: "What you were doing is exactly the same rhythm as you were playing originally…Play duh-duh duh-duh duh chuh."

Reg: "No, no more beats."

Tony: "You did it. You went dubbah-dubbah-dubbah-chuh."

Ronnie: "You can say that all fuckin' night, but you won't listen."

Tony: "We can keep on trying…"

Ronnie: [interrupting]: "Yeah – well just shut your fuckin' mouth for five minutes and give me a fuckin' chance to do it. Don't keep fuckin' rappin' down that fuckin' microphone. [In high pitched screeching voice –] dih-dih-dih dih-dih-dih. [In normal voice again –] Fuck me, Reg. Just fuck off in there…"

Reg: [interrupting] "Well, just fuckin' think then."

Ronnie: "Fuck off in there…and just keep going fuckin' through it just don't keep saying… Oi know it ain't fuckin' right. Oi can hear it ain't right, you cunt. Well, fuck me."

Reg: "You can hear it's fuckin' not right too."

Ronnie: "Oi fuckin' can, and Oi'm the cunt that's playing it, so Oi don't want to hear…fuck…fuck in me fuckin' head that's what Oi gotta fuckin' do, then Oi'll do it. Ya big pranny."

Tony: "Listen, let's keep on playing it."

[Bass guitar plays a couple of bars.]
Reg: "Fuckin' drummer. Oi shit 'em. ⌊sings⌋ Duh duh-duh duh derh. Duh duh-duh duh derh.
[Guitar joins in]
Reg: "One, two, a-one two three four... You're doing it fuckin' wrong."
Ronnie: "I know I am."
Reg: [laughs, then in time with the drums -] "Dubba dubba dubba chah, dubba dubba dubba chah, dubba dubba dubba chah, dubba dubba... You did it in the beginning. Bloody hell, Oi can't play to that."
Ronnie: "Nor can fuckin' Oi."
Reg: "Eh?"
Ronnie: "Nor can Oi."
Reg: "Well, you're fuckin' doing i'!"
Ronnie: "Well Oi can't fuckin' play to it either."
Reg: [laughs] "Why don't you just do what you fuckin' started out doing – dubba dubba durbba chah. On your top one, dubba dubba durbba chah. Dubba dubba durbba chah."
[Ronnie attempts to follow Reg's advice on tom-tom. It does not work.]
Reg: "Nooooo."
Ronnie: [agitatedly] "Why don't you fuckin'... You're talking out of the back of your fuckin' aaaarse because all you want then is the same fuckin' thing that Oi was playing fuckin' originally."
Reg: [loudly] "But on different fuckin' drums!"
Ronnie: [still agitatedly] "Then all you want, then, is fuckin' that one, and the fuckin' bass drum playing the same thing."
Reg: "You're the fuckin' drummer!"
Ronnie: "Yes you fuckin' do, 'cos that's all you're fuckin' doing. You ain't playing any fuckin' thing else. Orlroit, Oi'll play tha'. Oi'm goin' nah-nah-nah-nah-nah bomp, nah-nah-nah-nah-nah bomp, nah-nah-nah-nah-nah bomp... [thumps drums in accompaniment] You're changing the thing completely, 'cos you can't fuckin' do it. Nah-nah-nah-nah-nah bomp, nah-nah-nah-nah-nah bomp, nah-nah-nah-nah-nah bomp...[continues to thump drums in accompaniment]"
Reg: "Same thing on different fuckin' drums. You don't fuckin' listen, that's your trouble."
Ronnie: "Well, then change it round and do it the other way round."
Tony: [quietly] "I'm fuckin' going. We always get this..."
Reg: "Oi'm not asking you to do much. Oi'm only asking you to do

half of it on one drum, half of it on the other and the bang wherever you want the bang... Ronnie, can you 'ear me? Wha' abeou' tryin' i' not only just on that top skin, floor and then your floor tom-tom, but try it on...split your hands so's that one beat is doin' it on the top drum, one's doin' it on the floor tom-tom, then your bass."
[Drums begin. They do not sound right at all.]

Appendix

The Troggs British Discography

7" Singles

Lost Girl (RM Ball)
The Yella In Me (RM Ball)
CBS 202038 02/66

The first Troggs release: and the first and last to credit the composing rights to RM Ball. A driving, up-tempo, tambourine-tapping introductory disc which disappeared without a trace in the UK but charted in Holland.

The B-side is a 'Rocky, blues-orientated number', which confirms their R&B roots and is, even now, sometimes included in the stage set.

Wild Thing (Chip Taylor)
From Home (R Presley)
Fontana TF 689 04/66

Much imitated, but never surpassed. Every superlative in the dictionary has been used to describe this record. Basic, simple, but what a brilliant interpretation! This not only caught the mood of the time but has achieved cult recognition. In three weeks it climbed to Number 2 in the official UK charts. However, the two most respected music papers of the time actually showed it at Number One.

The theme of the B-track is of the 60's emancipated woman living 'her' life and her man trying to come to terms with the new lifestyles. Again, the B-side is still a favoured stage track.

With A Girl Like You (R Presley)
I Want You (L Page/C Frechter)
Fontana TF 717 07/66

The first UK 'Official' Number One. A compelling rhythmic, captivating classic Troggs track, which started the "bah-bah-bah" legend accompanying this classic.

Composing credits of this heavy, repetitive, drawling B-side go to two of the most important people in the Troggs' lives at that time, their producer and musical director.

I Can't Control Myself (R Presley)
Gonna Make You (L Page/C Frechter)
Page One POF 001 09/66

The first record on Larry Page's new Page One label. It stormed up the charts to Number 2 and was only kept from the top slot by The Four Tops' 'Reach Out I'll Be There'.

Airplay was totally banned in some countries, as the lyrics 'your slacks are low and your hips are showing' coupled with the final 'orgasmic' scream were felt to be too sexually explicit for the innocents of the 1960s! How could Reg's tongue-in-cheek performance be judged as pornographic?

The B-side is in a similar vein to the previous flip side, which again was written by their mentors, and can still be heard occasionally on stage.

Any Way That You Want Me (Chip Taylor)
66-5-4-3-2-1 (Reg Presley)
Page One POF 010 12/66

This is the very first Troggs ballad, written by the composer of 'Wild Thing', Chip Taylor. It was a complete departure from all of their earlier material and even incorporated the use of a string section. It was their fourth consecutive UK Top Ten hit and achieved a high of Number 8.

The flip side is a 'lyrically innuendo laden', wonderfully catchy ditty, with the throb of the drums pulsating assertively throughout the whole song and is yet another popular 1990s stage number.

Give It To Me (Reg Presley)
You're Lying (L Page/C Frechter)
Page One POF 015 02/67

A pounding, masterful, archetypal release which not only achieved a UK Top 20 place of Number 12, but was chanted around numerous football grounds throughout the UK.

In the USA it was released instead of 'Anyway That You Want Me', but failed to make any impact.

The theme of this B-side is of a lover who knows that his partner is cheating on him, and lying.

The bass guitar opens this track, with everybody participating on the vocals and is backed by bold drumming and innovative guitar work which works well with the flowing lyrics.

Night Of The Long Grass (Reg Presley)
Girl In Black (L Page/C Frechter)
Page One POF 022 05/67

A record of its time! This was a complete change of style for the Troggs. It was so atmospheric, with the eerie sound of the wind echoing over the airwaves. It was released at the time of the hippie movement and free love. Soft drugtaking had increased among the younger set so therefore the word 'grass' was assumed to be a reference to drugs and the single suffered restricted airplay, but it still managed to achieve Number 17 in the charts.

Another B-side that cites its credits to their producers. Full of drumming, crashing cymbals and strident guitar chords. It's a tale of unfulfilled love/lust: the girl in black ignores him and is with his brother! Then at long last, she dances with him, he wants it to be forever (aahhh).

Hi Hi Hazel (Martin/Coulter)
As I Ride By (Ronnie Bond)
Page One POF 030 07/67

This was a surprising choice for the next single. The track was lifted from their first album *From Nowhere* which had been in the shops for about a year.

American artist Geno Washington had also brought this number out as a single in 1966. But despite the odds The Troggs managed to climb three places higher than Geno's top chart position of Number 45.

It was the first of the B-sides to be penned by a group member other than Reg. As well as taking the composing honours on this song,

Ronnie Bond also took on the lead vocals.

It is an easy on the ear, up-tempo, flowing catchy melodic tune, which likens the loss of a lover to time moving on and the rivers flowing.

Love Is All Around (Reg Presley)
When Will The Rain Come? (Ronnie Bond)
Page One POF 040 10/67

The last record of 1967 and their penultimate sojourn into the Top 40. It achieved their highest chart position since September 1966, when it peaked at Number 5.

It was the year of flower power and the romantic ballad caught the public's attention. It is now recognised as a classic song. Not only did Wet Wet Wet prominently cover a song that was written after a Sunday lunch, but also international recording artists REM paid their homage on record.

The second Ronnie Bond-composed B-side. It has an Indian feel to it, which was very much the flavour of 1967. Experimentation was the name of the game, not only with drugs, but music as well. Different recording techniques, weird instruments that had not been used on pop records, they were all being tried at this time.

Little Girl (Reg Presley)
Maybe The Madman (Chris Britton)
Page One POF 056 02/68

This was the last UK chart entry of the 1960s for the Troggs. It only made Number 37. It's a lovely, gentle, and perhaps even mystical song, which caused mild controversy at the time.

The subject matter of the song was thought to be illegitimacy which outraged the guardians of morality! But in reality it's a love story, and was worthy of a higher place in the charts.

The very first of Chris Britton's compositions to be used as a flip side; much too brief, but full of psychedelia and deep-seated lines such as 'The raindrops are just condensation of tears cried for children that lied', which were spoken over not only the tune but technicians newly-found magic intermixed with the megaphonic sounding refrains.

Surprise Surprise (I Need You) (Reg Presley)
Marbles And Some Gum (Pete Staples)
Page One POF 064 04/68

A real honky tonk style rock'n'roll number. Colin Frechter is credited as the pounding pianist on the label. Reg growls his way through the up front lyrics, with the rest of the band harmonizing over the chorus of 'I Need You'. Finishes with a strangled throaty yowl. It failed to impress the fickle record buying public.

The first chance for Pete Staples to show his talents on a B-side. A very simple, catchy, sing-along country style number. The combination of the bass guitar and the drums give it a roll-along country feel. Could have been at home in a 1950s high school film.

You Can Cry If You Want To (Reg Presley)
There's Something About You (Ronnie Bond)
Page One POF 082 07/68

Was this an attempt by Reg to recreat the success of 'Love Is All Around' with another gentle ballad? With its ingenous lyrics, haunting harmonies and the inclusion of the string section, as the 1967 hit had. It seemed to have the hallmarks of another hit. But all to no avail as it failed to achieve the recognition it deserved.

Ronnie Bond once again took the honours on this surprising track. A smooth melodic ballad, well orchestrated and arranged, with a piano in prominence througout the number. You can almost imagine this as a big production number performed by The Walker Brothers.

Hip Hip Hooray (Geoff Stephens/John Carter)
Say Darlin'! (Chris Britton)
Page One POF 092 09/68

The last release of 1968 which was chosen as it was in tune with the 'bubblegum' music of the time. A happy up beat bouncy number, with the joint chorus of nah-nah-nahs and the pulsating drums backing and driving Reg's snarling lead vocals. Once again it fell upon the deaf ears of the record buying public.

An easy-going, flowing, blues-inclined track written by Chris. Pictures invade the mind of late nights and smoky clubs with a guitarist picking out this melody. It smacks of the laid-back Hendrix style of 'Hey Joe'.

Evil Woman (Larry Miles)
Sweet Madeleine (Reg Presley)
Page One POF 114 01/69

Only two single releases for the UK this year. The first A-side was
penned by the composer of 'Rhinestone Cowboy' which gave Glen
Campbell his first USA Number One in 1975. This is a track heavily
laden with atmospheric bass, an over-abundance of echo and
tambourines a-shaking in the background, and culminating with Reg's
vocal enthusiasms.

A different Troggs track on the flip with Reg's vocals accompanied
by a full orchestral backing. The band taped the backing track,
complete with tambourine and chorus of lah-lah-lah-lahs, and the
orchestration was recorded and added later.

Wild Thing (Chip Taylor)
I Can't Control Myself (Reg Presley)
Page One POF 126 03/69

The second 1969 single was a re-release of two of their biggest 1966
hits, back to back. This was an attempt by Larry Page to recapture
the hit making blueprint from 1966, but it made no impact on the
charts.

Easy Loving (H Spiro/V Avon)
Give Me Something (P Staples)
Page One POF 164 02/70

Three singles were released in the UK this year. This first one is a soft
gentle ballad, with The Troggs once again augmented with sections of
the orchestra.

This was arranged and conducted by Mike Batt now better known
for his Wimbledon Womble connections.

A piano backing is very much in evidence throughout this, another
gentle ballad credited to bassist Pete Staples, and is a farewell to his
Trogg days.

Noticeable by its omission is a named credit for production. The
label reads: 'A Page One production'...

Lover (Chris Britton)
Come Now (Presley/Britton/Murray/Bond)
Page One POF 171 05/70

This is the first A-side to be written by lead guitarist Chris Britton and
is much more in keeping with their past hit-making formula sound.

A durable, semi-rock number with Ronnie's drumming powering through the track and some complex guitar work from Chris. The production credit goes to one Phil Waller.

Again this is back to their early days with Reg delivering sexually suggestive lyrics and the rest of the band potently playing their parts.

A different touch was tried on the B-side with Reg speaking French in a seductive raunchy manner.

No named producer on the label. Again it reads: 'A Page One production'. The composing rights are shared between all four of The Troggs which now included Pete Staples' replacement, bass player Tony Murray.

The Raver (Reg Presley)
You (Presley/Britton/Bond/Murray)
Page One POF 198 10/70

The end of an era! This was not only their last single of 1970, but also the last released in the UK on Page One.

An unusual song, with just one refrain repeated over and over again. Incorporates not only the plentiful use of 'group harmonies' but a harmonica and a Jew's-harp; very atmospheric.

Another group composition for this B-side. This is plagiarism at it's most amusing. It's an amalgamation of segments taken from words and music of their own former recordings.

Lazy Weekend (Presley/Murray)
Let's Pull Together (Reg Presley)
DJM DJS 248 04/71

A new year and a new label, the only single to be released that year. It was produced by Dennis Berger and Clive Franks. A summer record which gently rolls along with a banjo strumming away throughout the song.

Essentially a Trogg-stylised record on the flip. On the same lines as Reg's earlier composition, 'The Yella In Me'. A semi-rock number which allows all of the band to showcase their talent.

Everything's Funny (Presley/Britton)
Feels Like A Woman (Reg Presley)
PYE 7N 45147 05/72

Another year and yet another label, this was the first of three singles for Pye. An up-beat number enhanced by orchestration, with a chorus of 'my my my, you know what it's like when you're high'. This was Chris Britton's last single before he went to Portugal.

Both of these tracks were produced by Rodger Bain who had formerly been a sound engineer for Black Sabbath. 'Feels Like A Woman' is a classic Troggs number, strong vocals, unbridled guitar work, solid drumming and loads of feedback, which all contribute to make this one of their strongest numbers.

It achieved the Number 1 spot in South Africa for four weeks, but made no impression in the UK.

Listen To The Man (Reg Presley)
Queen Of Sorrow (Richard Glenmoore)
PYE 7N 45244 05/73

A rhythmic harmonious lilting ballad, easy to listen to and very catchy. Produced by one David Reilly for Rare Records and released through Pye.

'Queen Of Sorrow' is a gentle, whimsical love song with Reg in soft mode lamenting his lost love. This is the debut single appearance for Richard Moore, Chris Britton's replacement.

Strange Movies (Reg Presley)
I'm On Fire (Richard Moore)
PYE 7N 45295 09/73

Specifically written by Reg Presley to shock and be banned; as it was by all of the radio stations. The theme is porn films and it is full of graphic grunts, groans and gropes. It is still a popular stage number which causes nudges and giggles through the audience.

Penned by the newest boy in the band, 'I'm On Fire' is a rocky raunchy number, heavily laden with wailing guitars and is ideally suited to Reg's voice.

Good Vibrations (Wilson/Love)
Push It Up To Me (Bond/Presley/Murray)
Penny Farthing PEN 861 01/75

Yet another label change and it was back to their original producer Larry Page on his new Penny Farthing label.

It was the full Trogg treatment for the Beach Boys' 1966 Number One hit, 'Good Vibrations'. With Reg half speaking the lyrics in an alluring breathless manner, over the backing harmonies and between a whistling passage. An immortal interpretation surely! It even received the recognition it deserved in Germany and Europe.

This flip side has a reggae, calypso rhythm to it and conjures up pictures in the mind of palm trees, hot sandy beaches and cool rum punch. Well worth a listen.

Wild Thing (Taylor)
Jenny Come Down (Presley/Bond/Murray)
Penny Farthing PEN 884 1974

Yes, this is the same song that The Troggs had a massive world wide hit with in 1966. But this 1974 performance tried a new slant – a reggae version, which unfortunately did not capture the record-buying public's attention.

'Jenny Come Down' was a much used track, credited to the same writing team as the last B-side. It was included on the 1975 album titled *The Troggs* (PEL 543) and was again the B-side on their next Penny Farthing single. It's an up tempo number, which has an American feel.

Summertime (Presley/Bond/Murray)
Jenny Come Down (Presley/Bond/Murray)
Penny Farthing PEN 889 07/75

This A-side was taken from their album *The Troggs* (PEL 543). It's a classic Troggs number which features Reg in full leering salacious flow, with stuttering innuendoes such as 'I like the summertime where the girls wear their dresses so high you can see the sun on their f-f-f—-aces'!!!!

The same B-side as on the last single.

(I Can't Get No) Satisfaction (Jagger/Richard)
Memphis Tennessee (Berry)
Penny Farthing PEN 901 1975

Yet another track taken from their *The Troggs* album. This time they gave their Trogg makeover to the Rolling Stones' 1965 Number One. The Troggs' rendition is a strong, powerful version with Reg's strident, grinding vocals pulsating over Ronnie's drumming. Still a very popular stage number.

'Memphis' is a good old Chuck Berry rock'n'roll number, which has been recorded by numerous artistes. The Troggs pay their respects to the old master with their innovative adaptation. This is again from the aforementioned album.

I'll Buy You An Island (R Presley/C Britton)
Supergirl (R Moore)
Penny Farthing PEN 919 1976

It's back to the soft side of the Troggs, with this gentle, fluent song. The sounds of seagulls and the ocean breaking gently on the seashore all add to the laidback atmospheric ambience.

'Supergirl' is the first single solo composing credit for guitarist Richard Moore since 'I'm On Fire' in 1973 and features a recurrent guitar break which predominates throughout the whole record.

Feeling For Love (Taylor)
Summertime (Presley/Bond/Murray)
Penny Farthing PEN 929 1976

A ballad, which is very much in the style of 'Anyway That You Want Me'. But with no orchestration, just the pure solid sound of The Troggs. Another little-known track which deserves a wider audience.

A surprising choice for the back up track on this single as it was released as an A-side in 1974.

Just A Little Too Much (Johnny Burnette)
The True Troggs Tapes? (Lee Wood)
Raw Records RAW 25 1978
(Play at 33 RPM)

The first Troggs single for almost two years, and another parting of the ways for the group and their erstwhile producer Larry Page. This is a cover of a Rick Nelson track which is given The Troggs 'punk rock' treatment. A really rocking record, worth watching out for.

The flip is not the infamous bootleg tape. It is a comedy sketch which pokes fun at the management side of the music business. The culprits on this very amusing lampooning recording are Reg, Ronnie, Tony Murray, Peter Lucas (also on piano) and Lee Wood, who is given the 'composing' credit.

Wild Thing (Chip Taylor)
With A Girl Like You (Reg Presley)
Old Gold OG 9001 1980

I Can't Control Myself (Reg Presley)
Give It To Me (Reg Presley)
Old Gold OG 9024 1980

Love Is All Around (Reg Presley)
Any Way That You Want Me (Chip Taylor)
Old Gold OG 9038 1980

These last three 'double hit' re-release singles were circulated via the oldie-orientated label 'Old Gold'.

The Troggs Tapes
DJM DJS 6 1981

A double pack of singles: Record 1 A side: Wild Thing, B side: I Can't Control Myself and Love Is All Around.
The second 7" comprises of Side A: The Troggs Tapes, Side B: The Troggs Tapes
A 'Limited Edition' two record pack with three of their biggest UK Top 10 hits re-released on the first single.
Record Two is the first official airing of the 'pirate' tape, that had been 'doing the rounds' of the music industry for about ten years.

Every Little Thing (Reg Presley/Arnie Treffers)
Blackjack And Poker (Chris Britton)
10 Virgin TEN 21 03/84

Every Little Thing (Reg Presley/Arnie Treffers)
Blackjack And Poker (Chris Britton)
Virgin 196324-100 1984

Every Little Thing (Reg Presley/Arnie Treffers)
Blackjack And Poker (Chris Britton)
Ten Records TEN 21 03/84
With A Girl Like You (Reg Presley)
(Picture Disc)

Both sides of this single were produced by The Troggs and co-written by Reg and Dutch composer Arnie Treffers.
The keyboard sound is predominant on this melodious catchy song, which deserved more success than it achieved. It was even promoted on national television with the addition of a fifth Trogg on keyboards.
'Blackjack And Poker' is another one of Chris's composing contributions. This is a very zippy, breezy, country-style number, which would be ideal for line dancing or just cruising in an open top car with the speakers up real high.

Wild Thing (Chip Taylor)
From Home (Reg Presley)
Fontana TF 689 1991

Twenty five years later, almost to the day, 'Wild Thing', complete with the same B-side was re-released in the UK on its original label and with its original catalogue number.
In the Official Gallop Chart of 31 March-6 April 1991 it achieved a chart position of Number 87.

Don't You Know (Reg Presley)
Nowhere Road (P Buck/B Berry/M Mills/P Holsapple)
Page One ESS 2014 03/92
(Available on 12" ESST 2014)

A momentous single, which preceded the release of an album of the amalgamation of The Troggs and members of the 1990s mega American hit making band REM. The whole project was produced by The Troggs' original producer Larry Page.

This single was record of the week on BBC Radio 1 and registered in the top hundred best selling singles.

'Nowhere Road' was written by the three participating REM band members and honorary member Peter Holsapple expressly for Reg's vocal talents, and was included in The Troggs' live stage set for quite some time.

Wild Thing (Chip Taylor)
Wild Thing (Chip Taylor) **(Tinchen GP Mix) Edit Version**
Lifetime LIF3.7 11/92

The Wild Man of acting, Oliver Reed, plus, The Wild Man of the snooker table, Alex 'Hurricane' Higgins combined their joint talents to assist The Troggs in recording a very different version of the international worldwide hit, 'Wild Thing'.

The edit version is a lighter dance mix, without all the snarls and screams of side one.

War (Whitfield/Strong) **Edwin Starr Featuring Shadow**
Wild Thing (Taylor) **The Troggs Featuring Wolf**
LWT WEEK 103 1993

This record was released due to the success of LWT's hit television show *Gladiators*.

Shadow featured 'War' as his theme song to build up an aura of excitement in the arena prior to his trials of strength. So it was a natural progression for him to team up with Edwin Starr, who had a massive hit with 'War'.

So The Troggs teamed up with Wolf who had used 'Wild Thing' in the same way as Shadow used 'War'. It was recorded very much in the traditional mould of the original hit single. But Wolf accompanies Reg on vocals and adds his own seal on the proceedings with wailing howls echoing in the distance.

Unreleased 7" Single

My Lady (Reg Presley)
Girl In Black (L Page/C Frechter)
Page One POF 022 1967

Copies do exist of this record. Larry Page decided to release 'Night Of The Long Grass' in place of this haunting, eastern-influenced tune. It was also seen on the album *Cellophane*, released in the same year.

Ex-Shadow Jet Harris also released it as an A-side on a 1967 single.

'Girl In Black' is a Trogg track written and recorded to suit the band's basic successful style. From the opening drum roll, this is a heavy, pounding number with the vocals powering throughout.

12" Singles

Wild Thing (Chip Taylor)
I Can't Control Myself (Reg Presley)
Love Is All Around (Reg Presley)
DJM DJR 6 1981

The Troggs Tapes

Every Little Thing
Virgin 10 Records TEN 21-12 1984
Side 1:   **Every Little Thing (Extended Mix)**
             (Reg Presley/Arnie Treffers)
Side 2:   **Blackjack And Poker** (Chris Britton)

Wild Thing
Lifetime LIF3.12 11/92
A Side: **Wild Thing** (Chip Taylor) **Oliver Reed and
             the Troggs with Alex 'Hurricane' Higgins
             (Tinchen GP Remix)**

B Side: **Wild Thing** (Chip Taylor) **(Tinchen GP Remix)
             Edit Version
             Wild Thing** (Chip Taylor)

NOTEWORTHY CD SINGLES

1 With A Girl Like You (Reg Presley)
2 I Want You (L Page/C Frechter)
Fontana UK TFCD 717 1991

A Limited Edition, No 000971 CD. This is one of a 12CD single set.

Together (Reg Presley)
Crazy Annie (Chip Taylor)
Tuned Into Love (Larry Page/D Boone)
Page One ESS X 2016 1992
(Also available on 12" vinyl ESST 2016 1992)

All three tracks taken from the album *Athens Andover*.

Wild Thing (Chip Taylor)
Wild Thing (Tinchen GP Remix) (Chip Taylor)
Wild Thing (Tinchen GP Remix) Edit Version
(Chip Taylor)
Lifetime LIF3.CD 1992

A CD version of the 12" vinyl release. This is The Troggs with a little help from Oliver Reed and Alex 'Hurricane' Higgins.

War (Whitfield/Strong)
Wild Thing (Taylor)
War-Battle Mix (Whitfield/Strong)
LWT CD WEEK 103 1992

This is a three track CD alternative to the 7" vinyl release of the Troggs' affiliation with 'Gladiator' Wolf.

Wild Thing (C Taylor)
With A Girl Like You (Reg Presley)
I Can't Control Myself (Reg Presley)
Old Gold OG 6164 1992

The oldie orientated 'Old Gold' label released this as a CD. It is of course the first three of The Troggs' British hits.

EPs

Trogg Tops No 1
Page One POE 001 1966
Side One: Wild Thing (Chip Taylor)
              From Home (Reg Presley)
Side Two: With A Girl Like You (Reg Presley)
              I Want You (L Page/C Frechter)

The first EP was on Page One and contained both sides of the second and third singles. It achieved its highest EP chart position of Number 8 in March 1967 and was in the EP charts for a total of four weeks.

Troggs Tops 2
Page One POE 002 1967
Side One: Any Way That You Want Me (Chip Taylor)
              I Can't Control Myself (Reg Presley)
Side Two: Cousin Jane (L Page/D Mathews)
              Gonna Make You (L Page/C Frechter)

The second EP comprised of both sides of their fourth single, the A-side of their fifth single and 'Cousin Jane' – an eerie, simple song of illicit love where Reg's vocals are accompanied by piano and unelaborate orchestration.

Unreleased EP

Track A Trogg
Page One POE 1967

Possible demonstration copies still exist.

The Troggs

Albums

From Nowhere The Troggs
Fontana TL 5355 07/66

Side One:	1 **Wild Thing** (Chip Taylor)
	2 **The Kitty Cat Song** (J Rouch/J Spindel)
	3 **Ride Your Pony** (N Neville)
	4 **Hi Hi Hazel** (B Martin/P Coulter)
	5 **I Just Sing** (Reg Presley)
	6 **Evil** (Shelby Singleton)
Side Two:	1 **Our Love Will Still Be There** (Reg Presley)
	2 **Louie Louie** (Richard Berry)
	3 **Jingle Jangle** (Reg Presley)
	4 **When I'm With You** (Reg Presley)
	5 **From Home** (Reg Presley)
	6 **Jaguar And Thunderbird** (Chuck Berry)

The Troggs' first UK album, which was in the album charts for 16 weeks and peaked at Number 6 at the end of July 1967. Five of the tracks were penned by Reg and only two of the tracks had been on previously released singles. A real showcase of a first album, which accentuates their R&B roots.

Reg takes lead vocals on all of the tracks except for 'Ride Your Pony' where Chris does the honours and 'Jaguar And Thunderbird' where Ronnie is the lead singer. The whole assembly of tracks is a potent and powerful introduction to The Troggs' music.

Trogglodynamite
Page One POL 001 02/67

Side One: 1 I Can Only Give You Everything
             (Scott/Coulter)
             2 Last Summer (Reg Presley)
             3 Meet Jacqueline (Albert Hammond)
             4 Oh No (Pete Staples)
             5 It's Too Late (Ronnie Bond)
             6 No 10 Downing Street (Page/Matthews)
             7 Mona (Bo Diddley)
Side Two: 1 I Want You To Come Into My Life
             (Reg Presley)
             2 Let Me Tell You Babe (Sherman/Weiss)
             3 Little Queenie (Chuck Berry)
             4 Cousin Jane (Page/Matthews)
             5 You Can't Beat It (Reg Presley)
             6 Baby Come Closer (T Dwyer/J Price)
             7 It's Over (Reg Presley)

This made Number 10 in the album charts in February 1967 and
stayed there for a total of 11 weeks. Another excellently varied album,
of which Reg composed four of the tracks, Ronnie one and Pete one.
Chris takes the credit for the vocals on 'Little Queenie', Ronnie on his
own composition; 'It's Too Late' and Pete on R'n'B exponent Bo
Diddley's 'Mona'.

The first track is still used on stage as a popular encore. 'Last
Summer' has the hallmark of the hippie era, and is an easy flowing
number. 'No 10 Downing Street' was also released as a single by The
Nerve.

Best Of The Troggs
Page One FOR 001 1967

Side One:	1 **Night Of The Long Grass** (Reg Presley)
	2 **Gonna Make You** (L Page/C Frechter)
	3 **Any Way That You Want Me** (Chip Taylor)
	4 **66-5-4-3-2-1** (Reg Presley)
	5 **I Want You** (L Page/C Frechter)
	6 **With A Girl Like You** (Reg Presley)
Side Two:	1 **I Can't Control Myself** (Reg Presley)
	2 **Girl In Black** (L Page/C Frechter)
	3 **Give It To Me** (Reg Presley)
	4 **You're Lying** (L Page/C Frechter)
	5 **From Home** (Reg Presley)
	6 **Wild Thing** (Chip Taylor)

This third album is essentially a collection of all the Troggs' hit records to date *i.e.* both sides of the singles, number two through to number seven.

This was the last Troggs album to make any impact on the UK album charts. The highest point it recorded in its five-week residency in the Top 40 polls was Number 24.

Cellophane
Page One POL 003 1967

Side One:	1 **Little Red Donkey**
	(P Staples/R Presley/R Bond/C Britton)
	2 **Too Much Of A Good Thing** (J Gillard/T Fogg)
	3 **Butterflies And Bees** (C Britton)
	4 **All Of The Time** (R Presley)
	5 **Seventeen** (R Presley)
	6 **Somewhere My Girl I Waiting** (Art Wayne)
Side Two:	1 **It's Showing** (R Presley)
	2 **Her Emotion** (R Presley)
	3 **When Will The Rain Come** (R Bond)
	4 **My Lady** (R Presley)
	5 **Come The Day** (R Bond)
	6 **Love Is All Around** (R Presley)

This album of new material was artistically a much superior collection of the Troggs' work, but unfortunately it did not sell particularly well.

Of the 12 tracks, ten were new Troggs recordings for the British record buying public.

Six tracks were written by Reg, one by Chris, two by Ronnie and 'Little Red Donkey' cites all four band members as composers. This track was covered by Freddie Garrity (aka Freddie & the Dreamers) in 1968. The remaining two songs were credited to outside composers.

Best Of The Troggs Volume 2
Page One FOR 007 1968

Side One:	1 I Can Only Give You Everything (T Scott/P Coulter)
	2 Meet Jacqueline (A Hammond)
	3 Jingle Jangle (R Presley)
	4 I Want You To Come Into My Life (R Presley)
	5 Cousin Jane (L Page/D Matthews)
	6 Louie Louie (R Berry)
Side Two:	1 Love Is All Around (R Presley)
	2 From Home (R Presley)
	3 Jaguar And The Thunderbird (C Berry)
	4 Hi Hi Hazel (B Martin/P Coulter)
	5 Evil (S Singleton)
	6 Mona (B Diddley)

This second *Best Of* compilation album has a selection of tracks taken from three of their earlier LPs. Six of the tracks were originally on *From Nowhere The Troggs*, five on *Trogglodynamite* plus 'Love Is All Around' which was not only a Top 5 hit single but on the last album, *Cellophane*.

Mixed Bag
Page One POLS 012 1968

Side One: 1 **Surprise Surprise** (R Presley)
               2 **You Can Cry If You Want To** (R Presley)
               3 **Say Darlin'** (C Britton)
               4 **Marbles And Some Gum** (P Staples)
               5 **Purple Shades** (R Presley)
               6 **Heads Or Tails** (C Britton)
Side Two: 1 **Hip Hip Hooray** (J Carter/G Stevens)
               2 **Little Girl** (R Presley)
               3 **Maybe The Madman** (C Britton)
               4 **Off The Record** (P Staples)
               5 **We Waited For Someone** (R Presley)
               6 **There's Something About You** (R Bond)

This is the rarest of the Troggs' albums, possibly due to limited promotion.

The band were now writing more and more of their own material. 'Hip Hip Hooray' is the only song which was not penned by a Trogg band member. Actually eight of the 12 tracks are the four singles of 1968.

'Purple Shades', which is one of the album's two new Reg Presley compositions, is a very different, psychedelic sounding song, which he wrote with the aid of nothing stronger than a cup of tea.

Another 'strange' track, which works well, is 'Off The Record', an amusing insight into studio banter between recording. It is also a very tame forerunner of 'The Troggs Tapes'.

Trogglomania
Page One POS 602 1969

Side One:	1 **Give It To Me** (R Presley)
	2 **Gonna Make You** (L Page/CFrechter)
	3 **LIttle Queenie** (C Berry)
	4 **Louie Louie** (R Berry)
	5 **Wild Thing** (C Taylor)
Side Two:	1 **I Can Only Give You Everything**
	(Scott/Coulter)
	2 **From Home** (R Presley)
	3 **Ride Your Pony** (N Neville)
	4 **The Yella In Me** (R Presley)
	5 **I Want You** (L Page/C Frechter)

This is a 'sampler' album, which as it suggests was released to tempt the record buying public. The selection of tracks has been taken from numerous sources: Two A-sides, four B-sides and four album tracks; two of which were on *From Nowhere* and two on *Trogglodynamite*.

Contrasts
DJM Silverline DJML 009 1970 (re-released 1974)

Side One:	1 **I Can't Control Myself** (R Presley)
	2 **The Raver** (R Presley)
	3 **Surprise Surprise (I Need You)** (R Presley)
	4 **Evil Woman** (L Weiss)
	5 **Lover** (C Britton)
	6 **Wild Thing** (C Taylor)
Side Two:	1 **Love Is All Around** (R Presley)
	2 **Little Girl** (R Presley)
	3 **You Can Cry If You Want To** (R Presley)
	4 **I've Waited For Someone** (R Presley)
	5 **Easy Loving** (H Spiro/V Avon)
	6 **Any Way That You Want Me** (C Taylor)

A budget release which encompassed no fewer than 11 of The Troggs' A-sides from 'Wild Thing' of 1966 through to 'The Raver' released in 1970.

Track four on side two, 'I've Waited For Someone' was a new Reg Presley experience for the British public. It still has the hallmarks of the hippie era. This album was re-released in 1974, the only changes were in the packaging: gone was the classic line-up 'Berlin Zoo' shot and animal print cover, replaced by a silver cover and an updated group picture which included Tony Murray.

With A Girl Like You
DJM Silverline DJML 047 1975

Side One:	1 Louie Louie (R Berry)
	2 With A Girl Like You (R Presley)
	3 Hi HI Hazel (Bill Martin/Phil Coulter)
	4 Let's Pull Together (R Presley)
	5 You Can Cry If You Want To (R Presley)
	6 Ride Your Pony (N Neville)
Side Two:	1 Give It To Me (R Presley)
	2 I Can Only Give You Everything (Scott/Coulter)
	3 Baby Come Closer (T Dwyer/J Price)
	4 Little Girl (R Presley)
	5 The Kitty Kat Song (J Roach)
	6 The Yella In Me (R Presley)

On this second DJM Silverline album there is a real assortment of Trogg tracks. Seven of the offerings were not only on A or B-sides of hit singles, but also on subsequent albums. The remaining five tracks were previously heard on the first two of the Troggs' albums – *From Nowhere* and *Trogglodynamite*.

The Troggs
Penny Farthing PELS 543 1975

Side One:	1 I Got Love If You Want It (Moore)
	2 Good Vibrations (Love/Wilson)
	3 No Particular Place To Go (Chuck Berry)
	4 Summertime (Presley/Bond/Murray)
	5 (I Can't Get No) Satisfaction (Jagger/Richard)
Side Two:	1 Full Blooded Band (Bond/Presley/Murray)
	2 Memphis Tennessee (Chuck Berry)
	3 Peggy Sue (Allison/ Petty/Holly)
	4 Jenny Come Down (Bond/Presley/Murray)
	5 Wild Thing (Taylor)

The first Penny Farthing album and back with Larry Page. Six of these recordings were drawn from the four 1975 Penny Farthing singles, including the new reggae version of 'Wild Thing'. But it was back to their roots, and their heroes of rock'n'roll, for the first airings of two dynamically powerful arrangements of 'No Particular Place To Go' and 'Peggy Sue', which was part of their live stage set for many years. To complete the diverse selection of material is Slim Harpo's salacious 'I Got Love If You Want It' and 'Full Blooded Band', a joint effort, in all ways, from all members of The Troggs, plus 'sideman' Peter Green (not the former leader of Fleetwood Mac), on acoustic guitar.

The Troggs Tapes
Penny Farthing PELS 551 1976

Side One:	1 **Get You Tonight** (R Moore)
	2 **We RodeThrough The Night** (R Presley)
	3 **A Different Me** (T Murray/R Bond)
	4 **Down South To Georgia**
	(T Murray/R Bond)
	5 **Gonna Make You** (L Page/C Frechter)
Side Two:	1 **Supergirl** (R Moore)
	2 **I'll Buy You An Island** (R Presley/C Britton)
	3 **Rolling Stone** (T Murray/R Bond)
	4 **After The Rain** (C Frechter/T Murray)
	5 **Rockin' And Rollin' LIttle Lady**
	(R Dunning)
	6 **Walking The Dog** (R Thomas)

This is the second and last Penny Farthing LP; it is unusual as there are temporarily five Troggs instead of the accustomed compliment of four. Colin Fletcher is the 'new boy' and contributes acoustic and electric guitars.

Another varied compilation with several brand new tracks to please British Troggs *afficionados* plus an electric rendition of Rufus Thomas' 'Walking The Dog'. Also on the release is the fifth Penny Farthing single with Richard Moore taking the vocals on 'Supergirl'.

The Troggs

Wild Thing
Chevron CHVL 155 1979

Side One:
1 Wild Thing (Taylor)
2 Rock'N'Roll Lady (Dunning)
3 No Particular Place To Go (Berry)
4 Memphis Tennessee (Berry)
5 Satisfaction (Jagger/Richard)

Side Two:
1 Good Vibrations (Love/Wilson)
2 I Got Loving If You Want It (Moore)
3 Walking The Dog (Thomas)
4 Gonna Make You (L Page/C Frechter)
5 Peggy Sue (Allison/Petty/Holly)

A budget release, which selects tracks from the last two Penny Farthing albums.

The cover is of special interest as Ian Amey, (Tich) from Dave, Dee, Dozy, Mick and Tich, plus Peter Lucas are pictured with Reg and Ronnie, although neither is named in any of the credits.

Black Bottom
RCA PL 30084 1981

Side One:
1 Black Bottom
2 Strange Movies*
3 Bass For My Birthday
4 Little Pretty Thing
5 Last Night

Side Two:
1 Hot Days
2 I Don't
3 Widge You
4 Feels Like A Woman*
5 I Love You Baby

All of the tracks were composed by Bullis, Bee Bee, Murray & Foote, except * which were by Reg Presley.

Chris Britton was back in the fold by this time with Reg, Ronnie and Tony Murray. This album was organised and arranged by the Troggs. It was recorded in London and released in co-operation with RCA and the French company New Rose Records.

The new Troggs compositions are in keeping with the tried and tested formulae of nearly 20 years. 'Hot Days' encompasses the melodic guitar work, prominent drums and suggestive lyrics which all make up the special Troggs sound.

Rock It Up
Action Replay Records Ltd AR LP103 1984

Side One:	1 **Got Love If You Want It** (Murray)
	2 **Good Vibrations** (Love/Wilson)
	3 **No Particular Place To Go** (Berry)
	4 **Summertime** (Presley/Bond/Murray)
	5 **Satisfaction** (Jagger/Richard)
	6 **Full Blooded Band** (Bond/Presley/Murray)
	7 **Memphis Tennessee** (Berry)
	8 **Peggy Sue** (Allison/Petty)
Side Two:	1 **Supergirl** (Moore)
	2 **I'll Buy You An Island** (R Presley/C Britton)
	3 **Rolling Stone** (T Murray/R Bond)
	4 **After The Rain** (C Fletcher/T Murray)
	5 **Rockin' And Rollin' Little Lady**
	(R Dunning)
	6 **Walking The Dog** (R Thomas)
	7 **Get You Tonight** (R Moore)
	8 **We Rode Through The Night** (R Presley)
	9 **A Different Me** (T Murry/R Bond)

All 17 tracks on this album are taken from the Page One original recordings for the Penny Farthing label, which were produced by Larry Page. Eight are from the first album, *The Troggs* of 1975 and nine from the second *The Troggs Tapes* of 1976.

Double Hit Collection
Platinum Music PRISM PLAT 3908 1989
Also on: CD PLATCD 3908 Cassette PLAC 3908

Side One: **THE TROGGS**
1 **Wild Thing** (Taylor)
2 **From Home** (Presley)
3 **With A Girl Like You** (Presley)
4 **I Can't Control Myself** (Presley)
5 **Anyway That You Want Me** (Taylor)
6 **Give It To Me** (Presley)
7 **Night Of The Long Grass** (Presley)
8 **Love Is All Around** (Presley)
9 **Little Girl** (Presley)
10 **Wild Thing '89** (Taylor)
Side Two: **DAVE DEE, DOZY, BEAKY, MICH & TICH**
1 **Hold Tight** (Howard-Blaikley)
2 **Hideaway** (Howard-Blaikley)
3 **Bend It** (Howard-Blaikley)
4 **Save Me** (Howard-Blaikley)
5 **Touch Me, Touch Me** (Howard-Blaikley)
6 **Okay!** (Howard-Blaikley)
7 **Zabadak!** (Howard-Blaikley)
8 **Legend Of Xanadu** (Howard-Blaikley)
9 **Last Night In Soho** (Howard-Blaikley)
10 **Wreck Of The Antoinette** (Howard-Blaikley)

A budget end of the market production. Prism Leisure has brought about the alliance of the two biggest West Country 60s bands. It's essentially a showcase for both groups' hits. But as an additional bonus it includes the new mix of 'Wild Thing', which was featured in the 1989 baseball film *Major League* starring Charlie Sheen.

Wild Things
See For Miles Records Ltd SEE 256 1989
Also on CD SEE CD 256

Side One:	1 I Got Love If You Want It (Moore)
	2 Good Vibrations (Love/Wilson)
	3 No Particular Place To Go (Berry)
	4 Summertime (Presley/Bond/Murray)
	5 Satisfaction (Jagger/Richard)
	6 Full Blooded Band (Bond/Presley/Murray)
	7 Memphis Tennessee (Berry)
	8 Peggy Sue (Allison/Petty)
	9 Wild Thing (Taylor)
	10 Get You Tonight (Moore)
Side Two:	1 A Different Me (Murray)
	2 Down South To Georgia (Murray/Bond)
	3 After The Rain (Fletcher/Murray)
	4 Rock 'N' Roll Lady (Dunning)
	5 Walkin' The Dog (Thomas)
	6 We Rode Through The Night (Presley)
	7 Gonna Make You (Page/Fletcher)
	8 Supergirl (Moore)
	9 I'll Buy You An Island (Presley/Britton)
	10 Rolling Stone (Murray/Bond)

This is another album which is taken from the 1975/76 Penny Farthing reunion days with Larry Page. Track numbers one to nine are taken from the album *The Troggs*. The rest of this LP is *The Troggs Tapes* in its unedited entirety.

Au
New Rose Records ROSE 186 1989
Also on CD ROSE 186 CD

Side One:	1 There's Always There To Remind Me (Bacharach/David)
	2 Strange Movies (Reg Presley)
	3 What You Doing Here (Reg Presley)
	4 I Can't Control Myself (Reg Presley)
	5 The Disco Kid Verses Sid Chicane (Reg Presley)
Side Two:	1 Wild Thing (Taylor)
	2 Walking The Dog (Rufus Thomas)
	3 Love Is All Around (Reg Presley)
	4 With A Girl Like You (Reg Presley)
	5 Maximum Overdrive (Reg Presley)

This is a True Troggs Album which is totally organised and produced by the band. All of the tracks are brand new recordings.

'Wild Thing', as on *The Double Hits Collection*, is the new mix which was used in the film *Major League*. The other three tracks from the halcyon hit heydays have had 'fairy dust' sprinkled liberally over them and stand up well to the test of time with the addition of orchestration. There is also a much slower re-recording of the 70s composition 'Strange Movies', which develops 'the blue movie tale' in a graphic, sexually explicit manner, aided by a strong brass section. A surprising inclusion is the Bacharach/David composition, 'There's Always Something There To Remind Me', but the Troggs' adaptation works very well.

Three brand new Reg Presley compositions are featured. The first, 'The Disco Kid Versus Sid Chicane', is an amusing paradoxical anecdote that pits disco music against rock, of course rock wins the day! The second new track 'Maximum Overdrive' is a vigorous, strident number, in true Trogg fashion. The last new number 'What You Doing Here' is a gentle, tender love story of an illicit passionate affair and tells of the pain in choosing between a lover and a partner – an outstanding composition, with Reg vocalising in a hushed, breathy tone.

Athens Andover
Page One ESS LP 180 1992
Also on CD ESS CD 180
Also on Cassette ESS MC 180

Side One:	1 **Crazy Annie** (Chip Taylor)
	2 **Together** (Reg Presley)
	3 **Tuned Into Love** (L Page/D Boone)
	4 **Déjà Vu** (Tony James Shevlin)
	5 **Nowhere Road**
	(P Buck/B Berry/M Mills/P Holsapple)
	6 **Dust Bowl** (Reg Presley)
Side Two:	1 **I'm In Control** (P Holsapple)
	2 **Don't You Know** (Reg Presley)
	3 **What's Your Game** (Reg Presley)
	4 **Suspicious** (Reg Presley)
	5 **Hot Stuff** (L Page/D Boone)

An album of great significance, with the amalgamation of 1960s cult band The Troggs and members of 1990s cult band REM. The coagulating agent in this enterprise was The Troggs' former mentor Larry Page, who had the vision to see the opportunities of a joint venture. He recognised that REM had always admired the Troggs, and 'Love Is All Around' was still part of their stage act.

All of the 11 tracks are brand new compositions, including a contribution from Chip Taylor, 'Crazy Annie', which is a really raunchy, sleazy number in classic Troggs style. 'Nowhere Road', which was released on a single, was written by REM's instrumental section with help from occasional member Peter Holsapple, while 'I'm In Control', an up-tempo number, with an echoing guitar riff and REM's hallmark of jangling guitar, was a solo Holsapple composition.

'Tuned Into Love' and 'Hot Stuff' were from Larry Page and Daniel Boone, who was also on electric guitar. Both songs are driving, rhythmic tracks, but 'Hot Stuff' is a much heavier number, with underlying hints of 'Feels Like A Woman'. The Tony Shevlin track is amusing; all aspects of the Troggs' history have been incorporated, *i.e.* song titles, verses, record labels etc into the words.

Reg Presley penned five tracks on this album. 'Together' is a virtuoso Troggs performance, with the pulsating drums and guitar chords harmonising with the lead and backing vocals. 'Dust Bowl' is environmental social commentary. 'What's Your Game' and 'Suspicious' complete the album in fine style, with Dave Maggs' uninhibited drumming, Peter Lucas' virtuoso bass and the irreplaceable guitar maestro Chris Britton all complimenting Reg Presley's unmistakable vocals.

NOTEWORTHY CD ALBUMS

Black Bottom
New Rose ROSE 4 CD NR 660 1982

The same format as the 1981 LP but with three bonus tracks added, which makes it of special interest:
'Troggs On 45s (Medley)', is a disco mix of numerous songs including, 'Louie, Louie', the McCoys 'Hang On Sloopy', 'Twist And Shout', 'Anyway That You Want Me' and 'Game Of Love' which was a bit hit for Wayne Fontana and the Mindbenders in 1965.
'Save The Last Dance For Me', which was a Number 2 UK hit for the Drifters, is again given The Troggs' 1980s disco treatment.
'I Do Do'. This was penned by Reg Presley, and a co-writer only known as Gem. It is still used as a stage number.
This CD was recorded in the spring of 1982, a year after the album, and again it was arranged and produced by The Troggs and released via the French company New Rose.

The Troggs Hit Single Anthology
Fontana 848 164-2 1991

1 Wild Thing (Taylor)
2 From Home (Presley)
3 With A Girl Like You (Presley)
4 I Want You (L Page/C Frechter)
5 I Can't Control Myself (Presley)
6 Gonna Make You (L Page/C Frechter)
7 Anyway That You Want Me (Taylor)
8 66 5 4 3 2 1 (R Presley)
9 Give It To Me (Presley)
10 You're Lyin' (L Page/C Frechter)
11 Night Of The Long Grass (Presley)
12 Girl In Black (L Page/C Frechter)
13 Hi Hi Hazel (Martin/Coulter)
14 As I Ride By (R Bond)
15 Love Is All Around (Presley)
16 When Will The Rain Come (R Bond)
17 Little Girl (Presley)
18 Maybe The Madman (C Britton)

The first major release from Fontana, through Phonogram, it incorporates both sides of all the nine British chart singles.

The Troggs Archaeology (1966-1976)
US Fontana 314 512 936-2 1992

Disc One:
1 Lost Girl
2 The Yella In Me
3 Wild Thing
4 From Home
5 With A Girl Like You
6 I Want You
7 Jingle Jangle
8 Out Love Will Still Be There
9 I Just Sing
10 I Can't Control Myself
11 Gonna Make You
12 Anyway That You Want Me
13 66-5-4-3-2-1
14 Give It To Me
15 I Can Only Give You Everything
16 You Can't Beat It
17 Last Summer
18 I Want You To Come Into My Life
19 Cousin Jane
20 Night Of The Long Grass
21 Girl In Black
22 Too Much Of A Good Thing
23 Seventeen
24 Her Emotion
25 My Lady
26 All Of The Time
27 Somewhere My Girl Is Waiting

Disc Two:
1 Love Is All Around
2 When Will The Rain Come
3 Little Girl
4 Maybe The Madman
5 Surprise, Surprise (I Need You)
6 You Can Cry If You Want To
7 Hip Hip Hooray
8 Purple Shades
9 Heads Or Tails
10 Evil Woman
11 That's What You Get Girl
12 I Don't Know Why
13 Easy Loving
14 Lover
15 Come Now

16 The Raver
17 Everything's Funny
18 Feels Like A Woman
19 Queen Of Sorrow
20 Strange Movies
21 I'm On Fire
22 Good Vibrations
23 Summertime
24 I'll Buy You An Island
25 Get You Tonight

This is the ultimate Troggs collection. It was released in late 1992 as a two CD, 52 track, boxed set, complete with a 24 page booklet of sleeve notes and unique Trogg photos.

A third CD of the infamous 'Troggs Tapes' was included as a free gift with the first batch.

This well presented, assortment of material, covers the whole spectrum of The Troggs' recording history. Not only are all the British hit singles to be seen, but also a wide and varied selection of album tracks.

The Troggs Greatest Hits
Polygram TV 522 739 ñ2 1994
Also on Cassette 522 739-4

1 Wild Thing
2 Love Is All Around
3 With A Girl Like You
4 I Want You
5 I Can't Control Myself
6 Gonna Make You
7 Good Vibrations
8 Anyway That You Want Me
9 Give It To Me
10 Night Of The Long Grass
11 Girl In Black
12 Hi Hi Hazel
13 Little Girl
14 Cousin Jane
15 Don't You Know
16 Together
17 Nowhere Road
18 I'm In Control
19 Summertime
20 Hot Stuff
21 Dust Bowl
22 I'll Buy You An Island
23 Crazy Annie
24 Jingle Jangle
25 Déjà vu

This 25 track CD and cassette were released in the wake of the fantastic success of Wet Wet Wet's refashioning of 'Love Is All Around'.

The compilation encompasses all of the old hits, plus eight tracks from *Athens Andover*, intermixed with tracks from the 1970s and early material, some of which appeared on the first album *From Nowhere*. The album sold well and achieved a high of Number 27 in the album charts.

Troggs Trogglodynamite
Gone Beat TR 7708 1995

This is the first re-release of two of The Troggs' albums in their original form on CD. All 14 tracks from *Trogglodynamite* and all 12 from *Cellophane* are included on this CD as well as 'Marbles And Some Gum', 'There's Something About You' and 'Say Darlin''.

The Troggs & Special Guests
Music Club MCCD 242 1996

Athens, Georgia & Beyond
Another CD which encompasses all of the 11 tracks of the 1992 *Athens Andover* collaboration with REM.

The remaining seven tracks are sandwiched between the *Athens Andover* material and are all taken from the 70s except for 'Gonna Make You' which was first seen on the B-side of 'I Can't Control Myself' in 1996.

Also of interest are the sleeve notes, which were penned by Peter Doggett, the editor of *Record Collector* magazine.

The EP Collection
See For Miles Records SEECD 453 1996

1 Oh No
2 You're Lying
3 The Yella In Me
4 From Home
5 With A Girl Like You
6 I Want You
7 Jingle Jangle
8 Our Love Will Still Be There
9 I Can't Control Myself
10 Gonna Make You
11 Anyway That You Want Me
12 66-5-4-3-2-1
13 Give It To Me
14 I Can Only Give You Everything
15 You Can't Beat It
16 Night Of The Long Grass
17 Girl In Black
18 Love Is All Around
19 Hi Hi Hazel
20 Little Girl
21 Cousin Jane
22 Wild Thing

This collection is made up of twenty tracks from six French EPs plus two bonus tracks taken from French singles. All of the material was originally recorded in 1966 and 1967.

From Nowhere and **Trogglodynamite**
Beat Goes On Records BGO CD 340 1997

These first two albums of The Troggs have been re-mastered from the original master tapes onto CD.

Side one track six of the original *From Nowhere* was the song 'Evil', which was listed on this CD, but unfortunately the tune on the CD is actually the recording of the 1969 track 'Evil Woman'! Whoops, somebody didn't do their job properly. But other than that the sleeve notes are very impressive.

Cellophane and Mixed Bag
Beat Goes on Records BGO CD 343 1997

The next two albums to have been remastered for CD release are the 1967 *Cellophane* and the 1968 *Mixed Bag*, again both albums have been released in their original form.

Solo And Other Material

Ten Feet Five
Baby's Back In Town (John Porter)
Send Me No More Lovin' (Claydon/King)
Fontana FT 578 1965

This was Chris Britton and Pete Staples debut on vinyl with their pre-Troggs band, Ten Feet Five. Both sides of this record don't give even a hint of the Trogg sound yet to come! 'Baby's Back In Town' is a slow, sad 'folksy-style' lament of a song.
  'Send Me No More Lovin'' is quite a contrast in style with its energetic, yet melodic, country flavoured guitar sound.

Ronnie Bond
Anything For You (Ben Findon)
Carolyn (Fay-Stein)
Page One POF 123 1969

Neither side of this single was actually composed by Ronnie Bond, even though he wrote several tracks for The Troggs.
  Ronnie's very able vocal talents are backed by The Larry Page Orchestra on both sides of this record. 'Anything For You' is a sentimental ballad, whilst the B side is an up beat number.

Chris Britton
As I Am
Page One POLS 022 1970

Side One: 1 Sit Down Beside Me
             2 Will It Last
             3 That Was The Time
             4 No Sense In Fighting
             5 Maybe Time Will Change You
             6 Fly With Me
Side Two: 1 If You Really Care
             2 Run & Hide
             3 How Do You Say Goodbye
             4 Sleep My Love
             5 Why Did I Let You Go
             6 Evil Woman
             7 Learn To Love Life

Twelve of the thirteen tracks were composed by Chris Britton. The odd man out is track six on side two, 'Evil Woman', which was an A side release for The Troggs in 1969. Chris' rendition of the Troggs number has the backing of a full orchestra but retains the rawness of the original.

The album is an excellent representation of Chris' multi-faceted talents from the Eastern influences and big band sound on 'Sit Down Beside Me' through to the Spanish guitar work on 'That Was The Time' and on to R'n'B in 'No Sense In Fighting'. This album is now a rarity, but well worth searching out.

Reg Presley
Lucinda Lee (R Presley)
Wichita Lineman (J Webb)
Page One POF 131 1969

The A side is a haunting ballad in the best Presley tradition, which describes the pain and passion of a boy and girl falling in love.

'Wichita Lineman' was a Number Seven hit earlier that same year for Glen Campbell, and is most effectively covered by Reg. Larry Page took the producing credits on this single and his Orchestra provided the accompaniment.

'S Down To You Marianne (Cook/Greenaway/Stephens)
Hey Little Girl (Cook/Greenaway)
CBS Records S CBS 1478 1973

An up beat number with a strong, 'twangy' backing track over the vocals and harmonies.

Co-composers, Roger Cook and Roger Greenaway, are also know for their singing talents as David and Jonathan of 'Lovers Of The World Unite' hit fame.

'Hey Little Girl' is another up tempo number, with a tambourine tapping away, augmenting the strings and the clearly audible brass sections of the orchestra.

Joe Public Presents Wild Thing
Cindy Jackson and Reg Presley
Side One: 1 **Wild Thing** (Taylor)
              2 **Glad All Over** (Clark/Smith)
Side Two: 3 **Talkin' About The Weather** (Seedback/Jackson)
              4 **Gudbuy T'Luv** (Seedback/Jackson)
Limey Records LIME 1 1980s

Another different version of 'Wild Thing' with Reg guesting on the lead vocals, with Cindy Jackson on the first track of this very obscure single. The sleeve note credits give special thanks to David Bowie.

Suzi Quatro and Reg Presley
Wild Thing (Chip Taylor)
I Don't Want You (S Benham/J Sammes)
PRT 7P 367 1986
Also on 12" PRT 12P 367

Reg Presley and 1970s hit-making, hard-rocking, Detroit-born chanteuse Suzi Quatro, teamed up for this 1980s electronically contrived disco dance interpretation of the 1960s hit.

The Corporation (the Travelling Wrinklies)
Ain't Nothing But A House Party (Sharh/Thomas)
Ain't Nothing But A House Party (Instrumental) (Sharh/Thomas)
Corporation Records KORP 1 1988?

Yet another amalgamation of great talents were assembled for this single.

Tony Crane of The Merseybeats, Clem Curtis of The Foundations, Mike Pender of Searchers fame, Brian Poole of Brian Poole & The Tremeloes and Reg released this recording of the Showstoppers' UK

1969 Number Eleven hit. It charted in the lower reaches of the Top Hundred and generated many TV appearances for the five 'Elders of the 1960s scene'.

Chris Britton & Reg Presley
First Priority featuring The Troggs
Wild Thing '96 Remix
1st Priority Cassette only 1969

Side One	**1 Wild Thing '96 (Piano Extended Mix)**
	2 Wild Thing '96 (GTR Mix)
Side Two	**1 Wild Thing '96 (Dual Club Mix)**
	2 Wild Thing '96 (Piano Radio Edit)

A limited edition cassette produced and arranged by Mark Ballard and also Simon King, the sound engineer of The Troggs in 1996.

As the description of the tracks state, they are all 90s mixes of the 60s classic. And they most certainly would not be out of place when played in clubs or all night raves.

Index

Kidd, Johnny and the Pirates
26, 35, 104, 114
King, Jonathan 54, 69, 112
Kinks 36-37, 39-41, 44-45, 67,
71, 80, 88, 97, 120-121,
125-126

Loot 84-85, 94, 100
Lovin' Spoonful 54
Lucas, Peter 10, 32, 110, 113,
121, 128, 137, 154, 168, 173

Madhatters R&B Set 37
Maggs, Dave 10, 37, 73, 128,
168
Maggs, Reginald (see
Maggs, Dave)
Manfred Mann 13, 36, 58, 70,
77, 93, 120
Mansfield, Howard 'Ginger'
25, 27-28, 38, 46, 55, 61
Matthews, Mick 42, 61
Mayall, John 42
MC5 104
Melody Makers Dance
Orchestra 17, 26, 28, 31
Men Friday 42
Moon, Keith 91, 100, 116
Moore, Richard 107, 111, 114,
152, 167-171
Murray, Tony 94, 98-100, 107,
114, 119-120, 134, 139-143,
150-154, 166-168
Mystery, Pete and the
Strangers 25, 28, 32

Nerve 125
Nicholls, Johnny and the
Dimes 26
Oldham, Andrew Loog 51, 59
Overlanders 13, 64

Page, Larry 23-24, 44-45, 51,
53-55, 57, 59-67, 70-71, 73-81,
83-86, 88, 91-96, 99, 101-105,
112, 117, 129-130, 146-147,
150, 157-159, 162-163, 165,
167-169, 171, 173-174, 181
Peel, John 109
Penfound, Chris 30
Peters, Lee and his Dynamic
Electrons 24
Pfeiffer, Michelle 59
Phillips, Stan 38, 41, 47, 52,
62-64, 80, 88, 107, 117
Pitney, Gene 84-85
Plastic, Penny 81, 87, 94,
98-100
Porter, John 33, 46
Presley, Elvis 22, 25, 57-58, 84
Presley, Reg 13, 15-18, 20, 22,
25, 28, 37-39, 41, 48, 53-56,
59, 63-70, 72, 74-82, 85-89, 91,
94-99, 101-119, 120-136,
138-145, 147, 158-183
Pretty Things 36, 41, 53, 66

Quatro, Suzi 121, 124, 127,
182

Ray, Johnnie 19
Redwoods 30-33, 61
Reed, Oliver 125, 156-158
REM 129-130, 135, 173, 178

FIREFLY PUBLISHING
An association of Helter Skelter and SAF Publishing

New Titles

Opening The Musical Box: A Genesis Chronicle : Alan Hewitt
Compiled by the editor of the definitive Genesis magazine *The Waiting Room*, *Opening The Musical Box* is a detailed and informative chronicle of the band's career: from early beginnings at Charterhouse school through to worldwide stardom. It is also the first book containing a detailed documentary of the solo recording careers and offshoot bands of Genesis members. Drawing on new interviews, packed with insights and anecdotes, and featuring the definitive discography, gigography and a guide to collectables, this is the ultimate compendium to one of the most successful and inventive bands of modern rock.
224 pages/8 photos/235 x 156mm ISBN 0-946719-30-6 UK £12.99

The Manic Street Preachers: Prole Art Threat: Ben Roberts
Drawing on new research and interviews with band insiders, Roberts charts the Manics' progress from Blackwood misfits to rock iconoclasts, through Ritchie Edwards' mysterious disappearance and its aftermath, on to the post-Ritchie mainstream pop stardom that culminated with hit singles such as 'A Design for Life,' and acclaimed albums *Everything Must Go* and *This is My Truth*.... Eschewing the more macabre and intrusive approach of most Manics' biographers, Roberts puts the emphasis back on the band's distinctive musical and cultural manifesto, documenting the rise and fall of The Manic Street Preachers' quest, in Ritchie's own words, 'to be the band that we never had when we were growing up'.
224 pages/8 photos/235 x 156mm ISBN 0-946719-25-X UK £12.99

Blowing Free: Thirty Years of Wishbone Ash: Mark Chatterton and Gary Carter
During the early 1970s golden era of progressive and heavy rock Wishbone Ash were one of Britain's most popular hard rock acts. Formed in 1969 around the twin-lead guitar attack of Andy Powell and Ted Turner, the group's music showcased blistering solos and a strong melodic sensibility. They became a staple favourite on the live circuit, and hit LPs quickly followed. In 1987, after a period in the wilderness, their original manager persuaded the band to reform and since then they have continued recording and touring to widespread international acclaim. The authors have produced a gripping account of the long and distinctive career of one of Britain's premier rock bands.
224 pages/8 photos/235 x 156mm ISBN 0-946719-33-0 UK £12.99

Soul Sacrifice: The Story of Santana: Simon Leng
This is the first ever biography of Carlos Santana – one of the most distinctive and influential guitarists of all time. His is a genuine 'rags to riches' story, and this book traces his life from a childhood spent playing Mariachi music on the streets of Tijuana through to worldwide superstardom. After receiving a Lifetime Achievement Award from *Billboard* magazine in 1996, Santana recently returned to the fray with his first studio album in seven years: *Supernatural* put Santana back at the *Billboard* number one spot, as did its first single, 'Smooth', and it won a multitude of awards at the first Grammy Award ceremony of the new millennium. Simon Leng has enjoyed unprecedented access to band members and associates, and most importantly Carlos Santana himself, .
224 pages 8 photos/235 x 156mm ISBN 0-946719-29-2 UK £12.99

Back Catalogue

Dancemusicsexromance: Prince: The First Decade: Per Nilsen
Documenting Prince's life from his humble Minneapolis beginnings to controversial, international stardom, before the artist's eventual rejection of his Prince persona and his adoption of a symbol instead of a name, *Dancemusicsexromance* is the first biography that gets to grips with one of the most contradictory geniuses of modern pop music. It is also the first in depth study of Prince's music during an extraordinarily creative ten-year period: from the funk-rock crossover platinum success of *Purple Rain* – which sold over 10 million copies in the US alone – to the intoxicating blend of soul, gospel, rock and dance that was *Sign O' the Times*. 'A serious and well-researched study.' *Publishers Weekly*
224 pages/24 photos/235 x 156mm ISBN 0-946719-22-5 UK £12.99

Jethro Tull: Minstrels in the Gallery: David Rees
The first ever biography of the band published on their 30th anniversary. This dates the band's career from the Rock 'n Roll Circus with the Rolling Stones in the 60s, through their megastardom in the 70s with platinum albums such as *Aqualung* and *Thick as a Brick*, and on to their place in the 80s and 90s as one of the great enduring rock acts. 'Brilliant, independently minded ... A fine read for Tull fans and non-believers alike.' *Mojo*
224 pages/24 photos/235 x 156mm ISBN 0-946719-22-5 UK £12.99

Poison Heart: Surviving the Ramones: Dee Dee Ramone with Veronica Koffman
The autobiography of the seminal New York punk band's bassist and songwriter, that documents his fifteen years with the band. 'Former junkie, alleged street hustler and bass playing, helmet-haired founder member of The Ramones, Dee Dee's done a lot of living in his time.' *The Guardian*
'One of *the* great rock books.' *Q******
192 pages/20 b&w photos/235 x 156mm ISBN 0-946719-19-5 Paper UK £11.95

HELTER SKELTER

New Titles

No More Sad Refrains: The Life and Times of Sandy Denny: Clinton Heylin
Drawing on fresh interviews with Sandy's closest friends and musical collaborators, and with unprecedented access to her journals, diaries and unreleased recordings, Heylin has produced a portrait of a complex, driven and flawed genius who may well have been this land's greatest ever female singer-songwriter. Clinton Heylin is a highly respected historian of popular music, whose book *Dylan Behind Closed Doors* (1996, Penguin) was nominated for the Ralph J. Gleason award. 'No female singer of the last ten years could touch her.'
Greil Marcus, *Rolling Stone*, May 1978
256 pages/8 pages b&w photos/235 x 156mm ISBN 1-900924-11-2 Hardcover UK £18.99

Like a Bullet of Light: The Films of Bob Dylan: C.P. Lee
Using archive research and fresh interviews, C.P. Lee traces Dylan's celluloid obsession from his teenage adulation of James Dean through his involvement in documentaries like *Dont Look Back* and his enigmatic appearance in Peckinpah's *Pat Garratt and Billy The Kid*. It looks at the genesis of Dylan's dramatic directorial debut, *Renaldo and Clara*, and his starring role in mainstream *Hearts of Fire*. The author also presents an analysis of all Dylan's major appearances on TV and video. 'There is no doubt that C.P. has done it again … thanks for getting it right.' Mickey Jones, drummer with Dylan during the *Dont Look Back* era.
192 pages/8 pages b&w photos/235 x 156mm ISBN 1-900924-06-4 UK £12.99

Rock's Wild Things: The Troggs Files: Alan Clayson and Jacqueline Ryan
The full sad, mad, funny story of the ultimate British garage band. While other bands of the *Sergeant Pepper* era were turning on and dropping out, the Troggs were knocking out raucously lascivious tunes like 'I Can't Control Myself'. Somehow, singer Reg Presley's mock-anthem 'Love is All Around' captured the spirit of the age. Respected rock writer Alan Clayson has had full access to the band and traces their history from 60s Andover rock roots to 90s covers, collaborations and corn circles. *The Troggs Files* also features the first-ever publication of the full transcript of the legendary 'Troggs Tapes', said to have inspired the movie *This is Spinal Tap*, together with an discography and many rare photographs.
224 pages/8 pages b&w photos/235 x 156mm ISBN 1-900924-19-6 UK £12.99

The Clash: The Return of the Last Gang in Town: Marcus Gray
Last Gang in Town is a fascinating study of the only band to fulfil punk's potential. It also paints an evocative picture of the mid-70s environment out of which punk flourished, as the author traces Strummer and co's origins from pub bands to US stadium rock status. This is a book to shelve next to Jon Savage's Pistols tome *England's Dreaming*. Previously published by Fourth Estate, this edition is fully revised and updated with a huge amount of new material. 'If you're a music fan … it's important you read this book.' *Record Collector* 'A valuable document for anyone interested in the punk era.' *Billboard*
488 pages/8 pages b&w photographs/235 x 156mm ISBN 1-900924-16-1 UK £12.99

Calling Out Around the World: A Motown Reader: Kingsley Abbott
Calling Out features articles on the legendary hit factory songwriting partnerships such as Holland-Dozier-Holland, portraits of key musicians like James Jamerson and interviews with behind-the-scenes players, as well as profiles of all the major artists on the Motown roster and label supremo Gordy himself. Contributors include top music critics like Dave Marsh, Geri Hirshey, Richard Williams and John Rockwell. With a foreword by Martha Reeves and a full discography of UK Motown releases, this is an investigation into how a tiny, Mafia-funded indie label from middle America could dominate the pop charts of the era.
256 pages/8 pages b&w photos/235 x 156mm ISBN 1-900924-14-5 UK £12.99

Emerson Lake and Palmer: The Show That Never Ends: George Forrester, Martin Hanson and Frank Askew
Prog-rock supergroup Emerson Lake and Palmer were one the most successful acts of the 70s and, in terms of sound, artistic vision and concept, operated on a scale far in excess of any rivals. ELP enjoyed a huge profile from the off. Though punk rendered acts like ELP obsolete overnight, they hung on for a couple of years before splitting. Lake and Palmer went on to enjoy massive success in the US charts before being lured back to reform ELP in the early 90s. Drawing on interviews with band members and associates, the authors have produced a gripping and fascinating document of one of the great rock bands of the 70s.
256 pages/8 pages b&w photos/235 x 156mm ISBN 1-900924-17-X UK £12.99

Animal Tracks: The Story of The Animals: Sean Egan: Newcastle's finest emerged from the early-60s blues scene, when Alan Price and Chas Chandler recruited gravel-voiced Eric Burdon to front their new combo. They signed to Columbia Records and released their #1 reworking of 'House of the Rising Sun,'. The Animals built a huge international following – briefly on a par with the Beatles and the Stones – and forged a reputation for legendary live shows, before ego problems resurfaced and they split up. The Animals will be revered as one of the ultimate 1960s groups. Sean Egan has produced a compelling portrait of a distinctive band of survivors.
224 pages/8 pages b&w photos/235 x 156mm ISBN 1-900924-18-8 UK £12.99

Dead End Street: When Rock's Greatest Talents Lost Their Way: Peter Doggett: While other artists are usually revered for their later, more mature work, rock 'n' roll's prime movers have burned more briefly, with career trajectories traditionally following an arc pattern. Witty, compellingly argued and always outspoken, this book takes a no-holds barred look at many of rock's most sacred cows, from Elvis Presley to Oasis, via Bruce Springsteen, the Rolling Stones, Bob Marley, John Lennon, Joni Mitchell, Led Zeppelin, R.E.M. and dozens more. Often drawing on fresh interview material, it offers thought-provoking broadsides which overthrow the popular view of rock's greatest acts. Peter Doggett is Editor in Chief of *Record Collector* magazine.
256 pages/8 pages b&w photos /235 x 156mm ISBN 1-900924-20-X UK £12.99

Razor's Edge: Bob Dylan and the Never Ending Tour: Andrew Muir
Bob Dylan began a short tour in 1986, and has toured every year since. In 1988 he began 'The Never Ending Tour'. Dylan fanzine editor Andrew Muir documents the ups and downs of this trek, analyses and assesses Dylan's performances year in year out and tries to get to grips with exactly what it all means. Part rock criticism and part cultural analysis, this is a telling portrait of a rock star stuck on the live treadmill and a mature audience still spellbound by his every utterance. 'You can press your luck. The road has taken a lot of the great ones: Hank Williams; Buddy Holly; Otis Redding; Janis; Jimi Hendrix; Elvis... It's a goddamn impossible way of life.' Robbie Robertson
256 pages/8 pages b&w photos/235 x 156mm ISBN 1-900924-13-7 UK £12.99

Save What You Can: The Tragedy of Dave McComb and The Triffids: Bleddyn Butcher
The music of Dave McComb's Triffids was infused with the wide open desert spaces and sweeping, treeless vistas of their Perth home on Australia's west coast. The Triffids failed to trouble the charts and in 1990 the band split. After an excellent solo album in 1994, he suffered serious illness, and in 1999 died following a car accident. Recently featured in *Mojo*'s Top Cult Artists, Dave McComb is due to enjoy a posthumous reappraisal that will set him alongside Nick Drake, Tim and Jeff Buckley. The author has had the full co-operation of the band and McComb's friends and family, producing an moving portrait of one of recent rock history's greatest and ill-fated talents.
256 pages/8 pages b&w photos/235 x 156mm ISBN 1-900924-21-8 UK £12.99

Back Catalogue

Waiting for the Man: The Story of Drugs and Popular Music: (Fully revised and updated): Harry Shapiro
First published in 1988, this is the definitive study of the association between drugs and popular music. Each development in music has brought with it a new fashion in drugs, though tragically, the heroes of one are so frequently the victims of the other. This edition is fully revised and includes new material covering the rise of Ecstasy and dance music; the links between rap music and 'crack' cocaine, and the return of the wasted, junky rock star. One of the 'twenty greatest music books of all time'. BBC's *Music for the Millennium*. The *Financial Times* voted it as one of its top 10 music books of 1999. Harry Shapiro has worked in the drugs field since 1979.
288 pages/235 x 156mm ISBN 1-900924-08-0 UK £12.99

Dylan's Demon Lover: The Tangled Tale of a 450-Year Old Pop Ballad: Clinton Heylin
This is a fascinating journey along the lesser-travelled byways of popular song into the heart of the ballad and investigates the tale of a 450-year-old popular ballad, spinning all the way from Dylan's 1961 recording of 'The House Carpenter' back to the origins of popular song. Heylin unearths the mystery of how Dylan knew enough to return 'The House Carpenter' to its 16th-century source, and looks at the development of folk song in the British Isles along the way.
'Clinton Heylin is the maddest muso currently writing.' *Time Out*
160 pages/235 x 156mm ISBN: 1-900924-15-3 UK £12.00

The Sharper Word: A Mod Anthology: Edited by Paolo Hewitt
Though the Mod phenomenon returned to the media spotlight with the rise of Britpop, Blur and Oasis, its heyday was undoubtedly the early 1960s. Mod was more than just a type of music or a style of dress, it was a religion, defined by Ace Face Pete Meaden as '...clean living, under difficult circumstances'. Paolo Hewitt, celebrated former *NME* scribe, has collected some of the best-ever writing on the original, and peculiarly British, cult of Mod, including hard-to-find pieces by Tom Wolfe, Nik Cohn, Andrew Motion, Colin MacInnes and Irish Jack. 'This is a great read.' *Mojo* 'An unparalleled view of the first world-conquering British youth cult.' *The Guardian*
192 pages/235mm x 156mm ISBN 1-900924-10-2 UK £12.00

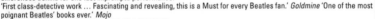

Get Back: The Beatles' 'Let It Be' Disaster: Doug Sulphy and Ray Schweighardt
Subtitled *Divorce, Drugs and the Slipping Image*, this is the no-holds barred account of the power struggles, bickering and bitterness that led to the break-up of the greatest band in rock 'n' roll. The *Get Back* recording sessions were an attempt by the band to return to their rock'n'roll roots, but carping and sniping and trudging through old hits, the Fab Four were coming apart. This puts the reader in the studio as well as reliving the glorious rooftop concert when they left their differences behind for one last impromptu performance.
'First class-detective work ... Fascinating and revealing, this is a Must for every Beatles fan.' *Goldmine* 'One of the most poignant Beatles' books ever.' *Mojo*
256 pages/235 x 156mm ISBN 1-900924-12-9 UK £12.99

XTC: Song Stories: The Exclusive and Authorised Story Behind the Music: XTC and Neville Farmer
The information fans have waited decades for! Following their evolution album by album, it looks at the band's early 70s foundation, and at their lyrics melodies, as well as containing photos from the band's archives. It features cameo appearances by famous XTC fans River Phoenix and Keanu Reeves. Co-written by one of the most popular cult bands of all time, this book is timed to coincide with their long awaited new album. 'A cheerful celebration of the minutiae surrounding XTC's music with the band's musical passion intact. It's essentially a band-driven project for the fans, high in setting-the-record-straight anecdotes. Superbright, funny, commanding.' *Mojo*
306 pages/100 b&w photos/235 x 156mm ISBN 1-900924-03-X UK £12.99

Bob Dylan: Like The Night: C.P. Lee
In 1966, at the height of his popularity, Dylan plugged in an electric guitar and merged his poetic lyrics with the sound of one of *the* great rock'n'roll bands. The rock world was delighted, but the folk scene felt outraged and betrayed. That summer Dylan toured the world, and every show was accompanied by frenzied booing and catcalls – culminating at the Manchester Free Trade Hall where fans called him 'Judas'. This book documents that legendary world tour where Dylan waged a nightly war with his audience, and reinvented rock 'n' roll with an incendiary zeal never subsequently equalled.
'Essential Reading.' *Uncut* 'C.P. Lee was there, but the point is that he can put you there too.' Greil Marcus
192 pages/24 b&w photos ISBN 1-900924-07-2 Paper UK £12.00

Born in the USA: Bruce Springsteen and the American Tradition: Jim Cullen
Born in the USA is an ambitious, myth shattering appraisal of one of America's most incisive, broadminded cultural critics.
'Cullen has written an excellent treatise expressing exactly how and why Springsteen translated his uneducated hicktown American-ness into music and stories that touched hearts and souls around the world.' *Q****
'This is a provocative look at one of America's cultural icons.' *Newsweek*
254 pages/b/w photos/200 x 135mm ISBN 1-900924-05-6 Paper UK £9.99

Back to the Beach: A Brian Wilson and the Beach Boys Reader: Edited by Kingsley Abbott
A collection of the best articles about Brian and the band, together with a number of previously unpublished pieces and some specially commissioned work.
Features Nick Kent, David Leaf, Timothy White and others, with a foreword by Brian Wilson.
'A detailed study and comprehensive overview of the BBs' lives and music, even including a foreword from Wilson himself by way of validation. Most impressively, Abbott manages to appeal to both die-hard fans and rather less obsessive newcomers.' *Time Out*
'Rivetting!' **** *Q* 'An essential purchase.' *Mojo*
256 pages/235 x 156mm ISBN 1-900924-02-1 Paper UK £12.99

A Journey Through America with the Rolling Stones: Robert Greenfield
By 1972, the Stones had become the number one musical attraction in the world: the only great band of the 1960s still around who played original rock 'n' roll. This is the definitive account of their legendary '72 tour, catching them at the height of their powers and excesses.
'A merciless, brilliant study of Jagger-power at full throttle.' Daily Mirror
'Filled with finely-rendered detail ... a fascinating tale of times we shall never see again.' *Mojo* 'Strange days indeed.' *Q* ****
192 pages/235 x 156 mm ISBN 1-900924-01-3 UK £12.00

Bob Dylan: A Biography: Anthony Scaduto
Along with Elvis and Lennon, Bob Dylan is one of the three most important figures in 20th-century popular music. Scaduto's book is his first and best biography.
'Scaduto's 1971 book was the pioneering portrait of this legendarily elusive artist. Now in a welcome reprint it's a real treat to read the still-classic Bobography.' *Q*****
'Perhaps the best ever book written on Dylan.' *Record Collector*
'I like your book. That's the weird thing about it.' Bob Dylan
312 pages/8 pages of photos/235 x 156 mm ISBN 1-900924-00-5 Paper UK £12.99

HOW TO ORDER OUR BOOKS

All titles available by mail order from the world famous Helter Skelter bookshop.
Please indicate title, author and price of each book, and give your full postal address

You can order by phone or fax your on the following numbers:
Telephone: 020 7836 1151 or Fax 020 7240 9880

Office hours Mon-Fri: 10:00am – 7:00pm, Sat: 10:00am – 6:00pm, closed Sunday

approx. postage per book:

UK and Channel Islands	£1.50
Europe and Eire (air)	£2.95
USA & Canada (air)	£7.50
Australasia, Far East (air)	£9.00
Overseas (surface)	£2.50

You can pay by Visa or Mastercard by giving us the following information

Name of cardholder . . . .

Card number . . . . Expiry date . . . .

You can also write enclosing a cheque, International Money Order or registered cash. Please DO NOT send cash or foreign currency or cheques drawn on an overseas bank.

Send to:
Helter Skelter Bookshop
4 Denmark Street, London, WC2H 8LL
UNITED KINGDOM

email: helter@skelter.demon.co.uk   website: www.skelter.demon.co.uk